AF624307

SECOND HANDBOOK OF PSYCHOLOGICAL AND SOCIAL INSTRUMENTS

SECOND HANDBOOK OF PSYCHOLOGICAL AND SOCIAL INSTRUMENTS

Edited and Compiled by
PROF. D.M. PESTONJEE

Research Assistance Provided by
Dr. S.N. Usmani

CONCEPT PUBLISHING COMPANY, NEW DELHI-110059

All rights reserved. No part of this work may be reproduced, stored in a retrieval system, or transmitted in any form or by any means, electronic, mechanical, photocopying, microfilming, recording or otherwise, without the prior written permission of the copyright owner and the publisher.

ISBN 81-7022-193-5

First Published 1988
Reprinted 2003

© **D.M. Pestonjee** (*b.* 1939-

Published and Printed by
Ashok Kumar Mittal
Concept Publishing Company
A/15-16, Commercial Block, Mohan Garden
NEW DELHI-110059 (India)

Phones : 25351460, 25351794
Fax : 091-11-25357103
Email : publishing@conceptpub.com

Preface

The most critical contribution of psychology as a social science is in the area of measurement of behaviour. Instruments are of great value not only to psychologists but to other behavioural scientists also. Instruments have been developed in India at a very fast rate. However, we do not have enough information about new developments. In 1974, Professors Udai Pareek and T.V. Rao prepared the First Handbook of Psychological and Social Instruments. The Handbook listed and described instruments developed and adapted in India in four areas, namely, Personality, Education, Organisational Behaviour and Social Phenomena. The book fulfilled a long felt need in psychology. Since 1974, a large number of instruments have been reported in journals and doctoral dissertations. It is necessary to update the efforts initiated by Professors Pareek and Rao.

This Handbook is in continuation of the First Handbook of Psychological and Social Instruments by Professors Pareek and Rao. The scope of this Handbook will be more or less the same as of the first one. Instruments of cognitive nature will not be included in the Handbook. The Handbook, therefore will not have intelligence tests, aptitude tests and achievement tests.

In order to make the Handbook as comprehensive as possible it was decided to contact Heads/Deans of Faculty of Psychology and Education, Directors of Institutes of higher learning, Professors and Teachers of Psychology and Education who are known for their contribution to the field of testing, and the research students engaged in researches in the field of testing. Some responded promptly while some others only after repeated reminders. Some authors sent information about their instruments but did not send copies of the instruments even after reminders. In several cases instruments received were in Indian languages.

Although we requested authors to send authorised translation of instruments in English, in most cases these were not received. Files of the several wellknown recent journals were also searched to get information about the new developments reported or cited in the papers. We have included a section on instruments about which limited or incomplete information is available.

On Using the Handbook

The coding system of the present Handbook is similar to the first Handbook. The coding is based on the following 3-tier classification :

Part indicates the field. The Handbook is divided into four parts :

1 - Personality
2 - Education
3 - Organisational Behaviour
4 - Social Phenomena

Each Part is further divided into sections. The first numeral of the code number of the instrument indicates the part and the second numeral indicates the section under that part.

Under each Section four categories of instruments are included :

A - Instruments reproduced with information
B - Instruments with technical information only
C - Citations
D - Adaptations.

The category is indicated by the letter codes mentioned above. In each category the instruments are serially numbered. Thus, in numbering an instrument, the Part number occurs first, followed by the Section number, and Category (A, B, C, or D explained above) which is followed by serial number of the instrument. For example 12A10 would indicate that the instrument is in Part 1, i.e., Personality, dealing with Adjustment (Section 2), is reproduced here with information (Category A) and has a serial number 10 in that category. Similarly, 31D2 indicates that the instrument is from organisational behaviour (Part 3), dealing with industrial organisation (Section 1), is an Indian adaptation (Category D) and has a serial number of 2 under that category.

Three indices are provided at the end of the Handbook namely, instrument index and author index. These may be used by the reader for locating a desired instrument in the Handbook.

Preparing the Handbook is a patently time consuming activity which depends on cooperation of several academic collaborators. Thanks should be given to authors and publishers of several tests and instruments whose works are included here. As a word of caution to users of this Handbook, it may be mentioned that the copyright of these instruments vests with the authors and/or test publishers, as the case may be, and no instrument, or its part, may be reproduced without their prior and specific permission.

The author would like to place on record thanks for the financial assistance provided by the Indian Council of Social Science Research for preparation of this Handbook. Without the generous support of the ICSSR it would not have been possible to undertake this project and bring it to fruition.

The American Psychological Association has very graciously allowed me to incorporate the "Standards for Educational and Psychological Tests (1974)" in the present Handbook.

I will be failing in my duty if I do not record my very sincere thanks to my friends and colleagues Professor Udai Pareek and Professor T.V. Rao (editors of the First Handbook) who were a source of constant help and encouragement since the inception of this project. Dr. S.N. Usmani very painstakingly worked on the project and brought many of his academic insights to bear on the Handbook. He deserves all praise and appreciation for his involvement. Ms. Tripti Sharma volunteered to proof read the script and deserves my thanks. I will also like to thank Shri M. Haridasan who typed the whole Handbook having had to read literally several hundred types of handwritings.

Ahmedabad
December 15, 1987

D.M. PESTONJEE

Contents

PART ONE

PERSONALITY

a single personality dimension. Some of the instruments are exclusively meant to cover a single or a select few dimensions, like extraversion, introversion, neuroticism etc. The different dimensions covered by these general personality instruments include : security-insecurity, mental health, altruism, non-violence, authoritarianism, frustration, manifest hostility, punctuality, stress and strain, social conformity, locus of control, racializm-conservatism, ego-identity, certainty of judgement, risk-taking, parental behaviour, menopausal symptoms, persistence and dominance etc. A few instruments for clinical diagnosis measuring psychiatric disability, psychosis, neurosis, paranoid tendencies etc. are also reported here. Out of 83 instruments 20 are adaptations. Only technical information about the other 36 instruments is provided here. 15 instruments are originally reproduced here. 12 titles are cited for which information or instruments could not be procured.

Table : 1

Break-up of Personality Instruments

Classification	Originals reproduced	Only Information	Citations	Adaptations	Total
General	15	36	12	20	83
Adjustment	5	8	1	3	17
Anxiety	-	5	-	1	6
Self-Concept	1	6	3	1	11
Motivation	5	7	-	-	12
Total	**26**	**62**	**16**	**25**	**129**

Instruments are available mainly for school and college students. A few instruments for special groups like Block-level personnel and Police Officers are also reported. Different techniques as scales, check-lists, questionnaires, inventories and tests, have been used in measuring the different dimensions of personality.

Regarding the standardisation measures, the reliabilities and validities of these instruments have been established. Split-half and test-retest are the most common forms of reliabilities.

The size of the sample on which the reliability coeffi-

Personality

Instruments dealing with personality dimensions have been included in this part of the Handbook. The instruments are reported under five sections:

i - general
ii - adjustment
iii - anxiety
iv - self-concept
v - motivation.

The classification system of the instruments is not based on theoretical distinctions, but it is a pragmatic one reflecting the number of instruments reported. The instruments measuring a particular dimension of personality, available in sufficient number are treated separately. Thus, adjustment, anxiety, self-concept and motivation emerge as separate dimensions. Anxiety and self-concept include instruments dealing exclusively with these variables whereas, the sections on adjustment and motivation report instruments dealing with several types of adjustment and motivation respectively. The section on adjustment reports instruments mainly related to personality adjustment and problems. The instruments dealing with the other personality dimensions have been grouped under the title of general instruments of personality. The instruments dealing with extraversion, introversion, authoritarianism, locus of control, frustration etc. have been included in this group.

In all 129 instruments have been reported in this part of the Handbook. 26 instruments are reproduced here, 15 of them are in general category ; 25 instruments are adaptations. Only technical information about other 62 instruments is provided here. 16 instruments have been cited and the information is not available. The detailed break-up appears in Table No. 1.

General Instruments :

In all 83 instruments are listed under this title. The instruments cover different personality dimensions. A few of these are multi-trait personality tests and cover more than cients are based, is mentioned only in a few instruments, hence no significant conclusions can be drawn on these. However, the coefficients in most of the cases are very high and thus, these instruments can be considered as well standardised instruments.

As regards the validity, most of the instruments are not validated. A quarter of the instruments available do not report any validity. A few of them simply report that validity is established without giving any details. Validity by correlating the instruments with other standardised instruments seems to be the popular type. Concurrent and validity by ratings are also commonly used. The validity coefficients wherever reported are fairly high and encouraging. More attention needs to be paid on application of systematic techniques of validation.

There are 15 original instruments which will be reproduced here. Multivariable Personality Inventory by Muthayya is meant for Block level administrative personnel and assesses the personality attributes among them. Psychoanalytic Personality Inventory by Rao, measures the personality structure of individuals of above 15 years of age. The Menopause Symptom Checklist by Sharma is a unique and well standardised instrument which screens women suffering from menopausal symptoms. It is useful to the middle aged women above 35 years.

There are some instruments which measure neuroticism and introversion. Two tests are reproduced here which measure the non-violent aspect of personality. Sentence completion test by Tiwari measures interpersonal as well as interpersonal conflicts. It needs to be well standardised as it has not reported any reliability and validity. Other tests reproduced here, measure reactions to frustration, security-insecurity, mental health, altruism, ascendence and submission among school and college students. Liar and criminal detection test by H.N. Singh seems to be a good instrument to detect the liar and criminals in a group. It requires further researches and standardization. A scale by Muttagi is also a significant contribution and is reproduced here as an anti-democratic and fascist scale.

A few of the instruments reproduced here have reported norms. Most of the instruments do not report any norms and a few of them do not report any reliability and validity. These instruments have been reproduced for benefit of further researches.

There are 20 adaptations of some of the standard instruments in this area. Most of these instruments are meant for adolescents and college students. The 16PF-test, Neyman-Kohlstedt Diagnostic test, short measure of Eriksonian Ego-Identity, Certainty of Judgement Scale and the Telic Dominance Scale, have been adapted in Hindi language. Junior Eysenck Personality Inventory is adapted in Bengali and measures introversion, extraversion, and neuroticism of school students. Another adaptation of this instrument is in Hindi. Eysenck's Personality Questionnaire and Wilson Patterson Conservative Scale have also been adapted in Hindi. The instruments are adapted in several languages as Hindi, English, Bengali and Urdu. Reliability and validity have been reported for most of the instruments. Indian norms are also provided for these instruments.

Information about the Indian norms for the Holtzman Inkblot Technique is provided here. The Indian adaptation of senior apperception test by Uma Chowdhury is a widely used projective type instrument. It is adapted with special emphasis on coping and adaptation between generations. It may be used on older people as well as on the younger generation above 16 years. Indian norms are also provided.

Adjustment and Problems :

There are 17 instruments which measure personality adjustment and problems. 5 instruments are available in their original forms and will be reproduced here. These are mainly to measure the adjustment of adolescents and college students. 2 instruments are meant for measuring marital adjustment. Information about the other 8 instruments is reported here which also measure adjustment. 3 instruments are adaptations of foreign instruments. Reference about one instrument is cited.

The adjustment inventories/scales are meant for measuring the adjustment in several areas like home, health, social, emotional and school adjustment of adolescents and college going students. Some other instruments are also available which measure neurotic tendencies and aggression etc. Reliabilities have been reported by 14 out of 16 instruments. Most of the instruments have reported both split-half and test-retest reliabilities. A few of them have reported only one type of reliability. The coefficients of reliabilities are quite high and are mostly above .70. Only for two instruments reliability data is not available.

7 Personality

As regards the validity, the instruments have reported validity by ratings, biserial coefficients of correlation and the correlation of the scores of the instruments with other standardised instruments. Some instruments have reported concurrent and construct validity. One instrument has reported more than one type of validity and no validity data is available for two instruments.

On the whole, the coefficients of validity reported by these instruments seem to be at an acceptable level.

Five instruments have been reproduced here. The Personality Adjustment Inventory by C.P. Sharma measures the maladjustive-adjustive behaviour reactions of individuals and reports highly significant reliability and validity data. Deshpande's Personal Adjustment Inventory is available in English and Marathi and measures the mental health of college going students. An Adjustment Inventory by B.A. Parikh and D.G. Das reporting high reliability and validity, is useful for measuring the adjustment of socially disadvantaged students.

There are two scales reproduced here which are meant for marital adjustment. The scale by Dhillan and others is available in Punjabi and English and assesses the marital adjustment of married men and women. The Marriage Adjustment Inventory by C.G. Deshpande is available in English and Marathi and is good for understanding the degree of adjustment and to help in counselling.

Other instruments reported here are mainly for High School and College students. These instruments have also reported high reliability and validity. Norms are also available for almost all the instruments.

There are a few other instruments which are adaptations. Bell's Adjustment Inventory is adapted in Hindi and Bengali languages. Norms are also prepared for Indian subjects. The Marital Adjustment Scale of Burgess and others is adapted in Hindi and Punjabi languages. No other details are available on the same.

On the whole, the adjustment inventories reported here seem to be fairly well standardised.

Anxiety :

There are only six instruments reported here which measure anxiety. No original scale is available which could be reproduced here. The scales are meant for high school and college students.

One instrument is available in Gujarati and measures the symptoms of anxiety relating physical health, sex, family and social relations etc. of adolescents and adult students. The other instrument is the Bengali version of State-Trait Anxiety. It is a self-reporting scale and measures two distinct types of anxiety (State and A-Trait). It can be used on both the normal and the pathological subjects. It can also be used for normal girls and women experiencing anxiety during menstruation. Another one is the shorter version of Sinha's Anxiety scale which is available in Hindi.

All the anxiety instruments have reported high reliability and validity coefficients. Three instruments have reported both the test-retest and split-half and the two only split-half reliability.

Three instruments have been validated by correlating with other instruments and yield highly significant coefficients of correlation. The validity of one instrument is determined in terms of indices of discrimination and internal consistency. The other one has also reported concurrent validity of .73. Norms in terms of °T' scores and °Percentile' are prepared for all the instruments.

Self-Concept :

There are 11 instruments available on this theme out of which only one instrument is reproduced here. The self-concept scale by H.M. Singh and S. Singh is meant for children. The scale contains descriptive adjective phrases which are rated on a 5-point scale. There are two other scales which also measure self-concept. They are also rated on a 5-point scale.

Information about two instruments are reported here which measure self-esteem. These scales are meant for under-graduate and university students. Another scale measures self-image of adolescent students.

Self perception scale by M.C. Agrawal is a good scale to judge the self confidence of supervisors. Information about the adaptation of the Texas Social Behaviour Inventory is reported here. It is adapted in Hindi and differentiates individuals on the dimensions of self-concept and self-esteem. 3 instruments have been cited.

Reliabilities have been reported for all the instruments. Both, the split-half and test-retest methods have been used and the values have been found to be very high. Validity is not indicated in case of three instruments. The other 5 instruments have reported validity coefficients. One instrument reports content validity established on the basis of experts' ratings. Other instruments have been validated by correlation methods.

Motivation :

There are 12 instruments listed on this theme. 5 instruments are reproduced along with full details. For the other seven only information is given. The instruments in this area measure prolonged deprivation, personality need, encouragement given by parents, level of aspiration, power motive, achievement motivation and fear of failure motivation. A few instruments are of projective type and a few are structured questionnaires. Majority of the instruments are for school and college students and a few are for others.

As far as the standardization is concerned, there instruments have not reported such data. A few have reported both the split-half and test-retest reliability and a few, only one type of reliability and all the values are fairly high. In only one TAT instrument inter-score reliability is established but the value is not reported here.

For validation of these instruments no good criterion has been adapted. Three instruments do not report any validity data. A few have been validated by correlational methods. One instrument has reported construct and predictive validity while the other one has reported content, construct, intrinsic and predictive validities, but details are not available. In all there seems to be enough scope for improving the validational components of the motivation instruments. More scientific rigour is needed in this area.

The first of these instruments reproduced here is a TAT instrument developed by Prayag Mehta which measures personal achievement motivation, social achievement motivation and influence motivation. The pictures used in this instrument are described here. This test is developed for adults and appears to be a fairly well standardized instrument. The next one is an approval motive scale which determines approval seeking of adolescents. This scale also seems to be well standardized. The Prolonged Deprivation Scale by Mishra and Tripathi is reproduced here for reference. Standardization data on this scale can be had from the authors. There is one personality need inventory by Sharma, meant for adolescents and measures psychological needs. Adequate standardization has been reported for this instrument. One instrument reproduced here assesses the degree of encouragement given by the parent and is useful for school, college and university students.

PERSONALITY

1. General Instruments

complete instruments A

11A1 MULTIVARIABLE PERSONALITY INVENTORY (MPI)

uthor : B.C. Muthayya
vailability : Agra Psychological Research Cell, Belanganj, Agra.
anguage : English
ses : To assess some of the personality attributes among the administrative personnel.
evel : Block level administrative personnel.
ain features : There are 50-items consisting of nine variables as empathy, ego-ideal, pessimism, neuroticism, introversion, need achievement, self-confidence, dogmatism and dominance. The answer categories provided are °yes' and °no' for each item.
eliability : The method of rational equivalence is preferred for assessing the reliability of the scale. All the variables studied are scored for their negative connotation for this purpose. The obtained reliability coefficient was found to be .52.
lidity : By using the percentage of the high and the low groups answering the item in a given direction, it was possible to find out the validity index of each item from the Flanagan's Table. The obtained validity indices of the items in the preliminary personality inventory ranged between 0 to .77.
rms : Mean and S.Ds norms are provided for each of the nine personality variables for the different developmental functionaries.
ference : Muthayya, B.C. and Gnana Kannan, I. Developmental Personnel, N.I.C.D. Hyderabad, 1973.

See preface for the meaning of the code number of the instruments.

11A1 MULTIVARIABLE PERSONALITY INVENTORY
(The following items have to be checked on °yes' or °no').

1. Most people can be trusted.
2. Are you repeatedly guided to action by high hopes of possible success?
3. Do you believe that life is just one worry after another?
4. Do you often feel lonely even when you are with other people?
5. Are you often troubled with feelings of guilt?
6. Do you enjoy doing work as much as play?
7. Are you easily hurt when people find fault with your work?
8. Do you find it difficult to speak in public?
9. Do you take the responsibility of introducing someone at a meeting or a party?
10. Do you think that other man's point of view is as important as your own?
11. Are you very talkative at social functions?
12. Do you think that no immediate compensation could console you for the failure of your highest hopes?
13. Do you work like a slave at everything you undertake until you are satisfied with the result?
14. When your own interests are in danger, do you entirely concentrate on your job and forget your obligations to others?
15. Does criticism discourage you in an argument even when you know you are right?
16. Do you try to take added responsibility on yourself?
17. After you have done something important, do you often come away feeling you could have done better?
18. Do you greatly dislike being told how you should do things?
19. Do you want some one to be with you when you receive bad news?
20. Do you set difficult goals for yourself which you attempt to reach?
21. Are you mostly quiet when you are with other people?
22. Are you easily discouraged when the opinion of others differ from your own?
23. Are you driven to ever greater efforts by a ceaseless ambition?
24. Do you often find that you cannot make up your mind until the time for action has passed?
25. Do you listen to your superior officer how-so-ever unreasonable he may be?

26. Do you think that nobody ever cares whatever happens to you?
27. Do you dislike people who reject authority?
28. Do you feel that there is little chance for getting promotion in one's job unless one has unfair pull?
29. Are people sometimes successful in taking advantage of you?
30. Do you feel so restless at times, that you cannot sit in a chair for a very long time?
31. Do you complain when you are served with poor quality of food in a hotel?
32. Do you ever that it is difficult to think clearly these days?
33. Are you in favour of very strict enforcement of rules no matter what the consequences are?
34. Are you often the last one to give up trying to complete any task?
35. Do you think that nobody ever offers help to you unless there is some ulterior motive?
36. Do you feel mad an innocent person is being accused for no fault of his?
37. Can you stick to a tiresome task for a long time without some one encouraging you?
38. Do you think that no one can demand for you as much as you demand from yourself?
39. Are you guided in most of your decisions by high ambition?
40. Do you take a subordinate/work-associate to task if he fails to complete the work on time?
41. Do you think that the country is heading for a disaster?
42. When some on the road pushes you unitentionally, do you try to understand the situation and not take him to task?
43. Do you suddenly feel deffident when you want to talk to your superior officer?
44. Do you prefer to shoulder responsibilities alone?
45. Do you feel that some big distant goal deserves your effort more than any daily duty?
46. Do you dislike having to adapt yourself to unusual situations?
47. Do you find it hard to take a °No' for answer?
48. Do you have difficulty in starting a conversation with a superior officer?
49. Do you often need understanding friends to cheer you up?
50. Are you free in expressing cordiality and good-will to others?

11A2 PSYCHOANALYTIC PERSONALITY INVENTORY

Author : Bishwanath Roy.

Availability : Author, Department of Psychology, NCERT, New Delhi.

Languages : English, Hindi, Bengali.

Uses : To measure the personality structure of the individual.

Level : Anybody who is 15+, that is, above fifteen years of age.

Main features : The inventory consists of 44 items, based upon the day-to-day activities of any individual. The items have been prepared by incorporating some of the assumptions of the psychoanalytic theory developed by Freud. It is aimed to arrive at a measure of the personality structure of the individual. The items of the inventory are based upon the following factors :

1. Identification
2. Tolerance
3. Narcissism
4. Lasting Cathexis
5. Object Cathexis
6. Libidinal Cathexis
7. Dependence
8. Sibling Rivalry
9. PAPI (Total)

Reliability : Split-half reliability : (1) F.H. vs L.H. : .833 Spearman-Brown method (2) Odd vs Even : .828 for the inventory as a whole.

Validity : There are factorial and face validities.

Time : Average 20 to 30 minutes.

Norms : Not available.

References : Roy, B. The philosophy of psycho-analysis (in Bengali), Chitta, 1372 (Bengali Saka) 158-166.

________ Sigmund Freud (1856-1939) (in Bengali), Chitta, 1380 (B.S.), 15(2), 37-46.

________ Ideal and Non-ideal in psycho-analysis (in Bengali), Chitta, 1383 (B.S.), 18(4).

________ A few days with Erik Erikson (in Bengali), Chitta, 1384 (B.S.), 19(2), 10-30.

11A2 PSYCHO-ANALYTIC PERSONALITY INVENTORY
(The following items have to be checked on
a 5-point scale of agreement)

15 Personality

1. People should like to leave the bed early in the morning than late morning.
2. People who drink wine are not good.
3. Smart people wear tight fitting clothing.
4. Classical music is liked by serious minded people only.
5. Pop or light music is liked by light minded people only.
6. There is something wrong with those who feel hungry immediately after boarding train for long journeys.
7. To eat a toffee one should chew it and not suck it.
8. Meals should be taken quickly and not slowly.
9. Humid climate is better than dry climate.
10. Summer season is better than winter season.
11. As a company one should like boys than girls.
12. One should remain alert in hearing anybody talking on anything.
13. One should not like buying painting materials.
14. Males should not wear colourful dresses.
15. One should greet a guest or a visitor by shaking hands.
16. People should not live in company of others but alone.
17. Instead of living in a village one should prefer living in a town or city.
18. Money should lavishly be spent on dress on clothing and decoration.
19. There is no embarrassment in using multicoloured clothings, e.g., shirts, slacks etc.
20. One coloured plain clothings are outdated.
21. One should not be camera shy for his/her own photograph.
22. People who like pet animals are better than the people who like flowers.
23. Film shows don't have much entertainment value.
24. Purchasing books, newspaper etc. are useless investments.
25. Every body should perform physical exercises everyday.
26. Any kind of hobby, e.g., stamp collection, books, painting, bird watching, etc. which involves expenditure is not good.
27. One should enjoy the excitement of travelling in a train by remaining awake instead of going to sleep.
28. When opportunities are given, one should like to practice music.
29. Whether one is capable or not but should try to help others.

30. It is better to take sweet food than salty food.
31. Money is earned to eat, drink and be merry.
32. A camera will be misused if it is used for shooting pictures of people, animals, birds etc., instead of shooting the pictures of natural scenery like sea, mountain, cloud etc.
33. It is not good to over hear others.
34. One should keep the living rooms perfectly neat and clean.
35. One should drink more water daily.
36. Everybody should use a strawpipe while drinking soft drinks like Coke, Fanta etc.
37. Whenever anybody gets money he/she should spend it immediately instead of saving it for sometime at least.
38. In comparison with academic works administrative works are much better.
39. The quantity of food served in home is not sufficient.
40. If somebody is in trouble he should face it and solve it.
41 People should not try to some how avoid any trouble.
42. Saying °Namaste' or °Namaskar' to a guest or a visitor has become outdated.
43. Days are gone for loose fitting clothings.
44. While in a group, those who remain silent and hear others are better than those who prefer to talk themselves without giving any chance to others.

11A3 VERBAL FRUSTRATION TEST (VFT)

Author : B.C. Muthayya.
Availability : Agra Psychological Research Cell, Agra.
Language : English.
Uses : To assess the reactions to frustration of adolescents.
Level : Adolescents (13+ to 17+ age group).
Main features : The test consists of 15 situations representing incidents of every day life as expressed by the High School Population. These are depicted in the test in a dialogue form as °A' saying something to °B'. In each case one character is saying something of a frustrating nature to another. Frustrating situation covers five areas.
Reliability : Scorers (two raters) and the test (items and matrix) reliability worked out on a sample of subjects was found to be satisfactory. There was 89% agreement between the raters. The matrix reliability ranged from

.36 to .70 and the test-retest agreement ranged from 50% to 75%.

Validity : Experimental validation, the validation through trend analysis and as compared through a group of delinquents response, showed a trend which is supportive, if not adequate to the validity of the test.

Norms : Norms are available in terms of mean and S.D.

11A3 VERBAL-FRUSTRATION TEST (VFT)
(Respondents have to imagine the answer which °B' would have given)

1. A.... "You shall not go to the picture today. Does not matter if you have promised your friends".
   B....
2. A.... "Have you no sense? Don't play inside the house".
   B....
3. A.... "Sorry I couldn't come yesterday. Were you waiting for me?"
   B...
4. A.... "I can't afford to buy you a cycle to go to school".
   B....
5. A.... "You can't go to your friends house now. You will have to help me with the domestic work".
   B....
6. A.... "I can't issue a ticket to you. This is an °Adults only' picture".
   B....
7. A.... "Tell your teacher that I can't send you to The Excursion".
   B....
8. A.... "You are too young to attend parties. You stay at home and look after the baby".
   B....
9. A.... "I don't like you to act in the drama".
   B....
10. A.... "Don't be a bookworm. Let us go to a picture".
   B....
11. A.... "I don't want you to join the music or dance classes".
   B....
12. A.... "You can't have the foot-ball match today. The ground is very wet".
   B....
13. A.... "I think we will have to cancel out trip as I have not been permitted to go on leave".

B....
14. A.... "I can't afford to send you to the college".
B....
15 A.... "I can't take you in the team. There are better players than you".
B....

11A4 SECURITY-INSECURITY (S-I) INVENTORY

Authors : Govind Tiwari and H.M. Singh.
Availability : Agra Psychological Research Coll, Agra.
Languages : Hindi, English.
Uses : It is a tool for measuring inner conscious feelings. It may be used to discriminate people according to their feeling of security-insecurity in respect to their various aspects of life.
Level : School and College students.
Main features : The Inventory consists of 70 items related with security-insecurity. The items have been selected with the help of careful study of the relevant literature and for some popular tests in the field. The inventory is standardized on a sample of 789 school and college boys and girls students of urban and semi urban areas.
Reliability : Split-half reliability (Spearman Brown Correction Formula) = .67.
Test-retest reliability (N = 49) = .73.
Validity : Content and face validity is established to be very high. The inventory is validated against Maslow's S-I inventory and the correlation (N = 40) was found to be .67. Again it has been validated against teacher's rating, and the coefficient of correlation is found to be .78 (N = 34).
Norm : Percentile norms for boys and girls are given.

11A4 SECURITY-INSECURITY INVENTORY
(Respondents have to answer 'yes', 'no' or 'undecided').

1. Do you like more to live in the company of people than to live alone?
2. Do you have lack self-confidence?
3. Do you feel that you are more appreciated?
4. Are you engrossed with the feeling to rebel against this world?
5. Are you worried with a feeling of certain pressures?
6. Do you think that people like you as much as they like others?
7. Are you worried with a feeling of inferiority com-

plex for a long time?

8. Do you have a feeling of self pleasure?
9. Do you take yourself to be normally unselfish person?
10. Do you feel to be away from troubles?
11. Do you feel lonely even when you are in the company of people?
12. Do you feel that you have lack of enthusiasm?
13. When your friends criticise, do you always think it to be correct?
14. Are you easily disappointed?
15. Do you often have a feeling of friendliness with everybody?
16. Do you often feel that it is futile to live?
17. Do you ordinarily optimistic?
18. Are you feel yourself as a shy person?
19. Are you ordinarily a happy man?
20. Do you often think about self-consciousness?
21. Are you dissatisfied with yourself?
22. Do you often have low spirits?
23. When you meet with people for the first time, do you feel that they do not like you?
24. Do you have over confidence in yourself?
25. Do you feel that usually people can be trusted?
26. Do you think yourself a useful person in this world?
27. Do you spend most of your time in worrying about future?
28. Do you usually think yourself to be good and strong?
29. Do you feel difficulty in expressing your experiences?
30. Do you feel you are a burden on others?
31. Are you even disappointed?
32. Do you think yourself a suspicious personality?
33. Do you think this world to be a good place to live in?
34. Are you easily disturbed?
35. Do you think yourself to be a disappointed person?
36. Do you feel that you are living according to your own will rather than others?
37. Do you often think about yourself?
38. Do you feel pains when you make mistake?
39. Do you feel that you are successful in your work or profession?
40. Do other people take you to be what you are?
41. Do you feel that you are satisfied with your life?
42. Do you imagine that things take their correct form themselves?
43. Do you feel that life is a burden?

44. Do you suffer with inferiority complex?
45. Do you usually feel nice?
46. Do you feel nice in living alone with the opposite sex?
47. Are you worried with the thought that people are looking at you?
48. Do you easily feel nervous?
49. Do you feel that you are happy in this world?
50. Are you worried about yours wisdom?
51. Do you get fearfull thought about your future?
52. Do you behave in a normal manner?
53. Was your childhood happy?
54. Do you have many true friends?
55. Do you not feel comfort for a long time?
56. Is your home atmosphere happy?
57. Do you feel afraid of competition?
58. Can you work with others in a proper manner?
59. Do you often get angry with other people?
60. Does your mood change from extreme joy to extreme pain?
61. Do you feel that others give you proper respect?
62. Do you feel that you can't control your thoughts?
63. Do you feel that sometimes people laugh at you?
64. Do you feel yourself in strained positions?
65. Are you worried with the thoughts that the things are not real?
66. Do you feel that you could not get the respect which you should have?
67. Do you feel that people do not behave with you properly?
68. Do you feel that you are not getting proper comfort in your life?
69. Do you feel often that you can't control your motions?
70. Do you repent on your actions?

11A5 MENTAL HEALTH INVENTORY

Author : V.D. Augestine.
Availability : Author, Department of Psychology, University of Madras, Post-Graduate Centre, Coimbatore.
Language : English.
Uses : To measure the mental health among individuals.
Main features : 60 items, 'Yes', 'No' type inventory. The items are in form of simple statements which express the different ways in which people think, feel and behave in their life situations.
Reliability : Reliability coefficient (Rational

Equivalance)=.79. Test-Retest reliability=.92.
Validity : Validity is established among the adult population.

11A5 MENTAL HEALTH INVENTORY

1. I am quite content the way I am now.
2. I am not a good joker.
3. My job is quite dull and boring.
4. I am not good at judging others.
5. I prefer my habitual way of living.
6. I am a victim of fate.
7. I am in the habit of disobeying meaningless rules.
8. I experience a sense of well-being.
9. I have no fear in doing a task which society criticized.
10. Mine is a very happy family.
11. I don't care much for the happiness of others, because most of them care not for mine.
12. I feel loneliness.
13. I cannot fully express my affections and genuine feelings.
14. I try to win the feelings of others.
15. I am afraid to mix with strangers.
16. I am happy to have born on this earth, in my family.
17. I like myself.
18. To my failures, mostly other people were responsible.
19. My weakness, which are known to others, do trouble me.
20. I wish to be like him (her).
21. I am afraid that my decision may go wrong.
22. I feel sorry for beggers and the handicapped.
23. Ugliness and physical defects in others, repels me.
24. Most of the people are selfish and when possible they take advantage over you.
25. Getting ahead in life is just a matter of luck and pull.
26. To me life is over the same as before.
27. I lead a kind of life that is satisfying to me.
28. A sense of fear about future bites me.
29. I behave occasionally like children-crying, laughing, playing and moving etc.
30. I am afraid of people's criticism.
31. My life is meaningful.
32. I am habitually dependent on others for ideas and decisions.
33. I am a good worker, in my little sphere.

34. I am well-rounded, square in behaviour and expressions.
35. As a mature individual I withhold my emotions from free expressions.
36. I feel that the most important thing in life is money.
37. I, in the final state, trust my own decisions than others.
38. To me, my small achievement is greater than my father's glory.
39. I am so afraid that, how I am going to manage all my family problems.
40. While introducing myself I emphasise my occupation and status.
41. I feel that most people are so unreasonable, it is hard to talk to them.
42. I have never completely revealed about myself to another.
43. I have no deep attachment with anyone.
44. I try to shape my own future and I have faith in that.
45. I do not act in ways just to please others.
46. I rarely value other peoples arguments when it contradicts mine.
47. I feel helpless.
48. In haste I decide and regret later.
49. New things about life rarely interests me.
50. To me mere material wealth is not enough for a full life.
51. I do my work just mechanically.
52. It is my habit to think about the past very frequently.
53. I wish to have a comfortable living free of all problems.
54. I have few talents to use.
55. I feel despirited.
56. I think that other people know more about me than myself.
57. There are some people I don't like.
58. I am adventurous, testing limits.
59. There is nothing real in this life.
60. If I were to be born again I would like to be the same person.

11A6 A MEASURE OF ALTRUISM

Authors : V.K. Kool and Manisha Sen.
Availability : Authors, IIT, Bombay.

Language : English.
Uses : Personality studies.
Level : Age groups above 17 years.
Main features : The final form of the questionnaire contains 23 items. The items are forced choice in nature.
Reliability : Guttman Split-half reliability = .60. Alpha reliability = .65.
Validity : The test was validated against the Buss Durkee Agression Inventory. A correlation of –.42 was obtained.

11A6 ALTRUISM TEST

1. I feel happy when I see others succeed.
2. Many times I have felt that I should not have told the source from where I had purchases some unique things e.g. bag, shirt material etc.
3. I am never happier than when alone.
4. I like to help other people who are less fortunate than I am.
5. I have often quarrels with others.
6. It is more important to work for the good of the team than to work for your own good.
7. In my school days, I offered my notes to my classmates without expecting anything in return.
8. I do not like to share my belongings or things.
9. Most people make friends because friends are likely to be useful to them.
10. Doing things for others should come before things you enjoy doing with others.
11. While waiting for a bus, if it suddenly starts raining, you would give shelter to the person next to you, who does not have an umbrella.
12. When I am in a great hurry I have often found myself pushing someone behind and making way for myself.
13. Many times I felt that I should not have helped to get change (smaller coins) while purchasing ticket in a bus, because I seldom received such help from other people.
14. I can easily make other people afraid of me and sometimes do so for the fun of it.
15. I have reason for feeling jealous of one or more members of my family.
16. One should be good to everyone, even his enemies.
17. People would be a lot better off if they could live far away from other people and never have anything to do for them.
18. I preferred to be all to myself at school.
19. I do not believe in giving donations as one never

knows where the money goes.
20. When given a task, I stick to it even if things I like to do better come along.
21. I help my friends even if I have to go out of my way to do so.
22. When I take a new job, I like to get a hint as to whom I should make friends with.
23. We should be prepared to undergo any sacrifice for the one who seeks our shelter.

11A7 ASCENDANCE SUBMISSION SCALE

Author : Kamal Dwivedi.
Availability : Agra Psychological Research Cell, Agra.
Languages : Hindi, English.
Uses : To assess the behaviour characteristics of ascendance and submission among students.
Level : University students, 15-18 years.
Main features : There are 25 statements in the scale rated on a 5-point scale.
Reliability : Test-retest reliability = .80. Internal consistency represents the reliability of the items.
Validity : The test has construct validity as has been determined by the discriminative power of items.
Norms : Percentile rank norms are available.

11A7 ASCENDANCE-SUBMISSION TEST
(The following statements have to be checked on a 5-point scale).

1. When other people talk about their abilities I also like to discuss my own.
2. I want to do much works that people may take me to a person.
3. I try to make myself important.
4. I want to do every work myself so that the credit comes to me.
5. I do not consider my friend's talk more important than mine.
6. I can accept my error only after being argumentatively proved.
7. I try to work better than others so that I may express them.
8. I try to complete my work quicker than others so that people may pay their attention to me.
9. At home I make my elders understand the dignity of my talk.
10. I can impress others as a leader.

11. I take the help of discussion to prove my ideas.
12. I am not influenced by discussions to prove my ideas.
13. I cannot bear being blamed.
14. I refuse to accept the wrong things of even my elders.
15. I can break my relations with those whose behaviour is not proper.
16. I can criticize people on their face.
17. I can not tolerate that people take me to be at all inferior than anyone.
18. I create acquaintances at important social places.
19. I can not withdraw the difference between the right and wrong just to satisfy others.
20. If I think something to be correct, I try to get it done by others also.
21. Even if circumstances compel me to do a work which appear wrong to me, I will not like to do it.
22. Without getting nervous I try to prove my ideas even people criticize me.
2 I can not accept any one's ideas without discussion.
24. Even when told, I will not like to do anything against my principles.
25. I can not ignore my wish to satisfy peυple at home.

11A8 LIAR AND CRIMINAL DETECTION TEST

Author : H.N. Singh.
Availability : Agra Psychological Research Cell, Agra.
Language : English.
Uses : To detect the liar and the criminal in a group.
Level : Schools, Colleges, Factories and Offices etc.
Main features : It is a diagnostic test based on the technique of free association. It consists of 100 words, fifty of them being detective words and the other fifty as ordinary words. Half of the detective words are related to religion and morality and the other half to prosecution and police department.

11A8 LIAR AND CRIMINAL DETECTION TEST

(The respondents have to write two response words of each stimulus word).

1. Book
2. God
3. Boy
4. Judge
5. Good
6. Moon
7. School
8. Dharamraj
9. Sleep
10. Kuran
11. Soap

12. Havalat
13. Future
14. Police
15. Doctor
16. Clock
17. Train
18. Hathkari
19. Government
20. House
21. Morality
22. Market
23. Prisoner
24. Sweet
25. Bible
26. River
27. Ganga
28. Dog
29. Prayer
30. Prosecution
31. Cheat
32. Aeroplane
33. Bushirt
34. Gita
35. Chowkidar
36. Rani
37. Habit
38. Evil
39. Love
40. Boby
41. Life
42. Taj Mahal
43. Soul
44. Fever
45. Church
46. Dhoti
47. Boat
48. Sin
49. Phansi
50. Pen
51. Gurudwara
52. House
53. Punarjanam
54. Gardan
55. Picture
56. Cycle
57. Bad
58. Mandir
59. Enemy
60. Citizen
61. Girl
62. Hell
63. S.P.
64. Thana
65. Flour
66. Theft
67. Mother
68. Murder
69. Car
70. Lie
71. Shoes
72. Military
73. Granthsahib
74. Constable
75. Father
76. Inspector
77. Ring
78. Jailor
79. Forgive
80. King
81. Heaven
82. News
83. Masjid
84. Tea
85. C.I.D.
86. Mango
87. Court
88. Marriage
89. Magistrate
90. Wine
91. Field
92. Soap
93. Prison
94. Charity
95. Bird
96. Lawyer
97. Bread
98. Lock
99. Imprisonment
100. Blue.

11A9 MENOPAUSE SYMPTOM CHECKLIST

Author : Vinod Kumar Sharma.
Languages : English, Hindi.
Availability : Author, Department of Psychology, Kumaun University Campus, Almora.
Uses : For measuring the extent of discomfort in middle-aged women as a result of the onset of menopause.
Levels : Middle-aged women above 35 years.
Main features : The check list consists of three category of symptoms—somatic, psychosomatic and psychic. There are 33 symptoms in all (11 somatic, 5 psychosomatic, and 17 psychic) related, directly or indirectly, to the menopause. Responses to each symptom are scored and quantified and over-all menopausal symptom score and three symptom sub-scorers are obtained. In this system of scoring, lower the score, lower the symptematology and vice-versa.
Reliability : Test-retest reliability corrected by the S-B prophecy formula was found to be .714 for overall menopausal symptom score and .822, .794 and .810 for psychic, psychosomatic and somatic symptom scores respectively.
Validity : Taking overall menopausal score as the base, index of reliability was worked out for the whole checklist. This work out to be .845 demonstrating how well the attained scores agree with their theoretically true values.
Time : About 15 minutes.
Norms : Available with authors.
References : Sharma, V.K. and Saxena, M.S.L. "Climateric Symptoms : A study in the Indian context" Maturitas, 1981, 3(1), 11-18.

11A9 MENOPAUSE SYMPTOM CHECKLIST
SECTION °A'

1. Hot Flashes/Flushes

(a) Have you experienced/or are experiencing hot flashes/flushes.
Currently Experiencing, Never Experienced, Stopped Experiencing.

(b) On which part of your body do you experience these.
Face or Neck, Variable Site, Over whole body.

(c) How often do hot flashes recur in your body?
Every Few Hours, Atleast once daily, Weekly or less.

(d) Since how long have you been experiencing these.

Less than six months, Between 6-12 months, More than one year.

2. Night Sweats

(a) Do You experience/have experienced night sweats. Currently Experiencing, Never Experienced, Stopped Experiencing.

(b) What is the intensity of night sweats in your body? Mild, Moderate, Severe.

(c) Since when have you been experiencing these. Less than six months, Between 6-12 months, More than one year.

3. Sleeplessness

(a) Do you experience/have experienced trouble sleeping? Currently Experiencing, Never Experienced, Stopped Experiencing.

(b) Since when have you been experiencing trouble sleeping. Less than six months, Between 6-12 months, More than one year.

(c) Which of the following symptoms accompanies sleeplessness in you. Hot and cold sweats, Sensation of falling/sinking, Fearful dreams.

SECTION 'B'
(The following statements have to be checked on 4-point scale-always to never).

1. Do you experience pounding of the heart?
2. Do you experience Dizzy Spells/Dizziness?
3. Do you suffer from Diarrhoea?
4. Do you suffer from constipation?
5. Do you generally feel tired?
6. Do you normally experience pains in the back part of the skull and neck?
7. Do you have fits of crying?
8. Do you experience black spots before the eyes?
9. Do you suffer from headaches?
10. Do you suffer from breast pains?
11. Do you experience cold sweats?
12. Do you experience numbness and tingling sensation in the hands and feet?
13. Do you suffer from swollen ankles?
14. Do you suffer from rheumatic pains?
15. Do you gain/loss weight?
16. Do you feel tense (mentally) within yourself?

17. Do you consider yourself to be a nervous person?
18. Is it generally difficult for you to concentrate?
19. Do you, without any particularly observable reason, consider your state as pathetic?
20. Is your temperament irritable?
21. Does your mind/attention fluctuate so much that you forget totally what you are doing?
22. Do you worry about something terrible and dreadful that is at hand?
23. Do you feel lonely and pent up (suffocated)?
24. Do you worry about losing your mind (being insane) in the near future?
25. Do you experience mood fluctuations?
26. Do you feel that you are getting afflicted with some dreadful diseases these days?
27. Are you worried over the possibility that in old age your physical energy would be very much reduced?
28. Do you feel restless and excited?
29. Do you feel depressed most of the time?
30. Do you feel that there are certain things in your heart which you are unable to expose?

SECTION °C'

1. Are you still menstruating?
2. When did your last menstruation take place?
3. Do you have menstrual periods smoothly or you experience some difficulty? (Please specify the difficulties, if any).

11A10 PGI HEALTH QUESTIONNAIRE N-2

Authors : N.N. Wig and S.K. Verma.
Availability : Agra Psychological Research Cell, Tiwari Kothi, Belanganj, Agra.
Languages : English, Hindi.
Uses : To measure neuroticism in our population.
Level : All educational levels, adults, Hindi or English Knowing Indians.
Main features : For neuroticism = 50 items.
For lie scale = 10 items.
Item selected from our own patients spontaneous complaints.
Reliability : Test-retest reliability = .82 KR_{21} = .92.
Split-half reliability = .92 KR_{20} = .92.
Index of reliability = .95 Flanagan Formula = .84.
Validity :
(1) Discriminated neurotics normals ($p < .01$),

(2) Each item discriminated neurotics normals ($p < .01$),
(3) Correlation with other scale (CMI, PEN, MHQ etc.) and
(4) Cross-validation from other centres in India.

Time : Five to seven minutes.

Norms : Available with authors.

References :

Verma, S.K. (1978) Construction and standardization of PGI Health Questionnaire N-2. Agra Psychological Research Cell, Tiwari Kothi, Belanganj, Agra.

Verma, S.K. (1978) Manual for PGI Health Questionnaire N-2. Agra Psychological Research Cell, Agra.

Verma,S.K. (1980) The index for PGI Health Questionnaire N-2. Indian Psychological Review, 19(4), 52-53.

Verma, S.K., Pershad, D. and Wig, N.N. (1979) Additional data on PGI Health Questionnaire N-2. Indian Psychological Review, 17(1), 47-50.

11A10 PGI HEALTH QUESTIONNAIRE N-2

1. I often get watering of the eyes.
2. I feel heaviness of the eyes.
3. I feel burning sensation in the eyes.
4. My appetite is not good.
5. My digestion is poor.
6. I belch a lot after eating.
7. I have often a bad taste in my mouth.
8. I often got wind formation (gas) in my stomach.
9. I feel heaviness of stomach and often it gets bloated.
10. I often have to go to toilet straight after meals.
11. I feel burning and pain in stomach.
12. I often feel sick (feel like vomiting).
13. I feel very thirsty.
14. I have got useless fears like—fear of dark, fear of crowds, fear of closed spaces etc.
15. I don't get proper sleep.
16. My health is getting weak.
17. I feel shaky in my body and limbs.
18. I suffer from backache.
19. I feel tired all the time
20. I want to do many a things but really I am unable to do anything.
21. I don't feel interested in doing anything.
22. I feel heaviness of the head.
23. I feel as if my head is going to burst.
24. I often get headaches.
25. I feel a great heat in my body.

26. I feel whatever is going to happen will be bad for me.
27. I feel sinking of my heart.
28. I feel nervous.
29. I feel that my mind is getting blank.
30. I find difficulty in passing water.
31. I get fainting fits.
32. I feel tense cor remain worried).
33. I feel my mind is getting weak and I cannot understand anything.
34. I am becoming foregetful.
35. I feel scared if some one speaks loudly.
36. I remain frightened all the time, not sure what will happen.
37. I feel mixed up when I talk to others.
38. I cannot tolerate loud noise.
39. I get easily irritated.
40. I have become superstitious.
41. Many bad (or, meaningless) ideas repeatedly come in my mind.
42. If something bad happens, I cannot get it out of my mind.
43. I don't feel like talking to or mixing with anybody.
44. I feel like crying.
45. I don't feel happy.
46. I have no feelings left even for my wife and children (or close family members).
47. I feel like running away from it all.
48. Sometimes I feel like ending my life.
49. I feel afraid that I may have got some incurable disease.
50. I find no relief even after consulting many doctors.
51. I have never lost my temper.
52. All my habits are good.
53. I always speak the truth.
54. I always remain calm and composed.
55. Nothing ever irritates me.
56. I never hide anything from anybody.
57. I never criticize anybody behind his back.
58. I never really like people praising me.
59. I never make loose talk.
60. I always like everybody.

11A11 GANDHIAN PERSONALITY (NON-VIOLENCE) SCALE

Author : Qamar Hasan
Availability : Author, Department of sychology. Aligarh Muslim University, Aligarh.

Language : English, Hindi.
Uses : As a research tool in experimental and correlational studies where non-violence is considered as a factor.
Level : Adults.
Main features : Number of items 58, selected on the basis of Likert's technique of Attitudes Scale Construction, Factor Analysis, for identification of dimensions of non-violence personality.
Reliability : Split-half r = .85.
Validity : Studies in progress.
Time : Thirty minutes.
Norms : Not yet prepared.
Reference : Hasan, Qamar & Khan, Shamsur Rehman. Measurement of Gandhian (Non-violent) Personality. 69th Session of Indian Science Congress, Mysore, 1982.

11A11 G.P. SCALE
(The following statements have to be checked on 6-point scale).

1. It is not possible for us to keep our emotions in check.
2. The life of birds and animals is not as important as that of man.
3. Forgiveness is the sign of weakness and revenge is the sign of courage.
4. Forgiveness is more manly than revenge.
5. Whatever may be circumstances running away from danger is better than putting one's life in danger.
6. It is impossible to distinguish between sinner and his sin. The sinner deserves as much hatred as his sin.
7. Life is valuable. If it comes to that, it is better to kill the other than to be killed by them.
8. Deep study of books of different religions reveal that basic principles of all religions are same.
9. There will be no peace in the world till the time when all humanity comes to believe in one religion.
10. With the use of impure means it is impossible to get at pure ends.
11. Society should make such arrangements as scientists, technicians and similar other well educated people have not to waste their time and energy in manual labour.
12. Disclosing his weakness and faults the individual looses his prestige.
13. Any fair or foul means should be adopted to realize a noble goal.

14. While talking about harsh facts there is no need of politeness of words and tone.
15. It is impossible for an individual to modify his understanding that he has once come to what is good and what is bad.
16. A man who follows his principles honestly can get respect from his opponents.
17. We inwardly dislike the pain we have to bear while extending helping hand to others.
18. This world is wholly governed by physical forces such as those of gravitation and chemical reactions.
19. An individual can change himself if he decides to do so.
20. Man is a toy in the hands of external forces.
21. There is always a selfish motive behind act of kindness and generosity.
22. It is natural and normal to go on living under all circumstances. There is something wrong with anyone who does not fear death.
23. Every person has a duty to keep others and not to do any thing which may harm them.
24. To understand this world personal experience is a must; knowing ideas of others and following their style of life is not enough.
25. Moral principles can only be believed in, but it is impossible to act according to these principles.
26. To get success it is important to conceal one's feeling and to manifest socially desirable behaviour.
27. It is foolish to think that international relations instead of being based on bargaining can be based on mutual trust and goodwill.
28. It is impossible for a polite person to be socially effective.
29. By spontaneous expression of one's dispositions and free talking about private affairs an individual comes down in the estimate of others.
30. No doubt fighting against one's enemy is bravery but to bear opponents' aggression without slightest relation or illwill is bravery of still more higher order.
31. Moving in accordance with prompting of inner voice an individual can face all sorts of dangers.
32. Truth and honesty are of no use in the field of trade and commerce.
33. Society is inconceivable without police.
34. Every individual has animal-like brutal tendencies concealed within himself which do not come out due

to fear of society.

35. Foreign relations are inconceivable without army, navy and air force needed to keep intact the term of treaties signed with foreign countries.
36. Weak and helpless individuals should seek the shelter with the powerful so as to avoid difficulties of life.
37. Politic is a game of power. Honesty and truth have no place in it.
38. It is useful to make an attempt to search out those social workers who serve people without considerations of personal gains.
39. °Tit for tat' is a realistic and practical principle of life.
40. No one can claim to be brave without taking arms.
41. I would not like to accept before others dirty thoughts coming in my mind.
42. When someone cheats me I feel that I should pay him in the same coins.
43. I like to do nursing.
44. Anyone would lie to get advantage and to get ahead.
45. The secret of honesty is that people are fearful of ignominy and punishment.
46. If I found that someone is being kind to me without any reason I become suspicious that he wants to get some advantage out of me.
47. I am not as much kind hearted as to be bothered by the sight of animal in trouble.
48. I have a plan to realize certain aims in my life and I continue to work according to that plan.
49. I can be friendly with people who do things which I consider wrong.
50. I do not like the games which I have not properly learned to play.
51. I think that anybody would tell a lie to keep out of trouble.
52. While extending helping hand to others people inwardly think that they unnecessarily involved themselves in trouble.
53. I firmly believe that there is only one true religion whose principle show the correct path of life.
54. I have no enemy looking for a chance to harm me.
55. When solving a problem I am enclined to consider all possibilities even though some are unrealistic and absurd.
56. There is possibility that country's economic growth would be blocked if people began to accept the view-

point that they should limit their needs.

57. Nature has created everything for human being. Man has, therefore, every right to use all the things in whatever way he lives.
58. A person can not adopt the same means for settling his disputes with remotely-related or unrelated people as he uses for setting his disputes with close relatives like father, mother, brother and sister.

11A12 THE NON-VIOLENCE TEST

Authors : V.K. Kool and Manisha Sen.
Availability : Indian Institute of Technology, Bombay.
Language : English.
Uses : Personality studies.
Level : Age Groups : above 17 years.
Main features : Yes-No type thirtyseven items.
Reliabilitv : Guttman split-half r = .78, Alpha reliability = .82.
Validity : Correlation of -.44 with Buss-Durkee Aggression Scale.
Time : No limit.
Norms : No.
Reference : Manisha Sen : Reduction of aggression in violent and non-violent individuals. Ph.D. thesis, IIT, Bombay, 1981.

11A12 THE NON-VIOLENCE TEST

1. A fast running car occasioned patches of water deposits on the road to fall upon passers-by. Some of them wanted to
   (a) compel him to cover the loss and apologise
   (b) make him understand that he should be more careful in future.
2. The more I think of the evils of a person present before me,
   (a) the more insight I get in human relationship for better adjustment with that person.
   (b) the more get irritated and tell the person off (if possible).
3. Despite my repeated requests, if a person keeps irritating me, I will
   (a) give him a hard slap
   (b) control myself.
4. When someone deserves criticism
   (a) I do not like criticizing him

(b) I enjoy criticizing him.

5. I believe in
   (a) forgive and forget is the best policy
   (b) a tooth for a tooth and an eye for an eye.
6. Your view on hunting is
   (a) you don't mind others hunting
   (b) you are against hunting.
7. Workers on an unlawful strike should be
   (a) approached and a compromise be negotiated
   (b) thrown out of job without any notice.
8. When a person is rude to him
   (a) I wait for an opportunity to give him back
   (b) I try to overcome the temptation to be rude.
9. It was found that some high officials were taking bribes. A number of steps were suggested
   (a) pardoned with minimum possible punishment provided they apologise
   (b) publically flogged and taken in a procession on a donkey with a blackened face and thrown out of job.
10. When people are rude or annoying I have
   (a) at times had to be rough with them
   (b) never been rough with them but are dealt with understanding.
11. A pickpocketer when caught should be
   (a) given a beating and deprived of all his possessions
   (b) put in a reformatory home or school.
12. Lawbreakers must be
   (a) Brought to justice but justice must be tempered with mercy
   (b) severely punished.
13. When I see a thief being beaten up by a few people
   (a) I think to myself that he deserves it to some extent
   (b) I like to disuade the people from beating the thief.
14. A boy was very mischievous and would beat other boys of the locality. They were angry and wanted to punish him. The suggestions offered were :
   (a) boycott him from the group
   (b) try to change his habits by way of goodwill and understanding.
15. When I hold a poor opinion of a person
   (a) I do not try to cover it so that he won't know how I feel
   (b) I try to cover it and try to make him better without his knowing it.

16. As far as teasing is concerned
    (a) I enjoy teasing
    (b) I do not tease until and unless I find out the reason why someone teased me and my teasing in return is essential.
17. When a person subordinate in rank refuses to carry orders you would
    (a) force him to do it or else fire him
    (b) convince him of its necessity so that he does it.
18. A person who commits a murder should be
    (a) given minimum punishment possible under the circumstances with an emphasis to rehabilitate him.
    (b) dealt with the principle "life for life".
19. When someone does me a wrong
    (a) I feel I should pay him back, if I can; just for the principle of the thing
    (b) I do not pay him back but try to show him his mistake.
20. All those who rebel should be
    (a) punished
    (b) given minimum punishment and treated in a human way.
21. In a restaurant, if a waiter is rude to you, you will
    (a) complain to the manager and see that some action is taken against him
    (b) explain to him as to how a waiter should behave.
22. If some one criticises me, I
    (a) do not present counter criticism but put forth my arguments in an effective and appealing manner
    (b) like to present counter criticism instantly.
23. Feeling of strength only comes when one can
    (a) force others into doing things one's own way
    (b) not forcing others into doing things one's own way but by convincing others to do it one's own way.
24. When a person makes fun of me, I
    (a) try and convince the person for sometime at least
    (b) retaliate immediately.
25. In politics, defectors from the party should be
    (a) made to understand the harmful effects of defection on the party
    (b) made to retire compulsorily from their political career.
26. Sex crimes such as rape and attacks on children, deserve :

(a) not mere imprisonment, such criminals should be given psychiatric attention first and then put in prison

(b) more than mere imprisonment, such criminals ought to be publically whipped or worse.

27. On some occasions, when scolded by my parents, I had :

(a) shown resentment

(b) tried to reason with myself to understand their position.

28. Efficient working is possible only when people are kept in

(a) a congenial atmosphere without terror

(b) some amount of terror.

29. When I am disturbed, say while studying

(a) my first reaction will be to get angry

(b) I will try to win over the person by explaining to him rather than getting angry.

30. At a lecture where a speaker seems unable to make up his mind as to what he really believes I would like to do the following :

(a) feel like helping him to improve his contention

(b) stop him completely and ask him to leave.

31. A man persistently gave false witness against his colleagues (in law courts). They met to do something against him.

(a) some suggested that he should go back to the court and admit his mistake

(b) some spoke of giving him a hard beating.

32. If a person jumps queue and stands ahead of me :

(a) I will bypass him and stand ahead of him

(b) I will persuade him to go back.

33. If students misbehave with teachers in school, they (teachers) should :

(a) give intermittent dozes of punishment as and when needed

(b) consider some of the ways in which they themselves might have been responsible for occurrence of such behaviour before any other step is taken.

34. If a person harms you and your family, you will

(a) wait for a suitable opportunity to retaliate

(b) ignore his act.

35. A poor man's land was forcibly occupied by his rich neighbours. The following suggestions were made to the person :

(a) forcibly occupy not only his own land but if possible some part of the rich man's land

(b) to move to the court when all other peaceful

methods fail.

36. When things go wrong because of others
    (a) I retaliate
    (b) I do not retaliate.
37. If a teacher cuts marks unjustifiably, you will
    (a) tell your low opinion about him
    (b) ignore it as it doesn't matter in the long run.

11A13 SENTENCE COMPLETION TEST (SCT)

Author : Govind Tiwari.
Availability : Agra Psychological Research Cell, Belanganj, Agra.
Languages : English, Hindi.
Uses : To measure interpersonal as well as intrapersonal conflicts of individuals.
Main features : The test has fifty items and covers interpersonal (home, school, work, neighbours, religion, political and economic) as well as intrapersonal (drive, environmental conditions, anxiety, aggression, etc.) conflict areas of an individual. The items have been collected from available tests and experienced psychologists.

11A13 SENTENCE COMPLETION TEST (SCT)

1. I feel proud when
2. Usually other people
3. My hope is
4. My past
5. My parents
6. My School/Home work
7. Usually My time
8. In My opinion quarrel
9. Our family
10. I feel
11. My friends
12. My Mother
13. Illness
14. When I was Child then
15. In my opinion, Religion
16. Thinking or doing of suicide
17. I like to see people as
18. At that time I feel angry when
19. My dreams
20. God
21. My neighbour
22. My biggest ambition is

23. Employment is absolutely necessary for livelihood
24. Modern Girls
25. The journey of life is pleasent if
26. I feel fear that my mother
27. If I
28. Childhood
29. I always think
30. Oftenly, I think
31. My
32. Sexual relation
33. On the inquiry of my family
34. People believe me or not
35. Sometimes such occasions arives
36. Talk ill at one's back
37. If there is domestic quarries
38. I
39. I hate too much that person
40. My heartiest desire is
41. I am with them
42. Economically
43. Sometimes worries
44. Reading and writing
45. The Laws of Government
46. During that period I am unable to control
47. Sometimes to be friend or to give up friendship
48. I never like to see
49. Mostly, I spent my time
50. I am interested to know

11A14 INCOMPLETE SENTENCE TEST

Author : C.G. Deshpande.
Availability : Author, Department of Psychology, University of Poona, Pune.
Languages : English, Marathi.
Uses : To analyse stressful or conflictive thoughts.
Level : College level and above.
Main features : Thirty items. It measures conflictive or stressful thoughts relating to (i) Past life, (ii) Present condition, (iii) Future life, (iv) Family life and (v) Social life.
Reliability : Split-half reliability is .87.
Validity : Validity measured against marital adjustment is .32 and against personal adjustment is .46.
Time : About 25 minutes.
Norms : Available with author.

11A14 INCOMPLETE SENTENCE TEST

1. Considering the future life I think that
2. As I look back to my life I feel
3. In my family
4. My parents are
5. My relatives
6. While living a life
7. In our society
8. In day-to-day life
9. My siblings are
10. My childhood recollections are
11. While living in a family
12. As I experience social life I feel
13. I shall
14. While living in a society
15. In my life
16. My relations with family members are
17. When I was a boy/girl
18. Regarding my school experiences
19. My life goal is
20. On the whole my family life is
21. While thinking about a society
22. Regarding my present life experiences
23. My future plans are
24. As I think about my friends I feel
25. At present my life is
26. My past life was
27. As I think about the next ten years
28. The important recollection of my life is
29. As I think to myself it appears to me
30. In the near future I shall

11A15 ANTI-DEMOCRATIC AND FASCIST SCALE

Author : P.K. Muttagi.
Availability : Tata Institute of Social Sciences, Deonar, Bombay.
Language : English.
Main features : The scale is a modified instrument based on the anti-semitism scale, ethnocentrism scale and politico-economic conservatism scale of the California studies. The scale consists of sixty items. These have been broadly divided into two categories. Thirty statements were supposed to reveal anti-democratic tendencies, remaining thirty fascist tendencies. These two scales were further divided into 3 sub-scales. The scoring is done on a 5-point scale. The scale reveals the following attitudes :

i Submissive attitudes, militancy.
ii Cynicism, conservation and reactionary tendencies.
iii Criminality, physical attack and fascist solution.
iv Segregation and suppression.
v Aggression toward religious minorities, and
vi Aggression toward linguistic minorities.

Reference :

Muttagi, P.K. An investigation into the cross community attitudes of students of under graduate and post graduate class in the University of Bombay. Unpublished Ph.D. Dissertation, University of Bombay, 1970.

Muttagi, P.K. Attitude Change : Impact of training for democracy. Indian journal of Social Work, 1974, 35(1), 47-56.

11A15 ANTI-DEMOCRATIC AND FASCIST SCALE
(The following statements have to be checked on 5-point scale of agreement)

1. People must have deep faith in supernatural forces.
2. India should be a theocratic state.
3. Religious preachings are to be obeyed uncritically and without questioning.
4. Parents and religious authorities should be looked upon as infallible.
5. India needs more autocratic leadership.
6. Military training must be compulsory for all.
7. No step taken is bad to wipe out socially useless people like the insane, the crippled etc.
8. Anti-social elements like criminals should be persecuted.
9. If necessary, sacrifice of a few individuals' lives for the benefit of the society should be encouraged.
10. There is no use wasting money on treating the very old people and those suffering from incurable diseases.
11. Compulsory sterilization of the criminals and mentally inferior people will prove good for the country.
12. Only people belonging to martial races can fight and defend our nation.
13. Caste system is created by God on the basis of virtues and past deeds. We have no control over them.
14. Untouchables are born inferior.
15. Only a few communities are capable of producing the

best in civilization.

16. Certain communities are fit for only manual labour and unskilled jobs.
17. There always will be inferior and superior communities. In the interest of all, superior community alone should rule.
18. The tribal people and Adivasis have not progressed because they are incapable of mental development.
19. People born in higher religious communities deserve preferential treatment, by virtue of their birth.
20. Sons of only rich people deserve higher education.
21. Since Indians are unfit for self-rule, foreigners should take over the administration.
22. War and conflicts are inevitable for the progress of mankind.
2 Persons belonging to higher castes alone should learn the religious scriptures.
24. Citizens should take permission of the government about the sale and purchase of their private properties.
25. Celebrations of religious festivals must be banned.
26. Intercommunity marriages should be declared illegal.
27. High court judges should always be selected from among the natives of the particular state.
28. There is nothing wrong in forced religious conversion.
29. There should be separate restaurants and cafes for the people of different religious communities.
30. Some people should be forced to do manual labour even if it is against their will.
31. Government being the supreme and final authority, an individual has no right to appeal against its decision.
32. All properties should belong to the state and no individual has any right to own anything.
33. Newspapers and magazines, criticising the government should be banned.
34. Freedom of political parties must be completely suppressed for all times.
35. Not all persons should be allowed to vote particularly when the large percentage is uneducated population.
36. Morchas, agitations and strikes should be crushed at any cost.
37. Trade Union Movement in India should be banned.
38. The government must be kept informed by all the citizens about the political activities.
39. Laws of the State should be exclusively in favour of

the poor people.

40. Women should take up feminine positions. They should not be allowed to compete with men.
41. There is nothing wrong in employing children and minors in factories, mines, hotels etc.
42. Government has every right to detain individuals in custody indefinitely without trial.
43. There is nothing wrong in creating chaotic conditions or disturbances leading to violence if it can establish justice and peace permanently.
44. Certain religious communities should be given favourable treatment due to their numerical superiority.
45. Persons not belonging to a particular linguistic state, even though Indians, should not be given the same rights and privileges as those belonging to the state.
46. Certain highly technical and skilled jobs should be reserved only for some religious communities to prevent the inefficient communities from entry.

For the sake of Unity of India there should be :

47. (a) only one language spoken by all.
48. (b) only one religion followed by all.
49. Reports of linguistic communalism or fanaticism in India are only exaggerations by the newspapers.
50. To prevent subversive activities religious minorities should not be employed in the establishments like atomic energy, aircraft factories.
51. If members from other states do not learn the local language, they should be sent back to their respective states.
52. A linguistic minority community should not be allowed to have a cultural organisation of its own.
53. High government offices should be reserved to a few selected religious communities.
54. Public harassment of some linguistic minorities is cometimes good as it teaches a lesson to them.
55. Place of birth should be an important factor in giving jobs and promotions.
56. It is a mistake to give the same educational facilities to all the linguistic communities in the state.
57. Beggars should be prosecuted.
58. Employment exchanges should be exclusively manned by people of linguistic majority community.
59. People of linguistic majority community should be given preferences in all government and private employment.

60. Military should take over the administration of India.

instruments with technical information **B**

11B1 THEMATIC APPERCEPTION TECHNIQUE

Author : S.C. Gupta.
Availability : Psychological Corporation, Shanti Sadan, Rai Beharilal Road, Lucknow.
Main features : There are 12 pictorial cards categorised on a 5-point scale. Cards portray certain common social situations and family relationships as observed in our culture. The cards are arranged for males, females and for both sexes separately. The nature of the contents on each card is as under :

IM -A boy engrossed in watching at a zoo park.
2M -Two young adolescents preoccupied with some common problem.
3M -An adult male on a bicycle.
4M -Two young men holding argument.
1F -A female child with background of a female shadow.
2F -An adolescent girl standing with support of a pillar.
3F -A village woman fetching water.
4F -An aged couple in presence of their two daughters-in-law.
IMF -A young man standing in a dilapidated house.
2MF -A young couple sitting preoccupied.
3MF -A Tonga carrying some children and adults.
4MF -Aged parents watching at their son and daughter-in-law leaving home.

11B2 MULTIVARIABLE PERSONALITY QUESTIONNAIRE

Authors : D.M. estonjee, A.P. Singh and U.B. Singh.
Availability : The Authors, Indian Institute of Management, Ahmedabad.
Language : Hindi.
Uses : To measure the general personality traits of individuals.

Level : Adolescents and Adults.
Main features : The questionnaire contains 153 items and measures such personality dimensions as alienation, dogmatism, extraversion, introversion, psychoticism, ego-ideal, self-confidence, dominance and empathy.
Reliability : In process.
Validity : In process.

11B3 WHAT KIND OF PERSON ARE YOU ? TEST.

Authors : Badrun Nisha and Kiran Gupta.
Availability : National Psychological Corporation, 4/230 Kacheri Ghat, Agra.
Language : Hindi.
Uses : To measure creative personality.
Level : From High School students to adults.
Main features : Fifty forced choice items.
Reliability : Split-half r = .96 (N = 200), K-R r = .94 (N = 200), and test-retest r = .68 to .90.
Validity : Validity coefficient against Torrance & Khatena is .68 (N = 100), against self ratings of 100 psychology students = .41, and against self ratings of 100 college freshmen = .33.
Time : There is no time limit for the test, but most Ss complete the test in 10 to 15 minutes.
Norms : T-Score norms available.

11B4 PUNCTUALITY SCALE

Authors : Q.G. Alam and Ramji Srivastava.
Availability : Authors, Department of Psychology, S.N. College, Azamgarh.
Language : Hindi.
Uses : To discriminate punctuals from non-punctuals in studies of personality.
Level : Adults.
Main features : Sixty positively and negatively worded items. A five point scale is used for obtaining responses.
Reliability : Test-retest reliability coefficient = .73, S.B. formula = .71.
Validity : Established.
Time : About 25 minutes.
Norms : Norms based on °T' scores available from authors.

11B5 SPORTSMAN SPIRIT TEST

Author : L.N. Dubey.

Availability : Agra Psychological Research Cell, Belanganj, Agra.
Language : Hindi.
Uses : To discriminate sportsman having high degree of sportsman spirit.
Level : School, College & University boys and girls of 16 to 26 years of age.
Main features : The test has 40-items each consists of three alternative responses.
Reliability : Spearman Brown Formula (Split-half method) = .896 and Kuder Richardson formula (R.E. method) = .877.
Validity : Predictive validity of the test is established by correlating the test scores with rating scores of the teachers, physical instructors and captains.
Norms : Classification according to range of scores, given in the manual.

11B6 RADICAL CONSERVATIVE ATTITUDE SCALE

Author : L.N. Dubey.
Availability : Agra Psychological Research Cell, Belanganj, Agra.
Language : Hindi.
Uses : To discriminate people according to their attitude towards conservatism or radicalism as a whole as well as in three areas - social, personal and religion.
Level : College students, 16-21 years.
Main features The scale consists of 60-items distributed into three areas - personal, social & religion. There are 20 items in each area. Each item has five alternative choices.
Reliability : Reliability coefficient by K.R. formula = .86, and by split-half = .91.
Validity : Item analysis validity coefficient was determined for each item by biserial correlation method. Intercorrelations among the three areas of the scale were found highly significant.

11B7 RADICALISM CONSERVATISM REACTION STUDY SCALE

Author : V.K. Mittal.
Availability : Department of Psychology, Meerut College, Meerut.
Language : Hindi.
Main features : This is a Likert type scale with 18-items representing varied areas.
Reliability : Split-half reliability = .73.
Validity : Besides content validity, the scale is validated

against Rural and Urban group iserial 'r' between the two group is .613.
Norms : Percentile norms are available.

11B8 LAW ABIDINGNESS SCALE

Author : V.K. Mittal.
Availability : Author, Department of Psychology, Meerut College, Meerut.
Language : Hindi.
Main features : A Thurstone type scale consisting of 14 items. Each item contains several alternative response statements. The respondent is required to check one of the alternatives most applicable to him. Items are selected on the basis of judge's ratings.
Reliability : Split-half reliability = .80.
Norms : Percentile norms are available.

11B9 SOCIAL PERCEPTION SCALE : A MEASURE OF RISK TAKING BEHAVIOUR

Author : S.M. Anwar Yousuf.
Language : Hindi.
Availability : Author, A.N. Sinha Institute of Social Studies, Patna.
Uses : To measure the tendency of risk.
Levels : For adult people.
Main features : Ten items. Four point scale.
Reliability : Split-half reliability is 0.67 and after applying Spearman - Brown prophecy formula the test reliability becomes 0.81.
Validity : The construct validity of the scale with CDQ AND BPS are 0.66 and 0.56 respectively.
Time : Thirty minutes (approximately).
Norms : No norms.
Reference : Anwar Yousuf, S.M. Social Perception Scale : A measure of risk taking behaviour. Journal of Social & Economic Studies, 1981, 9(1), 67-72.

11B10 PERSISTENCE QUESTIONNAIRE

Authors : Nisha Dhawan & Durgananad Sinha.
Availability : Department of Psychology, University of Allahabad, Allahabad.
Language : Hindi.
Uses : To provide a quick and reliable assessment of an individual's persistence level in the context of achievement, learning, and education.

Levels : Adolescents and young adults of the 14 to 25 age group.
Main features : The items on the questionnaire are based on a conceptualisation of °persistence' as a motivational component of behaviour and refers to the strength which sustains activity towards a goal, displayed through continuous string, adherence to target, and completion of task despite failure and obstacles. There are twenty items with forced choice (yes/no) responses.
Reliability : The test-retest reliability is .82 and the split-half reliability coefficient is .92 (N = 200).
Validity : The test has been validated against a projective test of persistence (developed by the author) with r = .49 (N = 200).
Time : Approximately 15 to 20 minutes.
Norms : Not available at present (are being prepared).

11B11 A TRAIT RATING SCHEDULE

Author : R.R. Tripathi.
Availability : Author, Department of Psychology, Banaras Hindu University, Varanasi.
Language : Hindi.
Uses : A quick screening instrument for selection, guidance and counselling.
Level : Meant for adults and college students.
Main features : Seven point rating instrument covering ten broad based personality traits such as ego-strength, emotional control, social adjustment etc.
Reliability : Internal consistency index (coefficient alpha) = .929, and stability coefficient = .82.
Validity : Validity coefficient ....79.
Time : Takes around 10 to 15 minutes for individual administration.

11B12 A MEASURE OF MANIFEST HOSTILITY

Author : V.K. Kool.
Availability : Author, Indian Institute of Technology, Bombay.
Language : Hindi.
Uses : Personality studies, to measure hostility.
Level : Above seventeen years.
Main features : Yes-no-tvpe as prepared by Siagel.
Reliability : Test-retest reliability = .67.
Validity : Established.
Time : No limit.
Norms : No.

Reference : Kool, V.K. Measures of authoritarianism and hostility.
Bombay : Himalaya Publ. House, 1980.
Kool, V.K. and John Ray. ^uthoritarianism across cultures. Bombay : Himalaya Publ. House, in press.

11B13 A COMPOSITE SCALE OF AUTHORITARIANISM

Author : V.K. Kool.
Availability : Author, Indian Institute of Technology, Bombay.
Language : Hindi.
Uses : Personality studies, to measure authoritarianism.
Level : Above seventeen years.
Main features : Likert type 23-items.
Reliability : Test-retest is .80.
Validity : High correlation (.33) with a personali+v --s-re of authoritarianism.
Time : No limit.
Norms : No.
Reference : Kool, V.K. Measures of authoritarianism and hostility. Bombay : Himalaya Publ. House, 1980.
Kool, V.K. and John Ray Authoritarianism across cultures. Bombay : Hlimalaya Publ. House, in press.

11B14 A PERSONALITY ORIENTED MEASURE OF AUTHORITARIANISM

Author : V.K. Kool.
Availability : Author, Indian Institute of Technology, Bombay.
Language : Hindi.
Uses : Personality studies, to measure authoritarianism.
Level : Above seventeen years.
Main features : Yes-no-type items.
Reliability : ‾est-retest is .62 (N = 52).
Validity : External criterion validity = .26 (N = 252).
Time : No limit.
Norms : No.
Reference : Kool, V.K. Measures of authoritarianism and hostility. Bombay : Himalaya Publ. House, 1980.
Kool, V.K. and John Ray : Authoritarianism across cultures. ‾ombay : Himalaya Publ. House, in press.

11B15 INDIAN F-SCALE

Author : L.I. Bhushan
Availability : M/s National Psychological Corporation, Kacheri Ghat, Agra.

Language : Hindi.
Uses : To measure authoritarianism.
Level : Adolescents & adults.
Main features : Seven point Likert type scale contains 35-items including six negative items.
Time : About thirty minutes.
Reference : Bhushan, L.I. Cluster analysis of the Indian F-Scale. Indian Journal of Psychology, 1978, 53(4), 177-182.

11B16 FRUSTRATION SCALE (FORMS A & B)

Author : R.P. Gupta.
Availability : Psychological Centre, 569 Ch/26K-2, Prem Nagar, Alambagh, Lucknow.
Language : Hindi.
Uses : To study the frustration states through verbal statements.
Level : Literate Hindi knowing adolescents and adults.
Main features : Twenty-one items in the main body of each form A & B, preceded by two similar practice examples.
Reliability : +.87 (The details are given in the manual).
Validity : +.61 (The details are given in the manual)
Time : About one hour though there is no time limit.
Norms : Percentile norms, in the manual.
Reference : Sinha, Mukul : Unpublished M.Ed. Thesis, Department of Education, Lucknow University, Lucknow, 1981.

11B17 FRUSTRATION TEST

Authors : N.S. Chauhan & Govind Tiwari.
Availability : Agra Psychological Research Cell, Belanganj, Agra.
Language : Hindi.
Uses : To study the effect of frustration upon the quality of a persons behaviour as a whole
Main features : The scale consists of 40-items and measures four modes of frustration as regression, fixation, resignation and aggression. Each mode has 10-items. The items are presented in simple and brisk style. Each item has five answers (multiple choice) graded on five points scale.
Level : School & College students and adults. Literate as well as illiterate population.
Reliability : Test-retest reliability on a sample of thirtyfive adult has been found as under.

Regression	Fixation	Resignation	Agression	As a whole

.78 .92 .85 .87 .88

Validity : Not given.
Norms : Percentile norms are available.
Reference : Chauhan, N.S. and Tiwari, G.P. Interest modality as a function of frustration. Journal of Madras Psychological Society, Madras (Accepted, 1972).

11B18 SAMASYA-SAMADHAN-VYAVAHAR MAPNI

Authors : Om Prakash Srivastava & R.K. Naidu.
Availability : Authors, Department of Psychology, University of Allahabad, Allahabad.
Language : Hindi.
Uses : To evaluate the coping responses of physically handicapped subjects in terms of the immediate emotional reaction to the stressful situation as well as the whole range of subsequent responses to the stressful life event.
Level : Physically handicapped children and adolescents.
Main features : It consisted of 2 parts

i. Part-I List of Immediate Emotional Experiences which consisted of 11 items of which six were negative and five were positive emotional experiences related to stressful life events.
ii Part-II Schedule of Coping Responses which consisted of 59 items which dealt with the strategies used for handling stressful life events. Out of these 59 items, 17 were task-related (coping) items, forty were non-task-related (defensive) items and two were amb'guous items.

Reliability : Not reported.
Validity : Not available.
Time : Twentyfive minutes.
Norms : Not available.
Reference : Srivastava, O.P. (1981) Stresses and coping mechanisms of physically handicapped children. D.Phil thesis, University of Allahabad.

11B19 STRESS SCALE

Authors : Om Prakash Srivastava and R.K. Naidu.
Availability : Authors, Department of Psychology, University of Allahabad, Allahabad.
Language : Hindi.
Uses : To assess the stresses frequency of actual occurence and perceived significance to which physically handicapped subjects are exposed.
Level : Physically handicapped children and adolescents.

Main features : It consisted of 44-items covering the following ten categories of stressors : Interpersonal Relations, Economic Difficulties, Ego-related (threat), Bereavement, Perceived Personal Inadequacy, Separation and Isolation, Training and Work Related, Uncertainty regarding future, problems related to living conditions.
Reliability : Test-retest reliability was found to be .70.
Validity : Not available.
Time : Twenty minutes.
Norms : Not available.
Reference : Srivastava, O.P. Stress and coping mechanisms of physically handicapped children. D.Phil thesis, University of Allahabad, 1981.

11B20 STRAIN SCALE

Authors : R.D. Caplan & R.K. Naidu.
Availability : Authors, Department of Psychology, University of Allahabad, Allahabad.
Languages : Hindi and English.
Uses : To measure person-environment fit among.
Level : University students.
Main features : Consisted of 38 items designed to measure state of health (present) on a 4 point response scale : Never, Rarely, Often, Almost Always.
Reliability : Coefficient alpha - the coefficient of internal consistency was computed, correlation between items was also computed, ten indices were found and r values ranged from .30 to .75 and alpha ranged from .57 to .88.
Validity : Not available.
Time : On an average ten minutes.
Norms : Not available.
Reference : Caplan, R.D. & Naidu, R.K. Stress, coping and social support : A study of University students in India.

11B21 LOCUS OF CONTROL SCALE

Authors : R.D. Caplan & R.K. Naidu.
Availability : The Second Author, Department of Psychology, University of Allahabad, Allahabad.
Languages : Hindi & English.
Uses : To measure person environment fit among university students.
Level : University students.
Main features : It consisted of 8-items designed to measure the causes attributed by students for obtaining good grades. Subjects responded on a 5-point response scale.

Reliability : Coefficient alpha the coefficient of internal consistency was computed. Correlation between items was also computed. Two indices were found and r values ranged from .37 to .57 and alpha values ranged from .54 to .73.
Validity : Not available.
Time : Average five minutes.
Norms : Not available.
Reference : Caplan, R.D. and Naidu, R.K. Stress, coping and social support : A study of University students in India.

11B22 COPING AND DEFENSE SCALE

Authors : R.D. Caplan & R.K. Naidu.
Availability : Authors, Department of Psychology, University of Allahabad, Allahabad.
Languages : Hindi & English.
Uses : To measure person-environment fit among University students.
Level : University students.
Main features : It consisted of 48-items designed to measure coping and defense styles employed when examination results were not what was desired. Subjects responded on a 5-point response scale.
Reliability : Coefficient alpha - the coefficient of internal consistency was computed. Correlation between items was also computed. Indices were found and r values ranged from .32 to .87 and alpha values ranged from .56 to .83.
Validity : Not available.
Time : Average 15 minutes.
Norms : Not available.
Reference : Caplan, R.D. and Naidu, R.K. Stress, coping and social support : A study of University students in India.

11B23 IMPULSE CONTROL SCALE (I-C SCALE)

Authors : Anjali Srivastava and R.K. Naidu.
Availability : Authors, Department of Psychology, University of Allahabad, Allahabad.
Language : Hindi.
Uses : Self administering Scale to assess the level of impulse control of an individual.
Level : Male and female students.
Main features : It is a 5-point scale based on summated ratings. It consists of 70 items which encompass the

following 10 categories : control, anger control, disruption of needs, persistence, physiological tolerance, mental disturbance, separation reactions to injustice, patience.

Reliability : Split-half reliability was found to be r = .73 (N = 32), and Test-retest reliability was found to be r = .76 (N = 50). Intercorrelations among the different impulse control areas were computed.

Validity : In process.

Time : Twenty minutes approximately.

Norms : Not available.

11B24 SAHAYATA SAMBANDHI PRASHNAWALI

Author : Radha Rani Sharma.

Availability : Author, 209, Rouse Avenue, New Delhi, or C/o National Institute of Educational Planning and Administration, 17-B, Sri Aurobindo Marg, New Delhi.

Language : Hindi.

Uses : To ascertain amount and areas of help-seeking for normals and mental patients to identify the mental disease.

Level : Adults.

Main features : Total test 62 items. Sub-tests : Personal help (A) 23 items, psvchological help (B) 24 items, and material help (C) 15 items.

Reliability : Split-half reliability correlated with S.B. prophecy formula, .95 for the normals and .96 for mental patients. Test-retest .64 for total test and .65, .52 and .61 ABC respectively.

Validity : Validated against clinical diagnosis.

Time : Ten to fifteen minutes.

Norms : Norms are not available.

Reference : Sharma, R.R. Help seeking as a measure of mental illness. M.A. Dissertation, Banaras Hindu University, Varanasi, 1973.

11B25 PERSONALITY ASSESSMENT FOR THE PURPOSE OF SELECTING POLICE OFFICERS AT THE LEVEL OF SUB-INSPECTORS.

Author : Shridhar Sharma.

Availability : Author, Central Institute of Psychiatry, Kanke, Ranchi.

Language : English.

Uses : To screen the police personnel at the Junior Officer level and to screen the personality of the police officer regarding the discipline, integrity, ability to stand to stress, presence of neurotic traits, conformity, etc.

Level : Junior Officers at the level of sub-inspectors.

Main features : Initially ten broad areas were identified and after discussing with various police officials at different levels a scale was designed, which was administered initially to screen out some of the personnel. Some of the items were deleted and added after a preliminary screening.

Reliability : The test has been administered twice on more than 500 police personnel who came for interview for the selection of Sub-Inspectors. Total reliability data are still not available.

Validity : Not available.

Time : One and half hours.

Norms : Not available.

11B26 KUNDU INTROVERSION EXTRAVERSION INVENTORY

Author amanath Kundu.

Availability : Author, Department of Psychology, Calcutta niversity, 92, Acharya Prafulla Ch. Road, Calcutta.

Language : English.

Uses : To use for diagnosis, selection and career guidance, to measure introversion-extraversion.

Level : Adult.

Main features : Five blocks, 70 items.

Reliability : .72 to .82.

Validity : 150 (using E.P.I.).

Time : Takes less than 40 minutes (untimed).

Norms : Available in the manual.

Reference :

Kundu, R. Development of a new introversion-extraversion inventory (First Report), Psychologia, 1(4), 1958, 257-264.

Kundu, R. Development of a new introversion-extraversion inventory (Second Report) Psychologia, 2(2), 1959, 125-132.

Kundu, R. Item Composition of Kundu Introversion-Extraversion Inventory, 4, 1976, 33-41.

Kundu, R. Standardization of Kundu Introversion-Extraversion Inventory, Manas, 24(1), 1977, 65-73.

11B27 BENGALI VERSION OF KUNDU NEUROTIC PERSONALITY INVENTORY (KNPI)

Author : Ramanath Kundu.

Availability : Author, Department of Psychology, University of Calcutta, 92, Acharya Prafulla Ch. Road, Calcutta.

Language : Bengali.
Uses : To assess neuroticism for the purposes of selection, guidance, diagnosis, etc.
Levels : Adolescent and adult levels.
Main features : Same as the original version developed by the same author.
Reliability : Normal .85 to .88, and Neurotic .73 to .81.
Validity : Biserial coefficient of correlation = .92.
Time : Takes less than 30 minutes (Untimed).
Norms : From the manual.
Reference : Bengali version of Kundu Neurotic Personality Inventory, Manas 1976, Vol. 23, No. 1, pp. 49-53.

11B28 N.I. SCALE

Authors : Padma Agrawal & Purnima.
Availability : Rupa Psychological Centre, Varanasi.
Languages : English and Hindi.
Uses : To measure neuroticism and introversion.
Level : High School and College students are ranging 14 to 18 years and may be used on adults also.
Main features : The scale is a two trait inventory measuring neuroticism and introversion. It is a 50-items inventory. 25 items descriptive of neuroticism and equal number of items descriptive of introversion.
Reliability :

	N	Neurotics	Introversion
Test-retest	200	.79	.71
Split-half	200	.78	.71
Rational Equivalence	1000	.98	.96

Validity : Validity coefficients for the two traits are worked out by correlating the inventory scores with neuroticism and introversion scores respectively obtained on Maudsley Personality Inventory, Hindi version by Jalota & Kapoor (1971). Values are .76 for neuroticism and .69 for introversion.
Time : Ten to fifteen minutes.
Norms : Stanine, percentile and T-score norms are worked out for both boys and girls of certain age group and for adults also.
Reference : Sampurna, T.V. A study of personality patterns in psychosomatic disorders through Rorschach Techniques. Unpublished Doctoral Dissertation, Banaras Hindu University, 1977.

11B29 PGI HEALTH QUESTIONNAIRE N-1

Authors : N.N. Wig and S.K. Verma.
Availability : Authors, PGI Medical Education & Research, Chandigarh.
Language : Hindi.
Uses : To measure neuroticism in psychiatric patients.
Main features : The scale consists of 38 questions divided into A (Physical) and B (Mental) sections.
Reliability : High reliability.
Validity : High Validity.

11B30 PSYCHIATRIC DISABILITY SCALE

Authors : R.S. Murthy, D. Anuradha, D. Pershad and N.N. Wig.
Availability : Department of Psychiatry, PGI Medical Education & Research, Chandigarh.
Language : Hindi.
Main features : It is a 27-item scale divided in three areas (Personal, Social and Occupational) of life.
Level : Male and female patients of 16-60 years.
Reliability : Kuder-Richardsons (formula-21) reliability and test-retest reliability for personal, social and occupational scales were found to be .65, .88, .77, and .60, .64 and .68 respectively.
Validity : Validity was compared against the independent and blind clinical evaluation by a psychiatrist. Contingency coefficient of correlation between scale's score and clinical evaluation was found to be .47, .52, and .71 for personal, social and occupational scales respectively.
Reference : Murthy, S.R., Anuradha, D., Pershad, D. and Wig, N.N. Psychiatric Disability Scale : Preliminary Report. Indian Journal of Clinical Psychology, 1975, 2, 183-187.

11B31 P. QUESTIONNAIRE

Authors : M. Arora and V.K. Varma.
Availability : PGI Medical Education & Research, Chandigarh.
Language : Hindi.
Uses : Personality measure of psychotics and neurotics.
Main features : 70-items, yes-no type questionnaire measures Lie and Psychoticism.
Reliability : .88.
Norms : Mean & S.D. norms (N = 400) are available.

11B32 S.P.D. SCALE

Authors : S. Pasricha, N.N. Wig and S.K. Varma.

59 Personality

Availability : PGI Medical Education & Research, Chandigarh.
Language : Hindi.
Uses : To measure three dimensions of personality as super-ego, paranoid and depression.
Main features : There are 45 items in the scale.

11B33 PGI LOCUS OF CONTROL SCALE

Authors : D.K. Menon, N.N. Wig and S.K. Varma.
Availability : PGI Medical Education & Research, Chandigarh.
Language : Hindi.
Uses : To determine Locus of Control.
Level : Children, adults and aged persons.
Main features : The scale contains seven items pertaining to the area of general fate and luck.
Reliability : Test-retest reliability (N = 100) = .76, and inter scorer reliability (N = 100) = .995.
Validity : Coefficient of validity by correlating the scale scores with psychiatrists rating (N = 25) = .792.
Time : Five to seven minutes.

11B34 A VERBAL TEST OF SOCIAL CONFORMITY

Author : S.K. Singh.
Availability : Kushinagar, Deoria.
Language : Hindi.
Uses : To measure conformity.
Level : College students.
Reliability : Split half reliability = .74.
Validity : Construct validity was established.
Time : No time limit.
Reference : Development of a self report measure of conformity : Proceeds 69th Session of Indian Science Congress, Part III, Mysore, 1982.

11B35 PARENTAL BEHAVIOUR QUESTIONNAIRE

Author : Hardep Ojha.
Availability : The author, Department of Psychology, T.N.B. College, Bhagalpur.
Language : Hindi.
Uses : To measure child rearing attitudes of parents.
Level : Adolescents.
Main features : The test has two forms Mother & Father forms. Each form consisting of 72 likert-type items.
Reliability : The internal consistency reliability of mother form is .752 and of father form is .812. The test retest reliabilities of mother and father are .682 and .701

respectively.
Time : Forty-five minutes maximum.

11B36 RATING SCALE FOR CHILD BEHAVIOUR

Authors : V.K. Bhat & A.K. Sinha.
Availability : Department of Psychiatry, Institute of Medical Sciences, Banaras Hindu University, Varanasi.
Language : Hindi.
Main features : The scale consists of 20 statements. Each statement has five possible answers. The scale measures general behaviour of children of both the sexes.
Reference : Bhat, V.K. & Sinha, A.K. A Rating Scale for Child Behaviour : Validation of the Hindi Version. Indian Journal of Clinical Psychology, 1978, 5, 25-28.

citations C

11C1 PERSONALITY TRAIT INVENTORY

Author : N.N. Sen.
Reference : Sen, N.N. Somatic Symptoms in Neuroses A cross cultural study. Indian Journal of Psychiatry, 1976, 18, 18(2), 103-108.

11C2 MYSORE PERSONALITY INVENTORY

Author : B. Krishnan.
Availability : Author, Department of Psychology, University of Mysore, Mysore.

11C3 SHORT EXTRAVERSION SCALE

Authors : O.N. Shrivastava & V.K. Bhat.
Availability : Department of Psychiatry, Institute of Medical Science, Banaras Hindu University, Varanasi.
Language : Hindi.
Reference : Srivastava, O.N. & Bhat, V.K. A short version of extraversion scale in Hindi. Journal of Clinical Psychology, 1975, 2, 63-66.

11C4 CONSERVATION RADICALISM SCALE

Author : Pramila Nath.
Availability : Author, Department of Psychology, Punjab University, Chandigarh.

11C5 HOME ENVIRONMENT SCALE

Author : S.L. Jani.
Availability : Author, Department of Education, Banaras Hindu niversity, Varanasi.

11C6 A SENSE OF RESPONSIBILITY SCALE

Author : Uma Rani Gaur.
Availability : Author, Department of Education, Banaras Hindu University, Varanasi.

11C7 AUTHORITARIAN SCALE

Author : C.K. Shah.
Reference : Shah, C.K. A study of prejudice in relation to conformity and personality. Proceeds 69th Indian Science ongress, Part-III, Mysore, 1982.

11C8 CASTE PREJUDICE SCALE

Author : C.K. Shah.
Reference : Shah, C.K. A study of prejudice in relation to conformity and personality. Proceeds 69th Indian Science Congress, Part-III, Mysore, 1982.

11C9 THE INDIAN CASTE PREJUDICE SCALE

Authors : S.N. Singh & R.N. Prasad.
Availability : Rupa Psychological Centre, B-19/608, Deoriaber, Bhelupura, Varanasi.

11C10 THE INDIAN CASTE-STEREOTYPE CHECK LIST

Author : S.N. Singh.
Availability : Rupa Psychological Centre, B-19/60 B, Deoriaber, Bhelupura, Varanasi.

11C11 DEATH ANXIETY SCALE

Authors : G.P. Thakur & Manju Thakur.
Language : Hindi.
Reference : Thakur, G.P. & Thakur, M. Development of an improved measure of death anxiety suitable to Indian conditions. Proceedings 69th Session of Indian Science Congress, Part-III, Mysore, 1982.

11C12 DYSFUNCTION ANALYSIS QUESTIONNAIRE

Authors : D. Pershad, S.K. Verma, A. Malhotra, S. Malhotra, K. Das, H.A. Khan and S. Khandelwal.
Availability : Department of Psychiatry, PGI Medical Education and Research, Chandigarh.

adaptation D

11D1 INDIAN ADAPTATION OF SENIOR APPERCEPTION TEST (SAT)

Author : Uma Chowdhury.
Availability : Manosamiksha, 76/A, Broad Street, Calcutta, and Manasayan, 32 Netaji Subhash Marg, New Delhi.
Language : English.
Uses : For understanding the problems of the aged people and the adaptation and coping with their children. It can be used as a successful tool in the area of cross-cultural researches.
Level : Aged people from 50 years and above and also among the younger generation from 16 years onwards.
Main features : It is the Indian adaptation of Bellak's Senior Apperception Test with a special emphasis on coping and adaptation between generations. There are 16 cards of Indian SAT. The situation have been drawn to reflect the feelings and thoughts of the aged population as well as the adaptation and coping between the generations. Details are given below :

1. Three elderly figures in discussion. The middle one is a male. Two elderly women are seen on his two sides.
2. An elderly man is sitting with a ball in his hand. On the right, at a distance, a figure of a woman is seen. Two children are eagerly coming towards the elderly man to take the ball.
3. The picture depicts an elderly man moving out of the house and a younger couple is seen in the background. In the middle an elderly woman is seen. She is in a dilemma.
4. An elderly couple is sitting in close proximity and engaged in discussion. A young couple is standing in close proximity.
5. An elderly woman carrying food on a plate. While serving the food to an elderly person she is dropping the food. The young girl standing at the corner is watching her activities.
6. A lonely figure is seen in bed in a sparsely furnished room. Purposely his room is drawn with a few environmental details only.

7. The figure of a lonely woman sitting in a sparsely furnished room.
8. A lonely man sitting alone in a room. He is in a pensive mood.
9. An unidentified figure in shadow standing in the midst of a storm with a bare tree in the background.
10. A young girl standing at a door and an elderly man sitting in a pensive mood.
11. An elderly woman standing at a door with an ambiguous expression and a young man standing in front with ambiguous gestures and expressions.
12. An elderly man is sitting and an elderly woman is standing beside him with a specific gesture. A young girl is standing behind them and a young boy is standing at the door and staring at them. Gestures and postures of all the figures are ambiguous.
13. A young boy is standing with an ambiguous expression by the side of an elderly man who is sitting. At a distance a woman is standing. All the figures have ambiguous expressions.
14. An elderly woman sits with a child on her lap. Her gestures and postures are ambiguous A young woman peeps from a window at a distance.
15. A young woman sitting with a child on her lap. An elderly figure is peeping from behind the door.
16. An elderly female figure is sitting with an ambiguous expression. A young man and a young woman in close proximity are standing in front of the elderly woman. All the figures have ambiguous expressions.

Reliability : The coefficient of reliability = .78.

Validity : Validity is established. Details are available in the manual.

Time : No time limit. The average time for exposure of each card is ten minutes.

Norms : Available in the manual.

Reference : Chowdhury, Uma. Indian Adaptation of Senior Apperception Test with special emphasis on coping and adaptation between generations (SAT). Calcutta, Manosamiksha, 1978.

11D2 16 PF TEST - A COMBINED STANDARDISED VERSION OF FORM C & D IN HINDI

Author : K. Suryanarayanan.

Availability : Author, Industrial Psychology Division, Central Labour Institute, Sion, Bombay.

Language : Hindi.

Uses : In counselling, industry, testing etc., to measure the complete coverage of personality.
Level : For adults of limited education, literacy or intelligence.
Main features : Measures 16 primary personality factors using 105 items and objectively scorable.
Reliability : Test-retest reliability after three months

Source	A	B	C	E	F	G	H	I
Trait	.84	.67	.76	.84	.79	.82	.81	.87
Source	L	M	N	O	Q_1	Q_2	Q_3	Q_4
Trait	.76	.71	.73	.76	.81	.83	.71	.79

N = 80.

Validity : Same as that of the original tests.
Time : No time limit (may be 30-40 minutes).
Norms : Norms (STEN SCORES) available from the author.
Reference : Suryanarayanan, K. "A Comparative Study of the Personality of Absentees and Regulars in an Industrial Setting". Unpublished Ph.D. thesis, 1979.

11D3 AN INDIAN ADAPTATION OF A SHORT MEASURE OF ERIKSONIAN EGO IDENTITY

Author Rakesh K. Srivastava.
Availability : Author, Department of Psychology, Degree College, Malikpura, P.O. Malikpura, Ghazipur.
Language : Hindi.
Uses : The scale measures not a 'foreclosed' identity with no real crisis but rather identity achieved as a reset of an identity crisis.
Level : Adolescents.
Main features : Twelve items with forced choice format.
Reliability : Split-half = .66 and test-retest = .64.
Validity : Validity = .61.
Time : No time limit, usually takes twenty minutes.
Reference :

Srivastava, R.K. An Indian adaptation of a short measure of Eriksonian ego identity and its relationship to certain socio-cultural variables. Paper presented at the 69th Annual Session of the Indian Science Congress, Mysore, January 3-8, 1982.

Srivastava, R.K. Certain social correlates of ego identity in India. Unpublished manuscript, Department of Psychology, Degree College, Malikpura, Ghazipur, 1982.

11D4 CERTAINTY OF JUDGEMENT SCALE : AN INDIAN ADAPTATION IN HINDI

Authors : C.N. Daftuar & L. Singh.
Availability : Authors, Department of Psychology, M.S. University, Baroda.
Language : Hindi.
Uses : To measure riskiness and ones confidence.
Level : High School and above. Students as well as others in industries, educational institutions, etc.
Main features : Likerts Scaling. 30 items.
Reliability : Internal consistency - .88 and test-retest -.76.
Validity : Intrinsic validity -.938, differentiate high and low school activities, and *r* with C.D.Q. -.423.
Time : Ten minutes.
Norms : No.

11D5 HINDI VERSION OF EYSENCK PERSONALITY INVENTORY

Author : L.I. Bhushan.
Availability : Author, Department of Psychology, University of Bhagalpur.
Language : Hindi.
Uses : In any study of adult's personality to measure extraversion and neuroticism.
Level : Adults.
Main features : 57 items with Yes - No responses. 24 items each for E and N scales and 9 items constitute the Lie-Scale.
Reliability : E Scale - split half-.78 and test-retest = .73. N Scale - split half = .69 and test-retest = .76.
Validity : Validated against original English version of EPI. Validity coefficient for E = .89, N = .84.
Time : About 30 minutes.
Norms : Available for male and female Post-Graduate & Under-Graduate College students.
Reference : Bhushan, L.I. A Hindi version of Eysenck Personality Inventory (Form °A'). Psychology Annual, 1969, 3, 27-30.

11D6 THE NEYMAN-KOHLSTEDT DIAGNOSTIC TEST FOR INTROVERSION-EXTRAVERSION (INDIAN ADAPTATION)

Author : Jai Prakash.
Availability : Agra Psychological Research Cell, Agra.

Language : Hindi.
Level : College & University students.
Main features : The present test is a Hindi adaptation of Neyman-Kohlstedt Test of Extraversion-Introversion consisting of 50 items. The are to be answered in °Yes' or °No' only.
Reliability : Test-retest reliability for male & female (N = 100 each) = .79 for under-graduate and .81 for post-graduate. Split-half reliability by Spearman Brown Prophecy formula = .82.
Validity : The test was validated against the original Neyman Test in English. coefficient of correlation (N = 75) = .87.
Norms : Average range score norm is available.

11D7 THE EYSENCK PERSONALITY QUESTIONNAIRE (PQ)

Authors : P.K. Chattopadhyay, P.K. Biswas, M. Chattoraj & A.K. Bhattacharyya.
Availability : Authors, Department of Psychology, Calcutta University College of Science, 92, A.P.C. Road, Calcutta.
Language : English.
Uses : Measurement of Psychoticism, neutoticism and extraversion of educated Bengalee individuals.
Level : Adult male and female individuals.
Main features : Original (Eysenck & Eysenck, 1975) scaling technique was followed and same number of items were retained.
Reliability : Split half reliability for the P.E.N. and L scales respectively are : (N = 304), P = .85, E = .98, N = .87 and L = .88.
Validity : Face validity.
Time : Forty minutes.
Norms : Available from the authors.

11D8 QUESTIONNAIRE FOR MEASURING PRESUMPTIVE STRESS

Authors : Musaddiq Jahan & Qamar Hasan.
Availability : Department of Psychology, Aligarh Muslim University, Aligarh.
Languages : Hindi and Urdu.
Uses : As a diagnostic tool for assessing intensity of stress experienced by a person.
Level : Adults.
Main features : It is the adaptation of life event questionnaire developed by orowitz, Schaefer, Hiroto, Wilner and Levin. Weights are worked out to indicate the inten-

sity of stress experienced after different periods (1 month, within 1-6 months, within 6-12 months, within 1-2 year, and over two years) of occurrence of the listed events. It have 42 items.

Reliability : The reliability of weight assignment was checked in subject groups that differed by sex, age and status.

Validity : Validity is indicated by the difference in the scores of patients and non-patients and also by decrease in the intensity of experienced stress with time.

Time : Twenty minutes.

Norms : Norms are to be prepared.

11D9 THE TELIC DOMINANCE SCALE

Authors : Afzal Kureshi and Rahat Ali Khan.

Availability : Department of Psychology, Aligarh Muslim University, Aligarh.

Language : Hindi.

Uses : The scale can be used for the purpose of screening out subjects and categorizing them into telics and paratelics, depending upon the extent to which they are serious minded, plan ahead and avoid arousal.

Level : The scale is appropriate for students of graduate and under-graduate classes and can also be used with literate adults.

Main features : The scale is the Hindi version of Murgateoyd et al. Telic Dominance Scale (1978). There are forty-two items in the scale, divisible into three sub-scale, each compriing fourteen items. Each of the 42 items is to be responded to by choosing one of the two alternative responses besides a °not sure' response.

Reliability : The split-half reliability of the Hindi version was found to be .63 (N = 200).

Validity : Validated against F.F. trait anxiety and anxiety defensiveness measure.

Time : About forty minutes.

Norms : Norms for Indian subjects are under process.

Reference : Kureshi, A. and Khan, R.A. Telic Dominance and Fear of Failure. A study under process.

11D10 AN ADAPTATION OF THE WILSON - PATTERSON CONSERVATIVE SCALE

Authors : P.K. Dhillon and Poonam Bahl.

Availability : First Jesus and Mary College, Chanakyapuri, New Delhi.

Language : English.
Uses : To assess the conservative-liberal attitude of college students.
Level : Literates : High school, and college students, adults married and single, in fact any age group above the high school level. It can also be used with illiterates of the same age groups with verbal instructions.
Main features : The same scaling technique as used by Wilson and Patterson (1968) was followed that is, presenting a list of brief labels or catch-phrases representing various familiar and controversial issues. The scale consists of 36 items.
Reliability : The split-half reliability (odd-even) of the adapted scale was .80 and the test-retest reliability was .95.
Validity : Validity was obtained by two techniques. The correlation coefficient obtained between self rating on conservation and scores on the Wilson Patterson Scale was .64 and the correlation coefficient obtained between self and friends ratings on conservatism was .83.
Time : Approximately 6-8 minutes.
Norms : Norms are available with the first author.
Reference : Dhillon, P.K. A Research Project submitted to the University of Delhi.

11D11 BENGALI VERSION OF JUNIOR EYSENCK PERSONALITY INVENTORY

Author : Ramanath Kundu.
Availability : Author, Department of Psychology, Calcutta University, 92, Acharya Prafulla Ch. Road, Calcutta.
Language : Bengali.
Uses : To assess Introversion-Extraversion and neuroticism of school students in regional language.
Level : Boys and girls of adolescent state (10-15 years).
Main features : Same as original English version number of items : 60 (same as English version).

Reliability :

	E	N	L
Male	.50-.75	.51-.65	.51-.59
Female	.59-.77	.81-.84	.62-.74

Validity : Sufficiently valid.
Time : Takes 35 minutes (Untimed).
Norms : orms are available with the author.
Reference : Kundu, R.N. Bengali adaptation of Junior Eysenck

Personality Inventory, Indian Psychological Review, 1976, Vol. 13, No. 1, pp. 17-21.

11D12 CHOICE - DILEMMAS QUESTIONNAIRE : A HINDI ADAPTATION

Authors : C.N. Daftuar & L. Singh.
Availability : The Authors, Department of Psychology, M.S. University, Baroda.
Language : Hindi.
Uses : To measure riskiness in decision-making.
Level : High School & above (including students).
Main features : Likert, proportion categories, 3 items.
Reliability : Internal consistence rtt =.80 and test-retest = .83.
Validity : High intrinsic validity. Validity tested against certainty of judgement scale was .423.
Time : Five minutes.

11D13 MEASURES OF RISK TAKING BEHAVIOUR : BEHAVIOUR PREDICTION SCALE

Author : S.M. Anwar Yousuf.
Availability : Agra Psychological Research Cell, Agra.
Language : Hindi.
Uses : To measure unethical risk taking behaviour.
Level : Under-Graduate.
Main features : A multidimensional scale having 16 items. There are four components manipulated in this measure : (i) Reinforcement value of gain (ii) Expectancy of gain (iii) Negative reinforcement value of censure and (iv) Expectancy of censure.
Reliability : Reliability coefficient by Kender Richardson formula = .90, and split-half reliability = .82.
Validity : Construct validity was established by correlating in with CDQ, a negative significant high correlation was found (r = -.60).
Time : Forty minutes.

11D14 MEASURES OF RISK TAKING BEHAVIOUR : CHOICE DILEMMAS QUESTIONNAIRE (CDQ)

Author : S.M. Anwar Yousuf.
Availability : Agra Psychological Research Cell, Agra.
Language : Hindi.
Uses : To assess risk taking behaviour under uncertain outcomes representing socially approved acts.
Level : Under-Graduate.

Main features : The test is semi-projective in nature. There are four situations considered as most risk oriented. One is asked how he would advise his friends in the situations described. The maximum possible score is 40, and the minimum is 4. The lesser the score, the greater will be the risk.
Reliability : Test-retest reliability (12 itemed) CDQ is found to be .78 for males, and .82 for females, and split-half reliability by applying SB formula = .70.
Validity : The construct validity was obtained by correlating it with BPS and coefficient of correlation was found negative (r = - .60)
Time : Approximately forty minutes.

11D15 CHILDREN'S REPORT OF PARENTAL BEHAVIOUR INVENTORY (CRPBI) :

Authors : Uma Saxena & N.K. Saxena.
Availability : Agra Psychological Research Cell, Agra.
Uses : CRBPI is an instrument mainly for measuring children's attitude toward their parental behaviour.
Level : Literate subjects and also as interview schedule in case of illiterate ones.
Main features : The present scale contains 108 items representing 18 different areas of children's perception. The scoring is done on a 3-point scale.
Reliability : Split-half reliability (N = 200) = .81 and test-retest reliability (N = 100) = .77.
Validity : Hundred Hindi and English knowing subjects were administered separately both the versions (English & Hindi). r was computed (r = .79) to find out concurrent validity.

11D16 INDIAN NORMS FOR THE COMPUTER SCORED HOLTZMAN INKBLOT TECHNIQUE

Author : Habib Ahmed.
Availability : Department of Psychology, Zakir Husain College, University of Delhi, Delhi.
Main features : The present study is a part of a major project on development of cultural norms for Holtzman Inkblot Technique. The test consists of 35 mm colour slides of 45 standard HIT inkblots of form 'A'. The test was administered on 200 Post-Graduate students of Delhi University (166 males and 134 females). The HIT records were scored by computer.
Norms : The means, standard deviations and percentiles for 17 HIT variables are prepared.

Reference : Ahmad, Habib : Indian Norms for the computer-scored Holtzman Inkblot Technique. University Psychology Research Journal, 1981, 2(2), 79-82.

11D17 INNOVATIVE PERSONALITY INVENTORY

Author : R.Venkatachalam.
Availability : Department of Psychology, University of Madras, P.G Centre, Coimbatore.
Language : English.
Main features : 20 items 'Yes-No' type inventory, measuring the way one behaves. The inventory has 2-point score for each statement.
Reliability : Reliability coefficient = .29.
Validity : Validated among adult population.
Time : Few minutes.

11D18 HEALTH QUESTIONNAIRE (HINDI ADAPTATION OF THE MIDDLESEX HOSPITAL QUESTIONNAIRE)

Authors : O.N. Srivastava & V.K. Bhatt.
Availability : Department of Psychiatry, Institute of Medical Sciences, Banaras Hindu University, Varanasi.
Language : Hindi.
Reference : Srivastava, O.N. & Bhatt, V.K. The Middlesex Health Questionnaire (MHQ) standardisation on a Hindi version. Indian Journal of Psychiatry. 1974, 16, 283-286.

11D19 MAUDSLEY PERSONALITY INVENTORY

Authors : N.N. Wig & Sanatam.
Availability : PGI Medical Education & Research, Chandigarh.
Language : Hindi.
Main features : Forty-eight items 'Yes-No' type questionnaires.

11D20 AN ADAPTATION OF MASLOW'S SECURITY-INSECURITY INVENTORY

Authors : Dhillon, P.K. and Beri, B.
Availability : An adaptation of Maslow's security-insecurity inventory on the student population of Delhi. A project submitted to the University of Delhi, 1977.

ADJUSTMENT AND PROBLEMS

complete instruments A

12A1 PERSONALITY ADJUSTMENT INVENTORY (PAI)

Author : C.P. Sharma.
Availability : Agra Psychological Research Cell, Agra.
Languages : English & Hindi.
Uses : To measure the maladjustive-adjustive behaviour reactions of the individuals.
Main features : The inventory consists of 54 'Yes', 'No' type items. The items have been selected on the basis of maladjustive behaviour reactions occurring in different dimensions of personality manifestations. Generally the items belong to maladaptive class of behaviour.
Reliability : Test-retest reliability (N = 150) coefficient was found to be .69 with reliability index of .83.
Validity : The scores were correlations with the scores of Asthana's Adjustment Inventory and a validity coefficient of .81 was found.
Norms : T scores norms are available.
Reference : Sharma, C.P. Need Structure and Maladjustment. Ph.D. thesis, Agra University, Agra, 1972.

12A1 PERSONALITY ADJUSTMENT INVENTORY (PAI)
(The following items have to be checked on 'Yes' or 'No').

1. Do you get excited soon?
2. Do you maintain the feeling of Disappointment?
3. When other people see you at work then do you get disturbed?
4. Do you feel some weakness in yourself?
5. Do you keep on thinking about your past?
6. Do you usually feel restlessness or physical tension?
7. Do you feel angry when other people cut joke among themselves?
8. Do you feel yourself lonely even when your friends are sitting with you?
9. Do you take yourself to be an accused?
10. Do you often pity yourself?
11. Are you lost among your thoughts?
12. Are you often disturbed when you dream evil and fearful dreams?
13. Do you sometimes think so much about yourself that

you feel crying on your own self?

14. Are you usually anxious about your health?
15. Do you get trouble to centre your attention?
16. Do you keep on changing sides for a long time while lying in bed?
17. Do you usually consider yourself happy or unhappy without any cause?
18. Do you usually feel exhausted?
19. Do you think that difficulties in future at sleeping in night?
20. Do you feel headache daily?
21. Do you feel fear when you are alone?
22. Do you feel fear by seeing quarrel?
23. Do you feel self-torture on not getting the correct answer of any problem?
24. Does your heart get hurt by the small things of others?
25. Do you feel any difficulty in giving speech infront of people?
26. Does aloneness hurt you?
27. Are you soon impressed by your praise or blame?
28. Do you feel inferiority complex to see better people than you?
29. Do you feel shy on getting less marks in class?
30. Do you usually feel trouble or take delay in coming to a decision?
31. Are you troubled when you have difference of opinions for others?
32. Do you usually get irritated on the members of your family?
33. Do you sometimes feel dejected?
34. Do you usually have trouble in recognizing people?
35. Do people usually think you to be a useless man?
36. Do you feel that some trouble is ahead?
37. Do you sometimes think to commit suicide?
38. Do you feel lack of self-confidence?
39. Do you think that you have no one in the world?
40. Do you often settle an account while walking on the road?
41. Do you often see day-dreams?
42. Do useless thoughts come into your mind?
43. Do you feel trouble in answering the questions in class?
44. Do you feel trouble in meeting and talking with unfamiliar persons?
45. Do you often had a feeling of sadness?
46. Do you have a feeling of suffering with some disease?

47. Do you cry very soon?
48. Do you wait to stay alone and leave with your friends?
49. Do you get nervous in petty things?
50. Do you curse your luck lot on ordinary things?
51. Do you feel nervous in meeting with people of opposite sex?
52. Do you feel anxiety in doing a work much earlier?
53. Do you loose temper soon while talking?
54. Do you feel that other people commit mistakes in understanding you?

12A2 PERSONAL ADJUSTMENT INVENTORY

Author : C.G. Deshpande.
Availability : Department of Experimental Psychology, University of Poona, Poona.
Language : English and Marathi.
Uses : (i) To know the mental health of the individual and (ii) Degree of personal adjustment.
Level : Adults _ age 20 and above, College students.
Main features : 20 statements. Subject has to see how far each statement is applicable to him on a three point scale.
Reliability : It is .81 as measured by split-half method using even odd scores.
Validity : It is measured against their marriage adjustment scores. Measured by biserial correlation, it is .35.
Time : About 20 minutes.
Norms : Norms prepared on the basis of range of scores.

12A2 PERSONAL ADJUSTMENT INVENTORY

(The following statements have to be checked on a 3-point scale of frequency : always sometimes and never).

1. You feel out of sorts in the company of strangers.
2. You feel perplexed when you meet acquaintances
3. You easily get bored with humour and entertainment.
4. You avoid attending public functions like speeches, ceremonies, etc.
5. You dislike being told how to behave.
6. You feel better when alone.
7. You feel that others have no affinity for you.
8. You do not like talking with others on your own.
9. You have vague fears and anxieties.
10. You are terribly disturbed in your sleep and cannot sleep henceforth.

11. A particular thought or idea takes hold of you.
12. You experience twitchings (e.g. of leg, hand or facial muscle).
13. You cannot control your laughing.
14. You experience dread of darkness, loneliness, corwds, injections or such other things.
1 . You constantly feel tired and exhausted.
16. You easily become angry even if a minor thing is not done systematically.
17. You cannot check your anger.
18. You avoid making acquaintances and friends.
19. You hate yourself.
20. You feel that people are gossiping about you.

12A3 AN ADJUSTMENT INVENTORY

Authors : B.A. Parikh & D.G. Das.
Availability : M.T.B. Arts College, Surat.
Language : English and Gujarati.
Uses : To measure general level adjustment, various types of adjustment of the socially disadvantaged students.
Level : High School, College students (scheduled tribes and backward classes).
Main features : Guttman Scale. 50 items.
Reliability : Test-retest = .84, alternate form = .84, and split-half = .79.
Validity : Scores validated against the opinion of teachers, close friends of the individual.
Time : Fifteen minutes.
Norms : Available with the authors.

12A3 AN ADJUSTMENT INVENTORY

(The following items have to be checked on °Yes' or °No').

Section I Family Adjustment.

1. Do you get love and affection in the family?
2. Do you feel that your parents are less or uneducated?
3. Do you feel that you would get more pleasure from elsewhere than what you get in your family?
4. Are you constantly painfully conscious that your parents belong to the backward class?
5. Do your parents or members of the family welcome your plans and ideas?
6. Do you feel that your family is inferior in comparison to your affluent friends?
7 Do you feel that the atmosphere of your house is

light and cheerful?
8. Do you feel that your parents are old fashioned an therefore you have conflict with them?
9. Do you feel that you are in conflict with you parents in certain matters?
10. Do you feel hesitant in taking your friends to you home?

Section II Social Adjustment

1. Do you ever try to conceal that you belong to back ward class/caste?
2. Can you develop contacts with other boys and girl without hesitation?
3. Do you feel that you are hesitant and a little con scious while talking with your teachers or othe elite persons?
4. Can you openly expose your name and surname befor others?
5. Do you feel ashamed and guilty that you have bee born in a backward class?
6. Do the people of your class approve and respect you studies?
7. Do people of other classes consider you les civilised and uncouth?
8. Can you develop friendship easily?
9. Do your co-students insult you by calling yc backward?
10. Do you feel that you have enough opportunities fo development of personality in your class?

Section III Educational Adjustment

1. Can you easily get co-operation of your co-students
2. Do you often worry whether you would be able to com plete your studies?
3. Do you feel disturbed and depressed when the teach asks you in the class?
4. Do you feel that your coeds are sympathetic?
5. Do your parents insist that you should join servi instead of studies?
6. Do your teachers downgrade you?
7. Do you feel that you cannot make good progress your studies?
8. Do you feel that you would have difficulty selecting a suitable mate?
9. Do you feel that because of your social class y cannot participate in common social cultur activities?
10. Do the people of your class look upon you wi

respect because you are inhigher education?

Section IV Financial Adjustment

1. Do you experience difficulties in maintaining the family?
2. Do you worry that you have incurred deeply for your studies?
3. Do you feel that you have no good clothes and therefore cannot impress others?
4. Do you feel that you have financial constrains or difficulties in normal life?
5. Do you feel that because of poverty you cannot enjoy the life?
6. Do you often feel dissatisfaction that you have no facilities in your house?
7. Do you believe that poverty and backwardness are a curse?
8. Do you feel like giving up studies because of financial difficulties?
9. Do you feel that your parents are put into hardship because of the burden of your studies?
10. Do you make efforts to hide before others that you are not well off?

Section V Emotional Adjustment

1. Can you speak without being conscious and feeling hesitant in public?
2. Do you often experience depressions?
3. Do you feel anxiety that you have not made a good show before others?
4. Can you tolerate small or big disturbance in your tasks.
5. Do you often feel that people are talking secretively about you?
6. Do you often feel that you are doing something improper?
7. Do you feel a sense of deprivation that you are not like others or you are lacking in something?
8. Do you feel that you are dragged by others suggestions or opinions?
9. Do you feel hesitant in front of the members of opposite sex?
10. Do you feel that you cannot express yourself clearly?

12A4 A SCALE OF MARITAL ADJUSTMENT

Authors : P.K. Dhillon, H.C. Ganguli & C.K. Basu.

Availability : The first author, Jesus and Mary College, New Delhi.

Languages : Punjabi and English.

Uses : To assess the marital adjustment of married men and women.

Level : Literate and illiterate adults who are married of all professions, religions etc.

Main features : Likert's scaling technique. The scale consists of 25 items.

Reliability : The split-half (odd-even) reliability of the scale was .97 and the test-retest reliability was .92.

Validity : The validity was calculated by the method of biserial correlation and r_{bis} was .91.

Time : No time limit.

Norms : Norms are available on 450 married men and women.

Reference : The Indian Journal of Psychology, 1975, Vol. 50, Part-I, 25-32.

12A4 A SCALE OF MARITAL ADJUSTMENT

1. If you could live your life all over again would you like to marry the same person to who you are now married?
2. Do you get as much affection (love) from your partner as you want?
3. Do you get as much understanding from your partner as you want?
4. In general, how do you feel about having sexual relations with your partner (husband/wife)?
5. Many spouses refuse to have sexual relations every time their partners want to. Do you ever refuse to have sexual relations apart from the times when you are sick?
6. In general how do you feel about the shortcomings of your spouse?
7. Is your spouse as sympathetic as you would like her or him to be?
8. Have you ever wished you were not married?
9. In general how do you feel about your home life?
10. Do you and your spouse agree as regards the care of the children (involving issues like schooling, playing, food etc.)?
11. Have you ever regretted your marriage?
12. Do you and your spouse agree about the philosophy of life?
13. How much satisfaction do you get from intercourse as compared to your partner?
14. Now which of these statements mentioned below comes

nearest to saying how well you and your spouse get along with each other?

15. Do you feel that your spouse cares more for his or her other relatives than you?
16. Do you and your spouse agree in dealing with in-laws?
17. Have you ever wished you were married to some one else?
18. Do you get as much respect from your spouse as you want?
19. Do you feel that the strength of your sex interest as compared with your partner is : (less, same. greater)?
20. Thinking about your family and children as they are now, which of these statements comes nearest to saying how you feel?
21. Have you ever been beaten or have you ever beaten your wife on any matter?
22. How do you feel about your husband or wife?
23. Does your spouse depend upon you rather than on other relatives and friends for advice on family matters?
24. Do you and your spouse agree in handling family finances?
25. When you were married who desired the children the most?

12A5 MARRIAGE ADJUSTMENT INVENTORY

Author : C.G. Deshpande.
Availability : Department of Experimental Psychology, University of Poona, Poona.
Language : English and Marathi.
Uses : To understand the degree of main adjustment and to help in counselling.
Main features : Rated items 5-point scale. 25 items.
Reliability : It is .83 as measured by split-half method using even-odd scores. Sample - 300 married individuals.
Validity : Measured against their personal adjustment scores (biserial correlation is .49).
Time : About forty minutes.
Norms : On the basis of range of scores available with the author.

12A5 MARRIAGE ADJUSTMENT INVENTORY

-A-

1. In-laws

As regards your relations with in-laws there are :

i No discussions or quarrels
ii Seldom references by your partner
iii Occasional disagreements
iv Heated discussions
v Frequent clashes.

2. Customs and traditions

As regards different customs and traditions followed :

i You never disagree
ii A few create disagreement
iii Occasionally you disagree
iv There are many differences
v It is the root of all trouble.

3. Food habit

Partner can take non-vegetarian diet

i Any time
ii Excepting certain religious occasions
iii Occasionally
iv Seldom
v Never.

4. Though your tastes are different you adapt yourself to your spouse's likes and dislikes :

i Every time
ii Almost every time
iii Occasionally
iv Seldom
v Never.

5. Social Participation

Your spouse permits you to attend festival speeches, dramatic performances and other social functions together :

i Every time
ii Almost every time
iii Occasionally
iv Seldom
v Never (always individually)

6. Bringing up of children

As regards bringing up of children you agree with your partner :

i Always
ii Almost always
iii Occasionally

iv Seldom
v Never.

7. <u>Temperamental differences</u>
Conflicts because of your different temperament take place :
i Never
ii Seldom
iii Occasionally
iv Usually
v Always.

8. <u>Mutual respect</u> :
Whenever there are differences or misunderstandings your spouse respects your views:
i Always
ii Usually
iii Occasionally
iv Seldom
v Never.

9. <u>Derision</u>
If you commit a mistake, your spouse ridicules :
i Never
ii Seldom
iii Occasionally
iv Usually
v Always.

10. <u>Personal daily activities</u>
As regards personal daily activities of your spouse :
i You are indifferent
ii You want to know only a few
iii You want to know details in some cases only
iv You are satisfied with an over-all information of them
v You insist on the detailed knowledge of each..

11. <u>Affection and love</u>
Your confidence in the love and affection of your spouse :
i Fullest
ii Not always
iii Not sure
iv Often doubtful
v Always doubtful.

12. <u>Sexual satisfaction</u>
In sex life with your spouse you are :
i Fully satisfied

ii Almost satisfied
iii Somewhat satisfied
iv Almost dissatisfied
v Always dissatisfied.

13. Confrontation and quarrels
You experience confrontations and quarrels with your spouse
i Never
ii Seldom
iii Occasionally
iv Usually
v Every day.

14. Success of Marriage
As regards the success of your marriage you are :
i Always confident
ii Usually confident
iii Doubtful
iv Usually worried
v Always worried.

15. Divorce
Regarding divorce :
i The idea never comes in your mind
ii The idea seldom strikes you
iii You occasionally think about it
iv Most of the time you feel so
v You feel that it would be good riddance.

(The following items have to be checked on 5-point scale of agreement)

1. Money matters
2. Study habits of children
3. Taste of food
4. Relation within the family
5. Kinship relationship
6. Rights of spouses
7. Purchases
8. Health of children
9. Political social discussions
10. Entertainment.

instruments with technical information B

12B1 YOUTH ADJUSTMENT ANALYSER (YAA)

Author : M.D. Bengalee.
Availability : Indian Psychological Corporation, R.B.L. Road, Lucknow.
Language : English, Hindi, Marathi and Gujarati.
Uses : To locate the areas of difficulty of maladjusted individuals.
Level : Individuals above 16 years of age; school and college going population.
Main features : The YAA consists of 140 items constructed by the author and 100 items borrowed from standardised personality inventories.

It consists of the following scales :

Part-I a. Parental Attitude Scale
Part-I b. Home Adjustment Scale
Part-II Agression, Neurotic and Lie Scale
Part-III Interest Scale (likes & dislikes)

Reliability : Reliability coefficient of the different scales is given below :

	N	Parent Attitude	Home Adjust.	Agre-ssion	Neu-rotic	Int.	YAA
Test-retest	100	.81	.87	.99	.91	.70	.97
Odd-even	100	.87	.90	.92	.96	.83	.97

Validity : Validity is established by four different methods i.e., significance of difference between the means of the adjusted and the maladjusted, Teachers' Counsellors' Ratings, Pupils' Rating by Guess-who Technique and correlation of YAA Test scores with Bell's Adjustment Inventory score, r Ranging from .29 to .66.
Norms : Norms are described in five-grades per scale, available in the manual.

12B2 ADJUSTMENT INVENTORY

Author : V.K. Mittal.
Availability : Department of Psychology, Meerut College, Meerut.
Language : Hindi.
Uses : To measure the adjustment of students.
Level : High School and College students.
Main features : Separate forms for boys and girls of high school and college students are available.

Reliability : Test-retest and split-half reliability are calculated and found to be high (above .93).
Validity : The inventories are validated against teachers ratings, parent's ratings and other inventories.
Norms : Percentile norms are available.

12B3 SAMAYOJAN SUCHIKA (AN ADJUSTMENT SCALE)

Author : R.R. Tripathi.
Availability : Author, Department of Psychology, Banaras Hindu University, Varanasi.
Language : Hindi.
Uses : To measure adjustment among individuals.
Level : Adults and college students.
Main features : It is a self-endorsement type of scale which has been rather than the rational method. The items are balanced for true-false keying (items = 82).
Reliability : Reliability coefficient calculated by K R formula 20 = .89, and index stability = .79.
Validity : Convergent validity coefficient = .87, and discriminate validity coefficient against three anxiety scales, .06, .12 & .1.
Time : 20 - 25 minutes.
Norms : Norms given in the manual.

12B4 ADOLESCENT ADJUSTMENT ANALYSER

Author : A. Pandey.
Availability : Indian Psychological Corporation, Shanti Sadan, Rai Beheri Lal Road, Lucknow.
Language : Hindi.
Uses : To segregate the poorly adjusted adolescents from normal adolescents.
Level : High School and Intermediate students.
Main features : It covers five areas home, health, social, emotional and educational adjustment. The analyser consists of 125 'Yes', 'No' and 'Cannot say' items equally distributed in five areas.
Reliability : Reliability calculated by test-retest (N = 80) method ranges from .72 to .93.
Validity : Construct, interitem consistency, and concurrent validity has been established.
Norms : Five-grade norms are available for high school and intermediate adolescent boys and girls.

12B5 SRIVASTAVA ADJUSTMENT INVENTORY

Authors : Ramji Srivastava & Bina Srivastava.

Availability : Prasad Trading Corporation, J-1/53, Daranagar, Varanasi.
Language : Hindi.
Uses : It is useful in diagnosis of maladjustment.
Level : College and Senior High School students.
Main features : 120 positively and negatively word items covering social, home, health, college, personal and emotional adjustment.
Reliability : Split-half reliability = .86, and Kuder reliability formula = .88.
Validity : The inventory has been correlated with Saxena's adjustment and Asthana adjustment inventory coefficient of correlation is found to be .85 and .88 respectively.
Time : Forty minutes.
Norms : Norms based on t-scores available from Authors/Publishers.

12B6 ADJUSTMENT INVENTORY

Author : M.C. Agarwal.
Availability : P.O. NITIE, Vihar Lake Road, Bombay.
Language : Hindi.
Uses : To determine the adjustment of students and help them improve.
Level : College students.
Main features : Three point weighted scoring procedure, 80 items (20 in each area of home, college, personal and health, and social adjustment).
Reliability : Test-retest reliability =.84.
Validity : Validity coefficient = .79 (with Asthana's inventory).
Time : Thirty minutes.
Norms : No.
Reference : 'Adjustment among college students'. Indian Psychological Review, 1970, 6(2).

12B7 ADJUSTMENT INVENTORY

Author : M.N. Palsane.
Availability : Department of Experimental Psychology, University of Poona, Pune.
Language : Marathi.
Uses : To assess the adjustment of School & College students.
Level : High School and College students.
Main features : The inventory consists of 375 items and measures five areas as home & family, social, personal and emotional, educational and health, adjustment.

Reliability : The test-retest (N = 200) reliability ranges from .79 to .93.
Validity : Data on cross-validation is not available. Content validity has been ensured as well as item validity index is available.
Norms : Percentile norms are available for male and female students.

12B8 SOCIAL ADJUSTMENT INVENTORY

Author : R.C. Deva.
Availability : National Psychological Corporation, Kacherighat, Agra.
Uses : To assess the emotional as well as social adjustment.
Main features : Equal appearing interval method used for scaling the items. The inventory has 100 items.
Reliability : Test-retest reliability = .91.
Validity : Validated against Saxena's Vyaktitva Parakh Prashnawali, the value came to be .80 and .79 for emotional and social adjustment respectively.
Time : About 45 minutes (no time limit).

citations C

12C1 MARITAL ADJUSTMENT RATING SCALE

Authors : V.K. Bhatt & S. Gauba.
Availability : Department of Psychology, Institute of Medical Sciences, Banaras Hindu University, Varanasi.
Language : Hindi.
Reference : Bhatt, V.K. & Gauba, S. A marital adjustment questionnaire in Hindi. *Indian Journal of Clinical Psychology*, 1978, 5, 29-32.

adaptations D

12D1 MOHSIN-SHAMSHAD HINDI ADAPTATION OF BELL'S ADJUSTMENT INVENTORY

Authors : S.M. Mohsin & Shamshad Hussain.

Availability : Aerovoice, Bari Road, Patna.
Language : Hindi.
Uses : To measure the adjustment of students.
Main features : The inventory consists of 135 **items** and measures four areas of adjustment as home, health, social and emotional as well as yields a composite score for overall adjustment. High scores on the inventory indicate low adjustment and vice-versa. Three response categories have been provided for answers to each item.
Reliability : The test-retest reliability ranges between .700 to .926 and the odd even reliability ranges between .738 to .938 for different areas as well as for the total test.
Validity : The test was validated against (N = 100) the Hindi version of the Eysenck's Personality Inventory. Significant positive correlations have been found.
Time : No time limits but it takes about 35 to 40 minutes.
Norms : Percetile norms have been developed.
Reference : Hussain, S. Hindi Adaptation of Bell's Adjustment Inventory and construction of norms for college students. Unpublished Ph.D. thesis, University of Patna, Patna, 1969.

12D2 BENGALI VERSION OF BELL'S ADJUSTMENT INVENTORY

Author : N.B. Mallik and P.K. Chattopadhyay.
Availability : Department of Psychology, Calcutta University, College of Science & Technology, 92, A.P.C. Road, Calcutta.
Language : Bengali.
Uses : To assess adjustment patterns with regard to (a) home (b) health (c) social and (d) emotional for both normal and pathological males and females.
Level : Individuals falling in the age range of 9 to 23 years.
Main features : It is an adaptation of Bell's Adjustment Inventory (Student Form) - 1962. The scale consists of 128 items excluding the items for occupation.
Reliability : Split-half (odd-even) 0.97, test-retest 0.84.
Validity : Concurrent validity = 0.77.
Time : No fixed time. But usually should take about sixty minutes.
Norms : Norms are available from the Authors obtained on 1309 subject.

12D3 BURGESS ET AL. MARITAL ADJUSTMENT SCALE

Authors : Vidhu Mohan & Arivinder Singh.

Availability : Department of Psychology, Punjab University, Chandigarh.
Languages : Hindi & Punjabi.
Reference : Mohan, V. & Singh, A. Hindi and Punjabi Adaptation of Burgess et al. Marital Adjustment Scale. Indian Psychological Review, 1980, 19, 33-38.

CORRECTION COMPLETE FROM HERE 26-9-87
CORRECTION START FROM NEXT LINE CONT.

3. Anxiety

instruments with technical information B

13B1 ANXIETY SCALE

Authors : D.N. Srivastava & Govind Tiwari.
Availability : Agra Psychological Research Cell, Agra.
Languages : English & Hindi.
Uses : To measure the manifest anxiety of students.
Level : School and College students.
Main features : The test consists of 100 °Yes' or °No' type items on following areas :
Psychological manifestations, ambition, future, family, relations, friendship, love, health, virtue and war, shame and guilt.
Reliability : Split-half reliability = .93, and test-retest = .91.
Validity : Validity was established by correlating the scores of this test with (i) Sinha's W-A Self Analysis Form; correlation = .71, and (ii) Sinha's Comprehensive Anxiety Test, correlation = .71.
Time : Twenty to twenty-five minutes.
Norms : Percentile norms for boys and girls are available.

13B2 SRIVASTAVA ANXIETY SCALE

Authors : Ramji Srivastava & Bina Srivastava.
Availability : Prasad Trading Corporation, J-1/53, Daranagar, Varanasi.
Language : Hindi.
Uses : To measure anxiety level of students.
Level : College and Senior High School students.
Main features : 100 items concerning hypochondriacal tendencies, paranoid suspiciousness, depression, insecurity, inferiority shame and physiological and

psychological manifestation of anxiety. The responses are obtained in one of the three categories—mostly, often, never.
Reliability : Split-half = .89, and K.R. 20 = .93.
Validity : Correlated with Sinha Anxiety Scale & Dutta Personality Inventory. The obtained coefficient was .78 and .76 respectively.
Time : No time limit but it takes around 40 minutes.
Norms : Norms based on T-scores available from Authors/Publishers.

13B3 SHORTER VERSION OF SINHA'S ANXIETY SCALE

Authors : Shamsur Rehman Khan and Qamar Hasan.
Availability : Department of Psychology, Aligarh Muslim University, Aligarh, UP.
Language : Hindi.
Uses : As a research tool to measure anxiety.
Level : Adults.
Main features : Number of items 30, selected on the basis of item-total correlation.
Time : About ten minutes.
Norms : T-score norms.

13B5 SWAMULYANKAN PRASHNAVALI : EK CHINTA MAPANI

Authors : R.R. Tripathi & Ambar Rastogi.
Availability : Raghubir Sharan Publications, Varanasi.
Uses : To measure state, trait and free floating anxieties.
Main features : Developed by Empirical-Criterion Method. Discriminating power of the items tested in terms of Standard Normal Deviates. The Z-values for all the items in the three sub-scales are significant. Item homogeneity tested by the Point Biserial 'r'.
Reliability : A—State Scale = .931 (Coefficient Alpha N = 200), A- Trait Scale = .892 (Coefficient Alpha N = 200), and Free-floating Scale = .869 (Coefficient Alpha N = 200).
Stability Coefficient : A-State Scale = .798 (N = 200), A-Trait Scale = .892 (N = 200), and Free-floating Scale = .901 (N = 200).
Validity : Convergent Validity Coefficients : Against IPAT Scale; A-State = .693 (N = 100), A-Trait = .799 (N = 100), and Free-floating = .528 (N = 100). Discriminant validity coefficients vary between .003 and .110 against the 15 sub-scales of the TPPS.
Norms : T-score and centile norms on a sample 800 males and 800 females respectively.

Reliability : Split-half reliability coefficient = .72.
Validity : Correlation with security-insecurity inventory (Maslow's adapted version) .535, and correlation with Cattell's Q_4 scale as measured by Hindi version of 16 PF = .531.
Time : Fifteen minutes.
Norms : Available with the authors.
Reference : Khan, Shamsur Rehman & Hasan, Qamar - A shorter version of Sinha's W.A. Self-Analysis Form. Psychological Studies, 1981, Vol. 26, No. 1, 8-9.

13B4 SELF ANALYSIS QUESTIONNAIRES

Authors : H. Badami & C. Badami.
Availability : Sujal Psychological Centre, 10/B, Janvishram Society, Behind Shajanand College, Ahmedabad.
Language : Gujarati.
Uses : To measure level of anxiety of students.
Level : Adolescents and adult students.
Main features : Fifty items scale indicating symptoms of anxiety. The items are concerning to physical health and fitness, material facility, friendship and sexes, family and social relations and approval and physiological manifestations. Items have been reduced simple sentences.
Reliability : Test-retest = .85, and split-half = .90.
Validity : Validity was determined in terms of indices of discrimination and internal consistency.

adaptations D

13D1 BENGALI VERSION OF STATE-TRAIT ANXIETY INVENTORY

Authors : N.B. Mallik, and P.K. Chattopadhyay.
Availability : Department of Psychology, Calcutta University College of Science & Technology, 92, A.P.C. Road, Calcutta.
Language : Bengali.
Uses : To assess anxiety for both normal and pathological subjects viz., patients suffering from various physical ailments, neurological complications and psychiatric problems; also normal girls/women experiencing anxiety during minarche and menstruation.
Level : Individuals falling in the age range of 9 to 13 years (Junior school students/children), 14 to 18 years

(High school students) and 19 to 23 years (College students/Under-Graduates; both male and female).

Main features : The inventory consists of 20 items in each scale.

Reliability : Split-half (odd-even) - Trait = 0.86, and State = 0.79. Test-retest - Trait = 0.83, and State = 0.32.

Validity : Concurrent validity = 0.73.

Time : No fixed time. But usually should take about ten minutes for each of the State and Trait scales.

Norms : Norms are available from the authors.

4. Self Concept

complete instruments **A**

14A1 SELF-CONCEPT SCALE FOR CHILDREN

Authors : H.M. Singh & S. Singh.

Availability : Agra Psychological Research Cell, Agra.

Languages : English & Hindi.

Uses : To measure the self concept of children.

Level : Children who understand the meaning of adjectives.

Main features : The scale contains 22 trait-descriptive adjectives. Each adjective is prefaced by the phrase and is followed by a five point rating scale.

Reliability : Test-retest reliability coefficient varies from .73 to .91 for boys and girls of different school grades.

Validity : Not indicated.

Time : Fifteen minutes.

14A1 SELF-CONCEPT SCALE FOR CHILDREN

(The following items have to be checked on a 5-point scale).

1. I am friendly.
2. I am happy.
3. I am kind.
4. I am brave.
5. I am honest.
6. I am likable.
7. I am trustful.
8. ~~I am~~ good.
9. I am proudly.
10. I am lazy.
11. I am loyal.
12. I am co-operative

13. I am cheerful.
14. I am thoughtful.
15. I am popular.
16. I am courteous.
17. I am jealous.
18. I am polite.
19. I am bashful.
20. I am clean.
21. I am helpful.
22. I am obedient.

information with technical information **B**

14B1 SELF-CONCEPT INVENTORY (SCI)

Authors : M.P. Uniyal & Beena Shah.
Availability : Authors, Department of Education, Garhwal University, Srinagar, Garhwal.
Language : Hindi.
Uses : To assess the level of self-concept.
Level : Teachers.
Main features : It is an inventory of 63 items to be answered on a 5-point rating scale. It has 8 dimensions.
Reliability : Test-retest reliability was found to be 0.873.
Validity : Validated against the Sagar Sharma's self-concept inventory and its value was found to be 0.682.
Time : No time limit, generally it requires about 30 minutes.
Norms : Norms are available with the authors.
Reference : Shah, Renu. "A Study of Job Satisfaction of Teachers in Relation to Their Self-Concept", M.Ed. Dissertation, Garhwal University, 1981.

14B2 SELF-CONCEPT SCALE

Author : Mukta Rani Rastogi.
Availability : Agra Psychological Research Cell, Agra.
Main features : The Scale consists of 51 statements. Each statement is followed by a 5-point rating scale.
Reliability : Reliability established by split-half method following Spearman-Brown Prophecy formula was found to be .87.
Validity : Content validity was established on the basis of the ratings by experts. Item discrimination value and homogeneity of items was also determined statistically.

Time : About 30 minutes.
Norms : Mean scores norms available.

14B3 SELF IMAGE QUESTIONNAIRE

Authors : Padma Agarwal & V.D. Misra.
Availability : M/s Indian Psychological Corporation, Shanti-Sadan, R.B.L. Road, Lucknow.
Language : Hindi.
Uses : To measure the adjustment of boys and girls.
Level : Fourteen to eighteen years (boys and girls).
Main features : Six point scale is used.
Reliability : Split-half r = 0.769.
Validity : Validity coefficient = .583.
Time : No time limit, but usually, forty minutes time is required.
Norms : Percentile and T-score norms are given in the Manual.

14B4 SELF PERCEPTION SCALE

Author : M.C. Agarwal.
Availability : Author, P.O. NITIE, Vihar Lake Road, Bombay.
Language : English.
Uses : To judge the self confidence of supervisors in their abilities.
Level : Middle level supervisors.
Main features : Likert method 5-point scale used number of items = 22.
Reliability : Correlational method of item analysis used. All the items found significant at 1% level.
Validity : As mentioned above.
Time : Twenty to twenty-five minutes.
Norms : No.
Reference : Agarwal, M.C. "Self Perception of Supervisors" - Perspective in Psychological Researches (Accepted for Publication).

14B5 SELF-ESTEEM INVENTORY

Authors : M.S. Prasad and G.P. Thakar.
Availability : Agra Psychological Research Cell, Belanganj, Agra.
Language : Hindi.
Level : Under-graduate students - 15-19 years.
Main features : The inventory has two sets of 30 identical statements but different instructions. One set assesses personally perceived self and the other, socially per-

ceived self. Each statement is scored on a 7-point scale.

Reliability : Split-half reliability (N = 400) = .82 for personally perceived self and .78 for socially perceived self. The test-retest reliability for both the tests were found to be .69 and .66 respectively for personally perceived self and socially perceived self.

14B6 SELF-ESTEEM SCALE

Authors : R.D. Caplan & R.K. Naidu.
Availability : Author, Department of Psychology, University of Allahabad, Allahabad.
Languages : English and Hindi.
Uses : For measuring person-environment fit among University students.
Level : University students.
Main features : Consisted of 5 items designed to measure experiences in study and examinations, on a 5-point response scale.
Reliability : Coefficient alpha - the coefficient of internal consistency was computed. Correlation between items was also computed. Two indices were found and r values ranged from .45 to .46 and alpha values ranged from .62 to .63.
Validity : Not available.
Time : Average three minutes.
Norms : Not available.
Reference : Caplan, R.D. & Naidu, R.K. Stress, coping and social support : A study of University students in India.

citations C

14C1 SWATVA BODH PARIKSHAN

Author : Pramod Kumar Goswami.
Reference : A study of self-concept of adolescents and its relationship to scholastic achievement and adjustment. Unpublished Ph.D. thesis, Agra University, Agra, 1978.

14C2 PERCEIVED PARENTAL BEHAVIOUR AND SELF CONCEPT RATING SCALE

Author : Shashi Kala.

Availability : Author, Department of Psychology, University of Mysore, Mysore.

14C3 SELF PERCEPTION SCALE

Author : K.G. Agrawal.
Availability : Author, Department of Psychology, Udaipur University, Udaipur.

FIG MS 139

adaptations D

14D1 THE TEXAS SOCIAL BEHAVIOUR INVENTORY

Authors : Afzal Kureshi and Rahat Ali Khan.
Availability : Department of Psychology, Aligarh Muslim University, Aligarh.
Language : Hindi.
Uses : To differentiate individuals on the dimensions of self-concept and self-esteem.
Level : College and University students, and also with non-student adolescents and adults.
Main features : The test consists of 32 declarative items to which subject has to respond in by showing his extent of agreement in either of the given five response categories.
Reliability : The split-half reliability of the Hindi version is .61 (N = 192).
Validity : Significant positive correlation reported between TSBI and the self-esteem scale of the CPI for males : .50 and for females : .52, significant positive correlation between TSBI and PAQ self rating scale, and TSBI positively correlated with a projective measure of fear of failure (r = .56).
Time : About 25 minutes.
Norms : For the Indian subjects under preparation.

5. Motivation

complete instruments A

15A1 TAT INSTRUMENT TO MEASURE PERSONAL ACHIEVEMENT

MOTIVATION, SOCIAL ACHIEVEMENT MOTIVATION AND INFLUENCE MOTIVATION.

Author : Prayag Mehta.
Availability : National Labour Institute, AB-6, Safdarjang Enclave, New Delhi.
Language : English.
Uses : To measure personal achievement, social achievement and influence motivation.
Level : Adults.
Main features : The set consists of six pictures :

1. A group of persons and a person walking aside the group looking at the group of workers.
2. Workers are entering in a factory and a chowkidar is standing outside the gate.
3. Man and a young boy. The boy is sitting on the floor with a book in his hand and the man is looking at him.
4. A line of people standing in queue. One person seen outside the line and other bending on knees sitting.
5. A woman sitting with child in her lap with one hand streaking slightly out. Besides it, a portion of car nd a man seen.
6. Few workers are working on lathe machine and others are looking at other work.

Reliability : Inter score reliability were found.
Validity : Construct and predictive validity established.
Time : Thirty minutes.
Norms : Scores are available for steel and coal employees.
Reference :

1. Mehta, Prayag : Scoring stories for motivational profile. A manual for personal achievement, social achievement and influence motivation, New Delhi, National Labour Institute, 1979 (Mimeo).
2. Mehta, Prayag : Employee motivation and work satisfaction in a public enterprise. Vikalpa, A Journal of Decision Makers, 1977, 2(3), 223-236.
3. Mehta, Prayag : Work motivation in Indian Public Sector. Some conceptualisation, National Labour Institute Bulletin, 1978, 90-99.
4. Mehta, Prayag : Motivational approach to organisation development. National Labour Institute Bulletin, 1980, 134-135.
5. Mehta, Prayag : A note on some suggested research in management of work organisations. Indian Journal of Industrial Relations, 1980, 16(2), 277-285.

15A1 T.A.T. INSTRUMENT TO MEASURE PERSONAL ACHIEVEMENT

MOTIVATION, SOCIAL ACHIEVEMENT MOTIVATION AND INFLUENCE MOTIVATION
Description of the pictures is given under main features.

15A2 APPROVAL MOTIVE SCALE

Authors : N.K.M. Tripathi & L.B. Tripathi.
Availability : National Psychological Corporation, Kacheri Ghat, Agra.
Language : Hindi, English.
Uses : To determine approval seeking.
Level : Adolescents.
Main features : The scale consists of 72- 'True', 'false' items distributed in 7 areas of approval motive-normative behaviour, social conformity, positive self presentation, defensiveness, dependency, social responsiveness and social approval.
Reliability : Test-retest reliability (N = 120) = .80 with an index of reliability of .89, and split-half reliability (N = 500) = .82 with an index of reliability of .92.
Validity : The scale has satisfactory content validity, construct validity, intrinsic validity and predictive validity.
Time : No time limit, but it takes about forty minutes.
Norms : Percentile norms are available for boys and girls.
Reference :

1. Tripathi, N.K.M. Cognitive complexity and approval motive. Journal of Education and Psychology, 1978, 36, 71-77.
2. Tripathi, N.K.M. Social perception as a function of approval motive. Psychologia, 1978, 21, 136-142.

15A2 APPROVAL MOTIVE SCALE

(The following statements have to be checked whether they are 'true' or 'false').

1. I am prepared to help people in trouble in all possible ways without any hesitation.
2. I don't consider the scenes of kissing, embracing etc. in the movies immoral.
3. Before extending my assistance to any one, I consider his suitability for it.
4. At times I have become stubborn so that every thing is done according to my wishes.
5. I remember that several times I have feigned illness in order to be exempted from difficulties.

6. I behave properly with the elders of the family under any circumstances.
7. Several times I have stopped working on many tasks presuming that I do not possess the necessary ability to do those jobs.
8. If, I get a chance to see a movie without paying for it, I take it.
9. I do not possess the necessary ability to do those jobs.
10. I do not consider it proper to jest and make fun with my elders.
11. If I am unsuccessful in a job, I do not beg help from my friends.
12. I am always ready to serve others.
13. I do good to even those people who are by nature wicked.
14. All the times, I consider it necessary to be very particular about my style of living, conversation and dress.
15. I think, it is proper to state my opinion about anything the way I feel it.
16. I do not endorse all appropriate Indian customs and styles of living.
17. No matter how big a crisis may be, I never lose my self-confidence.
18. Sometimes instead of forgiving and forgetting someone's offence, I try to take revenge upon him.
19. It is difficult for me to work until and unless someone encourages me.
20. I can never disagree with the opinions of prestigious people.
21. I even listen to those people whom I do not like.
22. I do not think that all poor men are thieves.
23. Under any circumstances, I wish to be known as wise, intelligent and a man of character.
24. I never set out upon a long journey without arrangements for my safety.
25. I do not consider it unethical to overhear other people's secrets sometimes.
26. I myself can evaluate my abilities and capacities, others can not.
27. On many occasions, I take advantage of others.
28. There have been occasions in my life when I have wanted to indulge in destructive activities.
29. I consider that even watching vulgar dances can be good entertainment.
30. At times I gossip and criticise others.
31. Unusually I do not feel jealous of others people's

good fortune.

32. When I do not know a thing, I always admit my ignorance of it.
33. I think that a person gets into trouble only because of his own faults.
34. In all circumstances, I try to observe the social customs.
35. If one's wife is not to his liking, then I think it is good to leave her.
36. Whenever I am conversing with someone I listen to him attentively.
37. There have been several occasions when I have thought of rebelling against authorities.
38. I never consider it proper to hurt any body.
39. I never think it proper to poke my nose into people's affair.
40. I do not want to maintain good relations with as many people as possible.
41. I think it is alright for some people to lead a different and open life from the ordinary people.
42. I like to meet new people.
43. Knowingly, I never utter a sentence which may hurt others.
44. Whenever a task is given to me, I like to begin it at once and continue it till it is done.
45. I like to be appreciated by others under all circumstances.
46. I have never hated any one too much.
47. I thoroughly investigate the capabilities of all the nominees before casting my vote.
48. I think that there may be other goals in life besides helping others.
49. Sometimes if needed I take help from my Juniors/Youngers or people of lower status as well.
50. Whatever people may say sometimes I do not consider it wrong at all to fulfill my desires by any means.
51. I always feel happy when others succeed and make progress.
52. Sometimes I have doubts about my capacities to succeed in life.
53. I am always careful about my appearance.
54. I take my meals at home in the same styles as I do with my friends or relatives.
55. I am always prepared to admit my mistakes.
56. I expect others to show opposite to the behaviour that I myself extend towards them.
57. I never get depressed on being unsuccessful.
58. On some occasions I do not think it wrong to be

jealous of others.

59. I always do what I say.
60. I often get annoyed with those people who want me to do injustice.
61. I like repaying someone's good deed.
62. I always show respect unhesitatingly towards my elders.
63. Sometimes I try to fulfill my needs by any means.
64. I always want to work according to the desires and suggestions of my elders.
65. I never think it proper to consider myself perfect.
66. Even in tense situations, I consider it proper to maintain good relations with the members of my family.
67. I never knowingly utter a sentence which might hurt others.
68. I do not find it difficult to work even with those who speak loudly and violently.
69. I do not consider it improper to secure a bob by any means.
70. I do not consider it improper to be partial to my relatives sometimes.
71. I never want others to suffer for my mistakes.
72. I think that people get into trouble because they deserve it.

15A3 PROLONGED DEPRIVATION SCALE

Authors : Girishwar Misra & L.B. Tripathi.
Availability : National Psychological Corporation, Kacherighat, Agra.
Language : English & Hindi.
Uses : As a quantitative measure of experimental deprivation.
Main features : The scale utilizes the techniques of interview, observation and rating. There are 96 items with 5-response-alternatives. It covers 15 areas of natural life along which members of the society enjoy different types of experiences. They are : residential accommodation, physical environment of home, economic status, food, clothing, educational experiences, rearing experiences, childhood experiences, parental characteristics, interaction with parents, motivational experiences, experience of reservation and travel, religious experiences, and miscellaneous quasicultural experiences.
Reference :

(1) Tripathi, L.B. & Misra, G. Cognitive activities as a

function of prolonged deprivation *Psychological Studies*, 1975, *21*, 54-61.
(2) Tripathi, L.B. & Misra, G. Some cognitive processes as functions of prolonged deprivation. *Indian Journal of Psychology*, 1976, *51*, 129-145.
(3) Misra, G. & Tripathi, L.B. The concept of prolonged deprivation and its measurement. *Indian Journal of Behaviour*, 1977, 1, 48-60.
(4) Misra, G. & Tripathi, L.B. Prolonged deprivation scale. *Indian Journal of Psychology*, 1978, *53*, 65-76.
(5) Misra, G. & Tripathi, L.B. Psychological Consequences of Prolonged Deprivation. Agra : National Psychological Corporation, 1980.

15A3 PROLONGED DEPRIVATION SCALE

1. In which type of house have you been living till now?
(a) Pucca cemented house
(b) Partly cemented, partly katcha
(c) Katcha house made with fire-bricks
(d) Partly katcha house and partly hut or thatched-roof
(e) Hut.

2. Is the house spacious enough for the number of persons living in it?
(a) More than sufficient
(b) Sufficient
(c) Tolerable
(d) Insufficient
(e) Extremely insufficient.

3. In what condition is your house? (Whether dilapidated, or strong-looking,in what physical condition is it?)
(a) Very strong
(b) Strong
(c) Average
(d) Weak and broken
(e) Very dilapidated.

4. What facilities (e.g. Courtyard, Verandah, Drawing-room with Windows, Lawn, Foreground, Latrine etc.) are available in the house?
(a) All facilities
(b) Most of the facilities
(c) Average

(d) A few facilities only
(e) Very few facilities.

5. What is the spatial location of the residence in the village/township?
(a) In the centre
(b) Near the central position
(c) Away from central position
(d) Far away from central position
(e) On the periphery.

6. Of what castes/socio-economic status (SES) are the residents of your neighbourhood?
(a) People of all castes/SES
(b) Of many castes/SES
(c) Of the same castes/SES
(d) Of all castes/SES
(e) Of very low castes/SES
(Note : Low is relative to the caste/SES of the subject).

7. What kinds of utensils are available in your house?
(a) Stainless steel, white-metal, china-pots and cups
(b) Some pots of stainless steel, white metal
(c) White metal and aluminium
(d) Brass and aluminium
(e) Mostly aluminium and earthen-pots.

8. What kinds of furniture are used in your house?
(a) Sofa, Chair, Table, Wall-Shelf, Bedstead etc.
(b) Some Chairs, Table, Charpoy
(c) Few Chairs, Table Charpoy
(d) Charpoy only
(e) Insufficient charpoys and straw mats.

9. What facilities are available for drinking-water in your house?
(a) Tube-well, Water-supply
(b) Hand-pump at a small distance
(c) Hand-pump at a long distance
(d) Well at some distance
(e) Well at a long distance.

10. What is the lighting arrangement in your house?
(a) Electricity
(b) Partly electricity and partly kerosin lamps
(c) Lanterns
(d) Indigenous earthen-lamps

(e) Controlled/occasional use of indigenous earthen-lamps.

11. What type of agricultural implements are available?
(a) Tractor,Tube-well and other implements
(b) Tube-well/Plough, Fodder machine
(c) Plough, Fodder machine
(d) Only plough
(e) Nothing.

12. What means of transportation are available?
(a) Car, Motor
(b) Motorcycle, Scooter
(c) Bicycle
(d) Occasional bicycle
(e) Dependence of foot.

13. How much printed literature (e.g., Books, Newspapers, magazines etc.) is available in the house?)
(a) Considerable number of books and daily supply of newspapers, and magazines
(b) Few books, occasional use of magazines and newspapers
(c) Newspapers, regular use of books
(d) Few books or occasional use of newspapers
(e) Nothing.

14. What are the mechanical gadgets available in the house?
(a) Radio, Clock, Refrigerator, Telephone etc.
(b) Radio, Clock, Gun etc.
(c) Radio, Clock, Torch etc.
(d) Torch and few photographs
(e) Few photographs only or nothing.

15. What are the sources of family income?
(a) Professional service, good agriculture/lucrative business
(b) Professional service only/good agriculture
(c) Average service (middle-class)/small agricultural holding
(d) Menial service/small landholding
(e) Daily wages.

16. Is the income of family sufficient to cover all expenditures?
(a) More than sufficient

(b) Sufficient
(c) Average
(d) Insufficient
(e) Very insufficient.

17. How much cultivated land have you in your family?
(a) More than sufficient (20 Bighas or more)
(b) Sufficient (10 to 20 Bighas)
(c) Average (5 to 10 Bighas)
(d) Insufficient (1 to 5 Bighas)
(e) Very insufficient (up to only 1 Bigha).

18. What is the cattle property?
(a) Ox, cow, buffalo, she-goat, hen
(b) Cow, one pair of ox
(c) One pair of ox, or 1 ox and one buffalo
(d) One ox/or cow
(e) Nothing.

19. What is the area of orchard in profession?
(a) Very big (several bighas)
(b) Enough (2-3 Bighas)
(c) Average (20-25 trees)
(d) Less than average (5 to 10 trees)
(e) Nothing.

20. What is the debt-position of your family?
(a) No debt
(b) Small amount
(c) Moderate amount
(d) Large amount
(e) Huge amount.

21. What is the general quantum of economic difficulties of your family
(a) Very little
(b) Little
(c) Average
(d) Fairly large
(e) Extremely large.

22. What is the daily meal programme in your family?
(a) Two daily meals with morning breakfast and evening snacks
(b) Two daily meals with morning breakfast
(c) Only two meals
(d) One meal in 24 hours with certainty
(e) Uncertainty concerning daily meals.

23. What are the items commonly included in food items?
(a) Rice, bread, dal, ghee, vegetables, meat, curd, sweets, etc.
(b) Everything but occasional use of meat, curd, etc.
(c) Rice and bread only
(d) Only rice or bread and coarse grains
(e) Coarse grains with uncertainty about quality and quantity.

24. To which extent nutritive material (e.g., milk, curd, fruits, meat, etc.) are used?
(a) Nearly regularly
(b) With sufficient frequency
(c) With average frequency
(d) Less than average frequency
(e) Occasionally.

25. What is the quantum of use of sugar and tea in your family?
(a) Nearly regularly
(b) With sufficient frequency
(c) With average frequency
(d) Less than average frequency
(e) Occasionally.

26. In general, what kinds of cloths are used in your family?
(a) All types of clothes, i.e., cotton, woolen, silk, synthetic fibre clothes
(b) Cotton, woollen, some synthetic fibre clothes
(c) Cotton, some woollen
(d) Mostly cotton, some synthetic
(e) Cotton only.

27. Do you have sufficient clothes?
(a) More than sufficient
(b) Sufficient
(c) Average
(d) Insufficient
(e) Very insufficient.

28. Since what age have you been using footwear?
(a) Use of footwear from early childhood
(b) From late childhood
(c) From adolescence
(d) Only after adolescence
(e) Only occasionally.

29. What kind of bed do you use?
(a) Bedstead, cushion, pillow, quilt, mosquito-net
(b) Mattress with cotton padding, chaddar, quilt, charpoy
(c) Mattress with cotton padding and quilt
(d) Rough mattress with cotton padding and either blanket or chaddar
(e) Either quilt or blanket or chaddar.

30. At what age did you begin study in school?
(a) Early childhood
(b) Late childhood
(c) Adolescence
(d) Adulthood
(e) Never.

31. What are your educational attainments?
(a) Graduate or more
(b) Secondary
(c) Middle high school
(d) Up to primary
(e) Illiterate.

32. How many years have you spent in educational institution.
(a) 13 years and above
(b) 10 to 12 years
(c) 6 to 9 years
(d) Up to 5 years
(e) Less than one year.

33. How regular were you in your school?
(a) Very regular
(b) Regular
(c) Average
(d) Less than average
(e) Very irregular.

34. How frequent was your interaction with teachers?
(a) Very frequent
(b) Frequent
(c) Average
(d) Infrequent
(e) Occasional.

35. How much interest did you take in extra-curricular activities?

(a) Extraordinary
(b) Sufficient
(c) Normal
(d) Insufficient
(e) No interest.

36. What castes of classmates were there in your school-days?
(a) Of all castes
(b) Of many castes
(c) Of your own caste
(d) Of lower castes
(e) Of lowest castes.

37. By whom you were brought up during childhood?
(a) By your own parents
(b) By your mother or your father
(c) By your own relation
(d) By your distant relation
(e) By person having very distant relation or uncertain.

38. In whose company did you spent most of your time during childhood?
(a) Father and mother
(b) Only mother or father
(c) Some class relation
(d) Some distant relation
(e) Uncertain.

39. How much attention did your parents/guardians paid to you during your childhood?
(a) More than sufficient
(b) Sufficient
(c) Average
(d) Insufficient
(e) Extremely insufficient.

40. How much affection did your parents extent to you during childhood?
(a) Sufficiently affectionate
(b) Very affectionate
(c) Moderately affectionate
(d) Insufficient
(e) No affection.

41. Under what type of discipline did your parents brought you up during your childhood?
(a) Highly disciplined (liberal)

(b) Fairly high
(c) Moderate
(d) Insufficient
(e) Extremely insufficient (less discipline).

42. How much time did you spend with children of your age groups?
(a) Most frequently
(b) Frequently
(c) Moderately
(d) Insufficiently
(e) Rarely.

43. What kind of friends did you have during your childhood?
(a) Of all castes
(b) Of many castes
(c) Of the same caste
(d) Of lower castes
(e) Of extremely lower castes.

44. How much opportunity did you have for play and recreation during childhood?
(a) Very frequently
(b) Frequently
(c) Occasionally
(d) Infrequently
(e) Rarely.

45. How frequently did you go to market-places (Bajaar) during your childhood?
(a) Most frequently
(b) Frequently
(c) Occasionally
(d) Infrequently
(e) Rarely.

46. With what frequency did you get opportunity to hear folklore from your elders during childhood?
(a) Most frequently
(b) Frequently
(c) Occasionally
(d) Infrequently
(e) Rarely.

47. How much opportunity did you have to go to religious and other places during childhood?
(a) Most frequently

(b) Frequently
(c) Occasionally
(d) Infrequently
(e) Rarely.

48. How frequently did you participate in household activities during your childhood?
(a) Most frequently
(b) Frequently
(c) Occasionally
(d) Infrequently
(e) Rarely.

49. How much educated are your parents/guardians?
(a) Adequately educated
(b) Father adequately educated
(c) Father moderately educated
(d) Father literate
(e) Father uneducated.

50. How sufficient is the income of your parents/guardians?
(a) More than sufficient
(b) Sufficient
(c) Average
(d) Insufficient
(e) Very insufficient.

51. What is the political status of your parents?
(a) Very high
(b) High
(c) Average
(d) Low
(e) Very low.

52. In general, what kind of reputation do your parents have in the community?
(a) Very high
(b) High
(c) Average
(d) Low
(e) Very low.

53. In general, what type of relation do your parents/guardians have with each other?
(a) Very good
(b) Good
(c) Average
(d) Bad

(e) Very bad.

54. In general, how much worry and anxiety do your parents/guardians exhibit?
(a) Least anxious
(b) Anxious
(c) Moderately anxious
(d) Very anxious
(e) Extremely anxious.

55. How healthy are your parents/guardians?
(a) Very healthy
(b) Healthy
(c) Moderately healthy
(d) Poor health
(e) Very poor health.

56. How easily do you express your opinions before your elders in the family or outside?
(a) Fully expressed
(b) Partially expressed
(c) Moderately expressed
(d) Occasionally expressed
(e) Rarely expressed.

57. To what extent, in general, do your views correspond to the views of your parents/guardians?
(a) Always
(b) Usually
(c) Moderately
(d) Occasionally
(e) Rarely.

58. What kind of expectations do your parents have from you?
(a) Extremely ambitious
(b) Highly ambitious
(c) Moderately ambitious
(d) Less ambitious
(e) Least ambitious.

59. In general, how much guidance did you get from your parents/guardians?
(a) Always
(b) Usually
(c) Frequently
(d) Occasionally
(e) Rarely.

60. How frequently do you involve to quarrel/hot argument with parents/guardians?
(a) Never
(b) Occasionally
(c) Moderately
(d) Frequently
(e) Very frequently.

61. To what extent or the average do you co-operate with your parents/guardians?
(a) Always
(b) Usually
(c) Moderately
(d) Occasionally
(e) Rarely.

62. To what extent is your need for social prestige fulfilled?
(a) Extremely well
(b) Well
(c) Average
(d) Very little
(e) Never.

63. To what extent is your need for getting company of others fulfilled?
(a) Fully
(b) Partially
(c) Moderately
(d) Slightly
(e) Least.

64. To what extent is your curiosity or need for knowing things satisfied?
(a) Fully
(b) Partially
(c) Moderately
(d) Slightly
(e) Least.

65. To what extent is your desire for making your own decisions
(a) Fully
(b) Partially
(c) Moderately
(d) Slightly
(e) Least.

66. To what extent is your desire for going to places, or act according to your own desire fulfilled?
(a) Always
(b) Usually
(c) Moderately
(d) Occasionally
(e) Rarely.

67. To what extent are your expectations from family members fulfilled?
(a) Always
(b) Usually
(c) Moderately
(d) Occasionally
(e) Rarely.

68. To which extent, in general, is your desire to dominate others fulfilled?
(a) Always
(b) Usually
(c) Moderately
(d) Occasionally
(e) Rarely.

69. To what extent is your desire for taking initiative satisfied?
(a) Always
(b) Usually
(c) Moderately
(d) Occasionally
(e) Rarely.

70. How dissatisfied and unhappy are you with your present mode of life?
(a) Extremely unhappy and dissatisfied
(b) Highly
(c) Moderately
(d) Partially
(e) Least.

71. How varied are your interests?
(a) Extremely varied
(b) Highly varied
(c) Moderately varied
(d) Partially varied
(e) Least varied.

72. How frequently do you think about future plans?
(a) Very frequently
(b) Frequently
(c) Sometimes
(d) Infrequently
(e) Rarely.

73. In general, how contented do you feel to be?
(a) Extremely
(b) Frequently
(c) Sometimes
(d) Infrequently
(e) Rarely.

74. How afraid or panicky do you feel, in general, from different types of objects, conditions and events?
(a) Extremely
(b) Highly
(c) Moderately
(d) Less than moderately
(e) Very little.

75. How neglected are you by others?
(a) Most
(b) Much
(c) Average
(d) Less than average
(e) Least.

76. How much sympathy do you get from others?
(a) Most
(b) Much
(c) Average
(d) Less than average
(e) Least.

77. How anxious and tense do you feel, in general?
(a) Most
(b) Much
(c) Average
(d) Less than average
(e) Least.

78. How much others praise you?
(a) Most
(b) Much
(c) Average
(d) Less than average

(e) Least.

79. How much of opportunity have you got in your life to get rewards?
(a) Always
(b) Frequently
(c) Sometimes
(d) Infrequently
(e) Rarely.

80. How healthy do you keep?
(a) Extremely
(b) Very
(c) Neither healthy nor unhealthy
(d) Slightly unhealthy
(e) Extremely unhealthy.

81. What facilities are available to you for your entertainments?
(a) Cinema, Radio, Playhouse, Games of choice
(b) Cinema, Radio
(c) Only Radio
(d) Only some sports and games
(e) Only talking with others.

82. How varied are your experiences of entertainment?
(a) Extremely varied
(b) Highly varied
(c) Moderately varied
(d) Slightly varied
(e) Least varied.

83. How much leisure time do you get?
(a) Least
(b) Less than moderate
(c) Moderate
(d) More than moderate
(e) Too much.

84. How much opportunity have you got so far of travels?
(a) Extremely
(b) Less than moderate
(c) Moderate
(d) More than moderate
(c) Too much.

85. How much time do you devote in religious rituals?
(a) Extremely

(b) Highly
(c) Moderately
(d) Occasionally
(e) Rarely.

86. How many rituals are observed in your family? (Such as rituals observed in your culture on religious days, and important days like birthday, marriage, etc.).
(a) Highly acquainted
(b) Almost all
(c) Some of them
(d) A few of them
(e) Very few of them.

87. How acquainted are you with other religions?
(a) Highly acquainted
(b) Fairly well
(c) Moderately
(d) Slightly
(e) Least.

88. People of what castes can take their meals in your family?
(a) Of all castes
(b) Of almost all castes
(c) Of some castes
(d) Of a few castes
(e) Of no other castes.

89. People of how many castes can touch your drinking-water?
(a) Of all castes
(b) Of almost all castes
(c) Of some castes
(d) Of a few castes
(e) Of no other castes.

90. People of how many castes can drink water brought by you?
(a) Of all castes
(b) Of almost all castes
(c) Of some castes
(d) Of a few castes
(e) Of no other castes.

91. People of how many castes can sit with you?
(a) Of all castes

(b) Of almost all castes
(c) Of some castes
(d) Of a few castes
(e) Of no other castes.

92. With which caste people can you sit on a charpai?
(a) Of all castes
(b) Of almost all castes
(c) Of some castes
(d) Of a few castes
(e) Of no other castes.

93. To what extent you participate in social activities of higher caste people?
(a) Of all castes
(b) Of almost all castes
(c) Of some castes
(d) Of a few castes
(e) Of no other castes.

94. How important do you find yourself in social activities of your mohalla/village/town?
a. Extremely
b. High
c. Moderately
d. Slightly
e. Least.

95. What kind of reputation do you have in the village/mohalla/town?
a. Extremely high
b. High
c. Moderate
d. Low
e. Very low.

96. How much contact do you have with city-life?
a. Very frequent
b. Frequently
c. Moderate
d. Slight
e. Least.

15A4 PERSONALITY NEED INVENTORY (PNI)

Author : C.P. Sharma.
Availability : Agra Psychological Research Cell, Belanganj, Agra.

Languages : English & Hindi.

Uses : To measure the psychological needs of personality variables.

Level : Adolescents 16 and above.

Main features : In the present test, 24-pairs of statement have been used to compare and measure the personality variables of n-achievement, n-affiliation, n-order and n-change. There are other 4-pairs of statements measuring the internal consistency of the test. The scale comprises of 28-pairs of statements arranged in random order.

Reliability : Test-retest reliability (N = 150) ranges from .54 to .79 for four needs. Reliability index is also calculated and found to be highly significant.

Validity : For the purpose of external validation, the need scores of PNI were correlated with need scores of the EPPS and validity coefficient was found to be ranging from .42 to .61 for the four needs (N = 150). The internal consistency has been found out by discrimination power of the test determined by point-biserial r.

Norms : T scores norms for male and female students are available.

15A4 PERSONALITY NEED INVENTORY (PNI)
(The respondent has to check one of the statements he likes more).

1. (a) I want to do deeds through best method.
   (b) I wish to help lame and poor people.
2. (a) I wish to share the joys and sorrows of others.
   (b) I want to do new works in an organised manner.
3. (a) I want to bring newness in my works.
   (b) I want to do my works in an organised way.
4. (a) I want to keep my things in a fine new way.
   (b) I wish to receive prestigeable place in the society.
5. (a) I want to get success in our works.
   (b) I want to get fresh news.
6. (a) I want to live faithfully with my friends.
   (b) I want to keep my things always organised.
7. (a) I want to do my works in best possible manner.
   (b) I want to help lame and poor people.
8. (a) I want to travel new place.
   (b) I wish to receive best to best places.
9. (a) I want to bring change in my life.
   (b) I want to be co-operative to others.
10. (a) I want to get good marks in examination.
    (b) I want to do my class-work daily regularly.

11. (a) I want to do work for good faith of others.
    (b) I want to get a good place in the class.
12. (a) I want to utilise my money in the best manner.
    (b) I want to share the sorrows of sorrow-stricken people.
13. (a) I want to do work through the organised manner only.
    (b) I want to read new books.
14. (a) I want to share joys and sorrows of others.
    (b) I want to do new works.
15. (a) I want to get success in my deeds.
    (b) I want to help lame and poor people.
16. (a) I want to get good marks in the examination.
    (b) I want to get fresh news.
17. (a) I want to get good position in the class.
    (b) I want to keep my things neatly and by new methods.
18. (a) I want to share joys-sorrows of others.
    (b) I want to do my works through best methods.
19. (a) I want to live faithfully with friends.
    (b) I want to do new works.
20. (a) I want to do work good for the others.
    (b) I want to keep always my things properly.
21. (a) I want to get a reform in my works.
    (b) I want to keep my things in an organised way.
22. (a) I want to bring novelty in my life.
    (b) I want to get best position.
23. (a) I want to do my work in a new manner.
    (b) I want to co-operate with others.
24. (a) I want to go excursion to new places.
    (b) I want to do works in an ordinary way.
25. (a) I want to make good use of my money.
    (b) I want to get good status in Society.
26. (a) I want to work according to my routine.
    (b) I want to share the worries of poor.
27. (a) I want to be regular in my class work.
    (b) I want to read new books.
28. (a) I want to keep my books in a new and orderly style.
    (b) I want to hold good position in society.

15A5 TEST OF ENCOURAGEMENT GIVEN BY THE PARENTS

Author : Mohana Sekhar.
Availability : Author, Department of Education, University of Bombay, Bombay.
Language : English.
Uses : To assess degree of encouragement given by the

parents.

Level : High School, Colleges, University students. Adult male and female and professional college students.

Main features : Likert type rating scale consisting of 18 statements to be rated on a four point scale. Summated score on the test gives degree of encouragement given both by father and mother.

Reliability : Test-retest reliability = 0.74.

Validity : Against an external criterion of a single question in the form of a four point rating scale gave a value of 0.33.

Time : No time limit but usually takes twenty minutes.

Norms : Percentile norms - available with the author.

Reference : Sekhar, M. "A study of creativity in relation to home environmental factors". Doctoral thesis in education. Bombay University, 1980.

15A5 TEST OF ENCOURAGEMENT GIVEN BY THE PARENTS
(The following statements have to be checked on a 4-point scale for mother and father separately).

1. My parents provide me with books of my choice.
2. My parents take interest in my hobbies.
3. My parents do not provide me with the materials I need for trying out a new idea.
4. My parents encourage me to contact people and find out about things.
5. My parents do not take me to film shows which are to my liking.
6. My parents forbid me from doing things which they cannot do.
7. My parents appreciate my out of pattern ideas.
8. My parents do not allow me to go for school trips excursions etc.
9. My parents even though they may not like the design or the colour of the pattern I have drawn, do not criticise saying that it is not good.
10. My parents take interest in accompanying me to fairs, exhibition etc.
11. My parents do not like me to take part in any games after school hours.
12. When I ask questions my parents do not put me off but try and explain to me what it is all about.
13. My parents do not allow me to take part in external activities of the school.
14. My parents do not allow me to freely mix with other children.
15. My parents encourage me to learn new things/try out

new ideas in any field.

16. In the event of failure my parents do not let me got discouraged but encourage me to make more efforts.
17. My parents do not assign any important work to me.
18. My parents buy me games like building blocks, combino, or other word puzzles to improve my imagination.

FIG MS P 167

instruments with technical information B

15B1 THE FF MOTIVATION TEST

Authors : Afzal Kureshi and Rahat Ali Khan.
Availability : Department of Psychology, Aligarh Muslim University, Aligarh.
Language : Non-language pictorial test.
Uses : This is a thematic apperception type, designed to measure fear of failure motivation constituting (a) defense against the less in self-estimate, (b) defense against punishment, (c) defense against a less in social value.
Level : Subjects from schools, colleges and from clinical, industrial and other social settings. Literate as well as illiterate.
Main features : The test consists of eight pictures to be used as items of a test eliciting themes of fear of failure that can be analysed and scored by means of the Hostile Press Scoring System.
Reliability : Internal consistency of the test as ensured by the split-half reliability method = .79 (N = 192).
Validity :

1. High FF persons more avoidant to take an achievement task.
2. FF and fear of death positively correlated.
3. External locus of control and FF positively correlated.
4. FF and anxiety positively related : r = .29, df = 191 FF motivation also positively related to Texas social behaviour inventory : r = .56; social desirability scale : .18; and the telic dominance scale : r = .396.

Time : 40 to 50 minutes.
Norms : In the process.
Reference :

1. Kureshi, A. AAPAS Motive Test, Rupa Psychological

Corporation, Varanasi, 1971.
2. Kureshi, A. and Khan, R.A. A study of certain personality correlates of fear of failure (communicated).
3. Kureshi, A. and Khan, R.A. FF social desirability, self-esteem and telic dominance - A study of relationship (under process).

15B2 THE POWER MOTIVE TEST

Authors : Afzal Kureshi and Bilquees Fatma.
Availability : Department of Psychology, Aligarh Muslim University, Aligarh.
Language : Non-language.
Uses : Can be used in the studies of individual differences. Its research uses include assessment of power motive as a dimension of personality.
Level : Can be used with subjects of all ages except small children, both literate and illiterate, and under clinical, industrial and experimental settings.
Main features : The eight pictures of the Power Motive Test may be treated as its eight items the responses to which in the form of stories can by analysed and scored according to Winter's Scoring scheme.
Reliability : Split-half reliability = .81.
Validity : A sample of known students leaders scored significantly higher on the Power Motive Test than a sample known non-leaders.
Time : About 40 minutes.
Norms : Are in the process of being worked out.
Reference :

1. Afzal Kureshi and Bilquees Fatma. Power Motive among student leaders and non-leaders : Testing the affective arousal model : AISCA, Mysore, 1982.
2. Fatma, Bilquees : Power Motive among University students in relation to certain social differentials. M.Phil Dissertation, Aligarh Muslim University, Aligarh, 1980.

15B3 MOTIVATION SCALE

Author : M.C. Agarwal.
Availability : Author, P.O. NITIE, Vihar Lake Road, Bombay.
Language : English.
Uses : To understand motivational level of supervisors.
Level : Middle level supervisors.
Main features : Likert method 5-points scale used, number of items 20.

Reliability : Correlational method of item analysis used. All the items found significant at 1% level.
Validity : As mentioned above.
Time : Twenty to twentyfive minutes.
Norms : No.
Reference : Agarwal, M.C. "Motivation of Supervisors" - Administrative Management, 1980, 15, (2) 7-9.

15B4 LEVEL OF ASPIRATION TEST

Author : V.P. Bhargava.
Availability : Agra Psychological Research Cell, Belanganj, Agra.
Language : English.
Level : Graduate and Post-Graduate students.
Main features : The test consists of coding work in English alphabet letters printed on 11 sheets. The task is simple. The subject has to fill up substitute letters below the English alphabet letters from a code on each sheet.
Time : The maximum time allotted for completing the whole work is 3 to 5 minutes.

15B5 LEVEL OF ASPIRATION TEST

Authors : H.M. Singh & G. Tiwari.
Availability : Agra Psychological Research Cell, Belanganj, Agra.
Main features : The test is based on Underwood's method. In the test-sheet there are five rows of forty-eight half inches squares. The subject is asked to work as per the instruction. The level of aspiration is determined on the basis of D-scores.
Norms : D-scores norms are given in the Manual.

15B6 SENTENCE-COMPLETION MEASURE OF LEVEL OF ASPIRATION

Authors : M.K. Verma & B.N. Sinha.
Language : Hindi.
Level : School and College students.
Main features : The form consists of 16 items covering both idealistic and realistic aspiration in social, educational, economic and occupational areas of students endeavour.
Reliability : Test-retest = .651, and split-half =.765.
Validity : Validity coefficient with G.D. scores on Finger Dexterity Test was recorded .282.

Norms : Percentile norms are available.
Reference : Verma, M.K. and Sinha, B.N. Development of a Sentence Completion Measure of Level of Aspiration. Proceeds 69th Session of Indian Science Congress, Part-III, Mysore, 1982.

15B7 TRIPATHI PERSONAL PREFERENCE SCHEDULE
(AAP KI PASAND : EK ANUSUCHI)

Author : R.R. Tripathi.
Availability : Raghuvir Sharan Publications, Varanasi.
Language : Hindi.
Main features : It is a multivariate scale of 15 normal personality variables, viz., achievement, deference, order, exhibition, autonomy, affiliation, interception, succorance, dominance, abasement, nurturance, change, endurance, heterosexuality, and aggression. The pairs of statements matched on the basis of their social desirability scale values have been prepared.
Reliability : Available in the Manual.
Validity : As mentioned above.
Norms : Centile and 'T' score norms available.
Reference : Tripathi, R.R. Diagnostic discrimination on the TAT. Indian Journal of Clinical Psychology, 1981, 8, 141-144.

PART TWO

EDUCATION

Education

This part of the Handbook reports instruments dealing with different dimensions of education. The instruments are reported under five sections : general instruments, student problems and adjustment, interests and preferences, attitudes, and institutional characteristics like climate etc. This classification is also based on the number of instruments reported in each area. The different sections reported here represent only a broad classification of the instruments. Some instruments which could not be clearly classified have been included in the general category.

In all, there are 70 instruments reported in this area of which 21 have been reproduced here. Technical information about other 33 instruments is given here. The detailed break-up of the instruments is given in Table-2, below.

TABLE 2
Break-up of Instruments on Education

Classification	Original Reproduced	Only Information Provided	Citations	Adaptations	Total
1. General	7	18	1	-	26
2. Student Problems & Adjustment	4	3	1	-	8
3. Interests and Preferences	4	8	3	1	16
4. Attitudes	5	4	8	-	17
5. Institutional Characteristics	1	-	1	1	3
Total	21	33	14	2	70

General Instruments :

There are in all 26 instruments reported under this category of which 7 are reproduced here. About the other 18 instruments only information is reported here. These instruments cover several dimensions related to teachers' job satisfaction, class room control and teacher leadership, teacher behaviour, school innovations, decision making styles of principals, teacher efficiency and effectiveness class teaching, purposes of higher education, teacher's morale, job motivation, job anxiety, social characteristics and family climate of students, leadership style of educational administrators, and student activism. Of these instruments 16 are meant for teachers, one for principals and others are for students and schools. Majority of these instruments are meant for measuring the job satisfaction of teachers.

As regards the standardization, most of these instruments report high reliability and validity. Only two instruments do not report such data. Test-retest and split-half methods have been used in majority of the instruments. A few have reported inter-rater reliability. The values of the reliability coefficients reported are fairly high. Validity has been reported by majority of the instruments. Face, content and concurrent validities have been reported for many of the instruments. A few have been validated against ratings and a few report inter-area coefficients of correlation.

Among the instruments reproduced here, one by S.P. Anand is a job satisfaction scale to locate satisfied and unsatisfied teachers in schools. There is one class room boundary questionnaire by Kiran Gupta and Badrun Nisa which measures the class room control and teacher leadership in the class room. There are a set of other instruments by J.K. Pillai and others which are good contributions to education. One analyses the verbal and non-verbal behaviours of teachers in action and the other one is an innovative index inventory. There is one rating scale to locate the traits of student activists. Another scale is meant to find out the decision making styles of principals of colleges. There is one checklist which is useful for finding out the purposes of higher education.

The other instruments reported here are mainly meant for teachers and measure job satisfaction and job anxiety of school teachers. A few instruments for students activism and social characteristics are also reported.

Student Problems and Adjustment

Instruments on students' problems and adjustment are included under this section. There are 8 instruments reported in this section of these 4 are reproduced along with information. Only technical information for other 3 is provided. 7 instruments have reported standardization data. Test-retest and split-half reliabilities have been reported by most of the instruments. Some have reported more than two reliability coefficients. All the values reported are fairly high. More attention is also paid on validation of these instruments. Only one instrument does not report any such data.

Among these instruments one is a study organisation inventory by Jayalakshmi Indiresan to identify and counsel the students regarding their study problems. The instrument is useful for senior high school and university students. This instrument measures the relative strength of the mechanical and motivational dimension of study. There is one D-I Scale by Ravi Wanger which may be used on university students both males and females. The scale reports fairly high reliability and validity and is a good instrument to identify disciplined and indisciplined students.

Another instrument is an adjustment inventory, meant for graduate and post-graduate students. It has also reported high reliability and validity and measures the adjustment in home, educational, emotional and social areas. The students' personal problem index by Wig and Nagpal does not report any standardization data but seems to be a good instrument to measure sources of stress of young people.

Other instruments reported here are also meant for school and college students and report fairly high reliability and validity data. These are also well standardized instruments and could be used to measure students' adjustment and problems in their respective ways. In general, the instruments reported in this section seem to be well standardized instruments and are useful contributions to educational research.

Interests and Preferences :

In this section, the instruments relating to curricular

interests, reading interests, vocational interests, study habits and preferences are reported. 16 instruments have been reported of which 4 are reproduced here. These instruments are available for high school, high secondary and college students. Majority of the instruments are on study habits and interests.

Reliability has been reported for all the instruments. 5 instruments report both split-half and test-retest reliabilities. The reliability coefficients wherever reported are fairly high. Validity has been established by different techniques. Face, content and construct validities seem to be commonly reported by the instruments. A few have used ratings and self criterion for validational purpose.

Four instruments are reproduced here of which 2 are study involvement and the other 2 are study habits inventories. The study involvement inventory by Indiresan is available in English and is useful for senior high school and university students. The other one is by Asha Bhatnagar and is available in Hindi and English. These instruments measure the involvement of students in their studies and report fairly high reliability and validity. Rao's study Habits Inventory is available in English. The other one by B.V. Patel is available in English and Hindi and seems to be a well standardized instrument useful for secondary school students.

The other instruments reported here are available in different languages and are meant for school and college students. These instruments measure students' liking, interest, mathematical and vocational interests, and study habits. Reliability and validity reported for these instruments are also fairly high. These instruments are useful for guidance and counselling purposes.

Attitudes :

The instruments dealing with attitudes of teachers and students about various issues of education are reported in this section. These instruments measure attitudes of students towards mathematics, internal evaluation, N.C.C., strike and violence/non-violence. A few instruments are for teachers also and measure their attitude towards their job.

In all 17 instruments have been reported out of which 5 have been reproduced here. These are all scales. Two scales are of Gutman type and 2 are of Thurston type. All the scales have reported reliability and validity data. Split-half and test-retest reliabilities have been reported for 4 instruments. For some scales more than one reliability coefficient has been reported. All the coefficients are fairly high. Validity is also worked out for all the instruments. A few have used teachers' ratings for validating the scales. One scale has reported factorial and cross-cultural criteria of validation and the other one has reported inter-area correlation.

The first two scales reproduced here are mathematics attitude scales. These are meant for high school students and measure their attitude towards mathematics. A scale by H.G. Desai is available in Gujarati. It is a Thurston type scale and reports fairly high split-half and test-retest reliability. This scale is validated against teachers' ratings. The other one by Tuli is available in Hindi and English and reports high reliability and validity. Norms are also available on these scales. There are two scales by B.A. Parikh, available in English, Hindi and Gujarati languages. One scale measures the attitude of students towards internal evaluation system in colleges and the other one towards NCC. These scales have also reported fairly high reliability and validity. There is one scale by Siddaramaiah and another is meant for college students and measures their attitude towards strike. This is a good contribution to this section.

The other instruments reported here are also well standardized instruments. Two instruments are meant for teachers and measure their attitude towards their job. The other one is a violence/non-violence reaction scale for college going population. Eight instruments have been cited here and details about them are not available.

Institutional Characteristics :

There are only three instruments available under this section. They mainly relate to the organisational climate of the institutions. One instrument is original and the other one is an adaptation and detailed information about its standardization data etc. is reported here. One instrument is cited and details are not available.

The instrument by S.Y. Kulkarni and Y.P. Singh is available in English and measures organisational climate of Agricultural Universities. The instrument has reported fairly high split-half and test-retest reliability coefficients. Validity is also established. The items of the instruments are rated on a 5-point scale.

The School Organisational Climate Description Questionnaire by Motilal Sharma is an Indian adaptation of OCDQ by Halpin and Crofts (1963). It is available in Hindi and English and can be used for other organisations also. Fairly high reliability and validity quotients are available and good references are also available on this instrument. Details are given in the manual.

Besides these, more standardized instruments are needed which may be utilized in other learning institutions. There is a need of systematic researches on educational institutions as organisations to bring out more well standardized instruments in this area.

EDUCATION

1. General Instruments

complete instruments **A**

21A1 DECISION MAKING STYLE SITUATION TEST

Author : J.K. Pillai & N. Muthiah.
Availability : Department of Education, Madurai Kamraj University, Madurai.
Language : English.
Uses : To find out the decision making styles of principals.
Level : Principals of Colleges.
Main features : The tool has twenty problems pertaining to college administration. Ten items deal with academic problems and the remaining ten deal with administrative problems. The tool speaks of three decision making styles, Vic Hernistic Routine and compromise.
Reliability : Chi square technique was employed to estimate the reliability of the tool. Test-retest method and split half-technique were used.
Validity : Validity was found out separately for the three different styles.
Time : Approximately 30 minutes.
Norms : Component norms were established.

21A1 DECISION MAKING STYLE SITUATION TEST
(The respondents have to select one of the three solutions which is best).

1. The DCE has written to you to take the responsibility of conducting a 21 day workshop in your college. Your staff members are very reluctant to have it in your college. You are expected to reply to the DCE. What action would you take?
   (a) I would seek the help of the interested persons in the locality and will try to conduct the workshop with their help.

(b) I would make an appeal to the staff through a circular explaining the significance of the workshop and their responsibilities.

(c) I would announce nominal honorarium for the service of the staff in the work and involve them in the workshop.

2. A set of staff members demand that the entire work schedule to be redrafted, since it has certain lapses. If you redraft, it is certain that you are earning the displeasure of the committee of professors who did the job. How would you solve the Problem?

(a) I would request the staff members who demand rescheduling to redraft the entire workschedule and convince the committee of Professors who did the job earlier.

(b) I would arrange a staff meeting, explain the difficulties involved and ask them to work according to the schedule atleast for the first semester.

(c) I would issue a memo to the staff members who demand rescheduling and warn them that disciplinary action would be taken for their gross misdeamenour.

3. Some miscreants encroach a promboke land adjacent to your College compound overnight. Inspite of your repeated requests, they, under the shelter of famous political party refuse to vacate the land. Emergence of a slum in front of your college reflects on your administration. What would you do?

(a) I would contact the popular leaders of the famous political party and persuade them to request the encroachers to vacate.

(b) On behalf of them I would make representation to the Government and plead for alternative accommodation of them elsewhere.

(c) I would send a written complaint to the Government authorities and make early arrangements to vacate them from the site.

4. Only at the time of University examination, you are given to understand that a particular staff member has dealt with an entirely different syllabus. What would you do?

(a) Since it would lead to trouble later, I would keep the news in the dark and I would move the university authorities later to consider our case sympathetically.

(b) I would request the students to study the other portion and sit for the examination.

(c) I would accept the mistake and request the Vice-Chancellor to give permission for arranging re-examination during the vacation.

5. The Principal issues orders not to dictate notes in the classes, it is against Educational Principles. But the staff continue their dictation of notes contending that in the days of strikes and closures it is the only method to complete the syllabus. How would you solve the problem?

(a) I would issue memos to those who do not follow my orders.

(b) I will try to convince the staff that dictating notes only makes the students cram and by citing many research studies I would say that the students are capable of learning by themselves if they have been trained to °learn to learn'.

(c) They would try to get as many staff as possible to resort to newer methods. Those who continue to give notes cannot be helped.

6. The Principal vested with the powers of sanctioning increments, has stopped increment to a staff member who is most inadanuate and inefficient. But the staff Association pleads for him. How would you solve the Problem?

(a) I would appoint the staff committee to consider the issue objectively.

(b) I would send him for some refresher course and give him time to improve himself.

(c) I will be firm in my action saying that he is inadequate and inefficient and refuse to sanction him increment.

7. A and B were friends and classmates. A, invirtue of his Ph.D. Qualifications became the Professor B has to serve under him. A exercises his authority, over B and inturn B is jealous of him. B is an efficient and popular teacher. The Social Climate in the department is affected. As a Principal what will you do?

(a) I would advise both A and B to shed all their differences inside the campus and save the Prestige of the institution.

(b) I would make an arrangement in consultation with other departments, that Department will be headed in rotation.

(c) I would have two sections in the department according to specialization and make B head of the section. So that both A and B could be free to contribute their best.

8. Staff Association passes resolutions which go against your stipulated College rules. For instance, they decide to be present in the college premises only during class hours. What would you do?
   (a) I would sit with the staff Secretary and request him to plead with his colleagues to withdraw the resolution.
   (b) I would encourage presenting of papers in seminar, writing articles to journals etc. and thereby I would make them stay in the college during working hours.
   (c) I would dissolve the staff Association immediately saying that it indulges in anti-college activities.
9. The staff members wish to enroll themselves as members in a Teachers' organisation. But you feel that the Organisation may go against management. You advise them not to join it. But some of the staff members join it against your wish and expectation. What would you do?
   (a) I would advise the staff members who have enrolled their names in the organisation to withdraw their membership.
   (b) I would convince a meeting and I would impress upon the staff that I am not against the Organisation and convince them that such organisation is not necessary since college itself takes effort to fulfill all their needs.
   (c) I would take steps in collaboration with my college staff to organise another organisation which may act according to my expectations.
10. All the staff go on mass casual leave according to the directions of their association. The students demand Classes etc. But the Government has already ordered that no college should be closed on account of the staff strike. How would you solve the problem?
   (a) I will arrange a filmshow for the students and invite the staff members present to see the show.
   (b) I would get the seminar students of each discipline to arrange an inter-disciplinary seminar and I would personally contact it.
   (c) I would ask the students to mark their attendance and go home.
11. Since their grievances are not redressed, the staff association, unanimously decides to boycott invigilation work. The University exams commence in a few days. How would you solve the Problem?

(a) I would circulate a notice that invigilation is compulsory.

(b) I would wait and if staff members do not turn up, I will get the non-teaching staff to invigilate.

(c) I will try to convince the staff members that by boycotting exams they are doing a disservice to the students and I will also try to educate the students that they should prove their integrity, honesty and maturity by doing the exams without the need of invigilators.

12. You have received a note from certain student leaders that they should go on strike, if the existing student union is not scrapped immediately. What would you do?

(a) I would contend that they want to have a role in the union activities and ask them to participate in union functions. I would fix that they will be like opposition parties in Parliament. I would say that they are the right persons to regulate the activities of the union.

(b) I would dismiss the student leaders from the college saying that their actions are against the Principal and norms of the college.

(c) I would convince a meeting of the office bearers of the union, selected student leaders and senior professors of the college and arrive at a compromising formula i.e. the existing student union should continue.

13. Two Prominent community students clash with each other frequently. They pick up quarrels even for petty things. They are highly unadjusted. Because of their ill feeling towards each other tension prevails always in the college. How would you solve the problem?

(a) I would arrange a meeting of parents belonging to prominent communities, the student leaders and college authorities and arrive at a compromising formula.

(b) I would organise a workshop on interpersonal relationship and pave way for the development of social virtues.

(c) I would identify the trouble-some students and take action against them according to college rules.

14. A young staff member moves freely with all other students who inturn like him most. The other colleagues resent saying that the new staff member does not maintain prestige and dignity, staff morale has

gone down etc. How would you solve the Problem?

(a) I would advise the concerned staff member to maintain dignity and preserve the honour of the staff group.

(b) I would convince a meeting of the concerned staff member, complaining staff and senior staff of the college, put the matter before them and reach an agreeable solution.

(c) I would expose the staff to new concepts like interaction analysis class room climate etc. and convince that good and cordial relationship with students would improve the climate and student achievement.

15 A group of students request you to declare a holiday in view of the local festival in a Temple. In case there is holiday for the present festival there is possibility for other religious students may demand holidays for their religious festivals also. How would you solve the Problem?

(a) I would declare a holiday for the present festival and in consultation with the organisors of festivals, I would send my students to do social service in the Temple.

(b) I would concede the demands of students and declare a holiday.

(c) I would hold classes in the forenoon and declare holiday in the afternoon for all festivals.

16. The admission committee decides not to admit a student in degree classes who was notorious in P.U.C. classes. The father of the student pleads that he may be admitted. As a principal what would you do?

(a) I shall seek admission for the student in a neighbouring college.

(b) Contending that the student would be trouble-some, I would refuse admission.

(c) I would willingly admit the student and contend that it is an opportunity to show my efficiency to tackle the so-called trouble-some students.

17. An there was a clash between busmen and students sometime ago, the busmen refuse to ply buses to your college which is not in the main route. Absence of buses to your college will lead to number of problems. As a Principal what would you do?

(a) I would send appeals to the concerned authorities to make early arrangements to ply buses to our college.

(b) I would close down the college due to the non-availability of transport facilities and I will make the bus operators feel the urgency of the Problem.

(c) I would go to the busmen and convince them that the students are young, immature, and request them to forget the unpleasant happenings.

18. Students demand certain physical comforts like fan in the class rooms, water cooler in the college etc. But management refuses to accord their request on the financial grounds. Since their demands are not met, tension is mounting among students. How would you solve the Problems?

(a) I would take steps to raise funds from the public for providing the required facilities in the college.

(b) I would persuade the management to meet the students demands in stages and reach an agreement with the students.

(c) I would emphatically tell the students that the college cannot offer these comforts and say that those who are not satisfied can quit the college.

19. You prescribe certain dress regulations to the students. They inturn feel that you interfere in their freedom and demand that your ruling must be withdrawn. How would you solve the problem?

(a) I would explain to the students the significance of uniform and make them realise that it lessens class feeling among students.

(b) I would come to an agreement that students should come in prescribed dress during functions in the college.

(c) I would serve suspension notice to the students who demand withdrawal of my ruling.

20. A popular Professor delegated his duty often to a junior member of his faculty without your knowledge. Since he has established his name among students, any action may prove to be harmful. But you realise his actions affect the faculty morale. How would you react?

(a) I would invite the concerned Professor and tell him to attend to his duty promptly.

(b) I would issue a circular saying that Junior members should handle classes of senior Professors only with my approval.

(c) I would allot additional non-academic activities of the college to him and make others feel that he is some-what engaged with the college work.

21A2 JOB SATISFACTION SCALE FOR TEACHERS

Author : S.P. Anand.
Availability : Regional College of Education, Bhubaneshwar.
Language : English.
Uses : To locate satisfied and unsatisfied teachers in schools.
Level : School teachers.
Main features : Likert Technique - 30 statements, 5 alternative choices for responses.
Reliability : Test-retest reliability = .952, and split-half = .81 and .83 for positive-negative and odd-even statements.
Validity : Established with expressed satisfaction and scores obtained on the scale.
Time : No time limit but usually 10 minutes are taken.
Norms : Teachers scoring a score of 80 and above are considered to the satisfied and vice versa.

References :

(1) Anand, S.P. A study of teacher-pupil relationship in higher secondary classes in Delhi. Unpublished Ph.D. Thesis, University of Delhi, 1971.
(2) Anand, S.P. School teachers and job satisfaction. Teacher Education, 1972, 7(1), 16-23.
(3) Anand, S.P. School teachers : Job satisfaction vs. extroversion and neuroticism Indian Educational Review, 1977, 12(2), 68-78.
(4) Anand, S.P. Job satisfaction vs. work role variables. Indian Educational Review, 1979, 14(4), 106-107.
(5) Anand, S.P. School teaching profession - reasons of joining and satisfaction. Quest in Education, 1980, 17(3), 260-266.
(6) Anand, S.P. Teachers' values and job satisfaction. Indian Educational Review, 1980, 15(4), 24-34.
(7) Anand, S.P. The quest of best quality teachers - an investigation. Educational Forum, 1981, 22(3), 49-54.

21A2 JOB SATISFACTION SCALE FOR TEACHERS
(The following statements have to be checked on a 5-point scale of agreement).

1. Teaching profession brings mental peace to the teacher.
2. Teaching even in Government schools is miserable.

3. Teacher because of the nature of his profession, should adhere to simple living and high thinking.
4. Teaching in a college is a boon while teaching in a school is a course.
5. Teachers can determine the future course of a nation.
6. Teachers if they want respect in the society because of their being teachers, will have to forgo some financial gains and work with a missionary spirit.
7. The teaching profession is a very degrading one.
8. One should dislike being called °Masterji' in the bazar by anyone.
9. I aspire for the day when I shall leave teaching in the school.
10. Teachers' success lies in the success of their students.
11. A teacher should feel proud of introducing himself to anyone as a teacher working in a school.
12. Teaching often becomes monotonous after a few years.
13. Thank God, I am a Teacher.
14. Teachers enjoy no appropriate rewards for their work.
15. Most pupils are considerate of their teachers.
16. One should not advise one's sons and daughters to become teachers.
17. Teaching profession is better than other professions in several respects.
18. Principals of the schools do not act as friends and guides but become masters of the teachers.
19. Teachers are responsible for knowing home conditions of everyone of their pupils.
20. Teaching is a respectable job.
21. One in teaching profession is in search of truth.
22. A teacher should not be expected to do more work than he is paid for.
23. The teaching profession opens field of knowledge for the adopter.
24. Teaching is the last refuge of those who are unemployed.
25. Teaching can be called an interesting profession.
26. One has to remain a school master because of his poor academic career.
27. Teachers learn throughout their lives.
28. Teachers live a dull life.
29. Teaching in schools sucks intelligence as well as initiative.
30. Very able people will be wasting time and energy in teaching profession.

21A3 CLASSROOM BOUNDARY QUESTIONNAIRE

Authors : Kiran Gupta & Badrun Nisa.
Availability : National Psychological Corporation, 4/230 Kacheri Ghat, Agra.
Language : Hindi.
Uses : To measure the classroom control and the aspect of teacher leadership in the classroom.
Level : Primary Schcol @Teachers.
Main features : 25 Multiple-Choice items with 3 or 4 alternatives.
Reliability : Split-half method = .88 (N = 200), rational equivalence method = .82 (N = 200), and test-retest method = .77 (N = 200).
Validity : 1. Against Morrison's CBQ Test = .70.
2. Concurrent validity established.
Time : There is no time limit for the test, but generally Ss took 20 to 30 minutes.
Norms : Percentile norms available.

21A3 CLASSROOM BOUNDARY QUESTIONNAIRE

1. After finishing his assigned seatwork.
   (a) a child should feel free to leave his seat in order to get materials from the classroom library or from another part of the room.
   (b) a child should be permitted to leave his seat only after requesting the teacher for permission to do so.
   (c) a child should stay in his seat until the teacher directs him to some other activity.
2. During a recitation lesson of the entire class.
   (a) every child should pay attention to the lesson.
   (b) a child who wishes to continue a seatwork project he has been working on should be given permission to do so.
   (c) a child who finds the lesson boring should feel free to do something else, as long as he remains in his seat and doesn't distract other children.
3. With regard to children's leaving their seats during class sessions.
   (a) children should not leave their seats unless they request permission from the teacher.
   (b) there should be a limit on the number of children allowed out of their seats at one time, but children should feel free to leave their seats as long as the limit is not exceeded.

(c) there should be no limit on when children can leave their seats, provided they have a reason to do so.

4. During a recitation
   (a) a child should feel free to leave his seat to sharpen his pencil.
   (b) a child should not leave his seat for purposes such as sharpening a pencil unless he first gets the teacher's permission.
   (c) a child should not bother the teacher with individual concerns such as the need to sharpen his pencil.
5. A child who comes late to class
   (a) should be permitted to enter only after obtaining permission from the principal's office.
   (b) should be permitted to enter only if he has a valid reason for his lateness.
   (c) should feel free to enter, and no explanation should be expected by the teacher.
6. With regard to attendance
   (a) if a child does not wish to attend class, he should seek permission from the teacher to use some other facility, such as the school library or gym.
   (b) all children should attend class at all times.
   (c) if a child does not wish to attend class he should be free not to come.
7. With regard to assignment of seats
   (a) the teacher should make the assignments of which seats are to be used by which children.
   (b) children should be free to agree among themselves to change their seats whenever they wish.
   (c) children should select which seat they want, and then this should be assigned as their permanent seat.
8. With regard to the area of the classroom near the teacher's desk
   (a) children should feel free to gather around the teacher's desk while waiting to speak to her.
   (b) there should be a rule setting the maximum number of children permitted in the area of the teacher's desk.
   (c) children should not approach the teacher's desk unless specifically given permission to do so.
9. A child finds that the sum shining on his desk interferes with his paper work
   (a) should request the teacher to close the window shade.

(b) should feel free to close the window shade.
(c) should do nothing; the height of the shades should be determined by the teacher.

10. With regard to physical contact in the classroom
(a) a child should feel free to touch the teacher in a friendly way, i.e., a tug on the arm, pat on the back, etc.
(b) children in the classroom should feel free to touch each other, but not the teacher, as long as they do not hit.
(c) children should not touch each other or the teacher in the classroom.

11. With regard to talking in class
(a) there should be periods of time set aside throughout the day when children can talk quietly with each other; at other times they should be working or engaged in activities.
(b) children in adjoining desks should be permitted to whisper quietly with each other when they have finished their work.
(c) children should not have casual conversations with each other in the class, but should wait until recess or lunch time for that.

12. A child who wishes to make a contribution to a class discussion
(a) should feel free to attract the teacher's attention by calling her name if necessary.
(b) should raise his hand and wait to be recognised.
(c) should say what he wants to say at the first opportunity; there is no need for him to wait to be recognised.

13. With regard to classroom supplies
(a) students should have direct access to the supply closet and should take whatever supplies (paper, etc.) they need for their work.
(b) a supply of paper should always be directly accessible to the children; other supplies should be requested from the teacher.
(c) the teacher should pass out supplies and children should use only what is distributed to them.

14. During a recitation, if a child wishes to move his chair forward so that he can see or hear better
(a) he should feel free to do so.
(b) he should do so only with the teacher's permission.
(c) he should tell the teacher, and she should arrange for a permanent change of seat.

15. With regard to language in class

(a) children should feel free to use the language that comes naturally to them, even if it is ungrammatical (i.e, colloquialisms, slang, "ain't", etc.) swearing, however, should not be allowed.
(b) children should feel free even to swear in class if this express how they feel.
(c) children should watch their language in the classroom : they should be polite and try to use correct English.

16. with regard to classroom dress
(a) there should be no dress code in class; it is up to the children and their parents to decide how the children should dress.
(b) there should be dress code in class, but it should be flexible and allow for popular fads in dress, with the stipulation that children be neat.
(c) children should be expected to conform to <u>conventional</u> dress code in class.

17. With regard to sleeping in class
(a) there should be no sleeping allowed in class.
(b) during seatwork, if a child feels tired, he should be permitted to put his head down on his desk and sleep - but only if he has finished his work.
(c) if a child feels tired he should feel free to rest (put his head down in his desk) for a while whether or not his work is progressing well.

18. With regard to seatwork assignments
(a) a child should feel free to work on his assignments in whatever order he wishes, provided he gets all his work done by the end of the day.
(b) when a particular seatwork lesson (e.g., Arithmetic or spelling) is assigned, the child should work only on that lesson until the teacher directs the class to a new lesson.
(c) a child should not have to turn in routine assigned work on time if he is working on something else that is interesting to him.

19. A child who wishes to leave the room during a class period (e.g. to go to the bathroom or get a drink of water)
(a) should feel free to get up and leave quietly.
(b) should be allowed to do so, but only after asking permission from the teacher.
(c) should be told to wait until recess or another scheduled break period.

20. When a child wants to ask the teacher about how to do his assignment
(a) he should raise his hand and the teacher should

permit him to come to the teacher's desk.
(b) he should feel free to leave his seat to approach the teacher's desk to ask the question.
(c) he should raise his hand and the teacher should go to his seat to answer the question.
(d) he should try to figure out the answer to his question himself.

21. If a child has a question about the directions for an assignment he should
(a) feel free to leave his seat and ask a child in another part of the room.
(b) not ask for help, but try to figure out the problem for himself.
(c) ask the teacher for help, not another child.
(d) feel free to ask a whispered question to another child in any adjoining seat.

22. When a child has finished his seatwork
(a) he should proceed with his next assignment.
(b) he should do something quietly at his desk, but it need not be work.
(c) he should feel free to talk quietly with a neighbouring child who has also finished.
(d) he should feel free to leave his seat to talk quietly with another child who has also finished his work.

23. When class is dismissed
(a) children should line up in an orderly way to leave the room and should only leave at the direction of the teacher.
(b) children need not line up, but they should all leave the classroom at the proper time.
(c) the teacher should dismiss the class row by row.
(d) children need not line up, and children who wish to stay behind in the room (e.g., to finish up work) should be allowed to do so.

24. When children enter the classroom
(a) they should take their seats and begin assigned work.
(b) they should take their seats but should be permitted to have quiet conversations until the teacher calls the class to order.
(c) they need not take their seats until the teacher calls the class to order.
(d) they should sit quietly, but they need not begin working.

25. With regard to eating in class
(a) there should be no gum chewing in class, but children should be allowed to eat small candies

such as Life Saver.
(b) chewing gum in class is permissible provided the child disposes of it carefully.
(c) not only candy but also soft drinks should be allowed in class.
(d) there should be no chewing gum or eating in class.

21A4 AFFECTIVE TONE ANALYSIS SYSTEM - OBSERVATION INSTRUMENT

Author : J.K. Pillai.
Availability : Department of Education, Madurai Kamaraj University, Madurai.
Language : English.
Uses : To assess the affective behaviour of teachers to students in any instructional setting.
Level : Primary School.
Main features : The tool consists of four components verbal positive, non-verbal positive, verbal negative and non-verbal negative. Thirteen (Ten) statements of the tool reveal the affective behaviour of the teacher.
Reliability : Inter rather reliability was found out. Value ranged from 80% to 90%.
Validity : Content validity was established.
Time : Fifteen minutes.
Reference : Pillai, J.K. Report of the 15th Annual Conference of Indian Association for Pre-School Education 28th December 1970.

21A4 AFFECTIVE TONE ANALYSIS SYSTEM (ATAS)

1. The Teacher praises the work of an individual child/group.
2. The teacher praises the ideas of an individual child/group.

VERBAL POSITIVE

3. The teacher praises the personal social behaviour of an individual/group.
4. The teacher uses the names of children.
5. The teacher personalizes remarks.
6. The teacher moves physically close to the students.

NON-VERBAL POSITIVE

7. The teacher maintains eye contact with the students.
8. The teacher criticizes the work of an individual/group.

VERBAL NEGATIVE

9. The teacher rejects ideas of an individual/group.
10. The teacher criticizes personal/social behaviour of students.

OBSERVER OPINION :

(The teacher should be rated °Yes'or °No' on the following).

The teacher appears to be :

Calm, confident, cheerful, organised, and on task.

21A5 RATING SCALE TO FIND OUT THE TEACHER PERCEPTION OF STUDENT ACTIVITIES

Authors : Sathiagiri Rajan and Esther Vijaya Rani.

Availability : Department of Education, Madurai Kamaraj University, Madurai.

Language : English.

Uses : To locate the traits of student activities.

Level : College Teachers.

Main features : The scale has twelve traits and it is a five point scale.

Reliability : Reliability was established by finding the relationship between judges rating and self-rating.

Validity : Content validity was found out.

Time : No time limit.

Reference : Esther Vijaya Rani : "Teacher Perception of student activities in colleges". M.Phil Thesis, Department of Education, Madurai Kamaraj University, Madurai, 1980.

21A5 TEACHER PERCEPTION OF STUDENT ACTIVITIES

(The teachers have to rate five activities and five non-activities among students on a 5-points rating scale i.e. always to never).

Traits

1. Carefree
2. Confused
3. Forceful
4. Enthusiastic
5. Happy
6. Ambitious
7. Suggestible
8. Relaxed
9. Shy
10. Nervous
11. Intolerant
12. Talkative

21A6 INNOVATION INDEX INVENTORY

Author : J.K. Pillai.

Availability : The Author, Department of Education, Madurai Kamaraj University, Madurai.

Language : English.
Uses : To find out the areas of innovations introduced in the schools.
Level : Schools.
Main features : The scale consists of three innovative areas viz. administrative innovations, curricular innovations, and methodological innovations.
Reliability : Test-retest reliability = .82.
Validity : The tool was administered to two groups of higher innovative schools and low innovative schools and °t° test was applied to find out the significant difference between them. C.R. = 2.2, p .05.
Time : No time limit.
Reference : Pillai, J.K. "Organisational Climate, Teacher morale and School quality". Unpublished Ph.D. Thesis, M.S. University, Baroda, 1973.

21A6 INNOVATIVE INDEX INVENTORY

(The following facilities and innovations should be answered whether introduced °Yes' or °No', year in which it was first introduced, and extent of adoption i.e. 100% to 75%, 75% to 50%, 50% to 25% and up to 25%).

1. Planned programme of school assembly.
2. Educational and vocational guidance.
3. Cumulative record card.
4. Work experience.
5. Work books for students.
6. Weekly periodical tests.
7. Unit planning and Unit test.
8. Weightage to periodical tests held in the course of the year to decide promotion.
9. New type of question paper.
10. Open shelf library.
11. Science club.
12. Language club-(school Magazine News letter literary association).
13. Social study circle.
14. Hobby centre-(art club, Music association).
15. N.C.C.
16. Boy scout Girl guides.
17. Organised games for all children.
18. School Cooperative Stores.
19. School museum.
20. Annual exhibition by children.
21. Uses of projected aids, films, filmstrips, slides.
22. Inclusion of school broadcast programmes in the

schedule.
23. Programme for gifted children.
24. Remedial programme for backward children.
25. Parent-teacher association.
26. Regular staff meetings.
27. Annual seminars of teachers.
28. Summer Institutes - (Refresher courses for teachers).
29. Experimental project developmental project and action research.

21A7 PURPOSES OF HIGHER EDUCATION - CHECK LIST

Author : P. Joseph Sathiaraj.
Availability : Department of Education, Madurai Kamaraj University, Madurai.
Language : English.
Uses : To find out the priorities of purposes of higher education by parents, teacher and students.
Level : College students, teachers and educated parents.
Main features : Twelve statements - purposes of Higher education are given in the tool. Both individual as well as national purposes of higher education are included.
Reliability : -0.83 - The test-retest method was used.
Validity : Content validity was established on the Jury opinion.
Time : Five minutes.
Norms : Nil.
Reference : Joseph Sathiaraj, P. "Purposes of Higher Education as perceived by Parents, Teachers and Students". M. Phil. Thesis, Department of Education, Madurai Kamaraj University, Madurai, 1980.

21A7 PURPOSES OF HIGHER EDUCATION - CHECK LIST
(The following items have to be ranked according to order of importance).

1. To get meaningful employment.
2. Pursuit of excellence.
3. To gain social status.
4. For social mobility.
5. To attain professional growth.
6. To foster the spirit of international understanding.
7. For character development.
8. To produce experts in various fields.
9. To develop leadership qualities.
10. For self-reliance.
11. For proper utilisation of human potential.

12. To have the rich experience in life.

instruments with technical information

B

21B1 JOB SATISFACTION SCALE (JSS)

Author : M.P. Uniyal.
Availability : Author, Department of Education, Garhwal University, Srinagar, Garhwal.
Language : Hindi.
Uses : To assess the level cf job satisfaction of teachers.
Level : Teachers.
Main features : It contains 43 items formed in negative and positive statements distributed in seven areas of job. The response scheme is of yes/no type.
Reliability : Test-retest and split-half reliability was found to be .887 and .713 respectively.
Validity : Inter-area correlations were found between 0.64 to 0.602.
Time : Twenty minutes.
Norms : Available with the author.
Reference : Uniyal, M.P. "Job motivation and Satisfaction of Teachers", D.Phil. (Edu.) thesis, Allahabad University, Allahabad.

21B2 TEACHER JOB SATISFACTION INVENTORY

Author : M.N. Wali.
Availability : Faculty of Education, Banaras Hindu University, Varanasi.
Language : Hindi.
Uses : To find out the factors responsible for job satisfaction among teachers.
Level : School and college teachers.
Main features : Fifty items inventory covering 15 areas of job as interesting, chance for progress, use of ability, authority, co-workers, chance to be creative independence, social status, security, relation with supervisors, variety in work, service conditions, personal recreation, moral values and identification. Statements are in positive or negative forms.
Reliability : The odd-even split-half reliability = .86, and test-retest reliability = .86.
Validity : Validity was established by correlating it with other tests. The correlation with Pramod Kumar's J.S.I. was .48 and with that of Allahabad JSI was .78.
Norms : T-score norms are available.

21B3 JOB SATISFACTION QUESTIONNAIRE (JSQ)

Author : S.B. Singh.
Availability : Department of Psychology, Jagdam College, Chapra, Bihar.
Language : Hindi.
Uses : To measure job satisfaction of teachers.
Level : High school teachers.
Main features : 75 items inventory, measuring ten dimensions of job satisfaction.
Reliability : Test-retest and split-half reliability has found to be .71 and .73 respectively. Full length reliability was found to be .96.
Validity : Face validity established.
Time : No time limit.

21B4 JOB SATISFACTION QUESTIONNAIRE (JSQ)

Authors : P. Kumar & D.N. Mutha.
Availability : Agra Psychological Research Cell, Belanganj, Agra.
Language : Hindi.
Main features : The questionnaire consists of 29 °Yes' or °No' type items classified into four different aspects of job satisfaction in teaching-work, salary, security and promotion policies, institutional plans and policies, and authority including school management.
Reliability : Split-half reliability = + .95 (N = 100) with an index of reliability of .97, and test-retest reliability = .73 (N = 60) with an index of reliability of .85.
Validity : Face validity very high. Content validity is ensured on the basis of judges ratings.
Time : No time limit but it takes about twenty minutes.
Norms : Percentile norms are given in the Manual.
Reference : Kumar, P. & Mutha, D.N. Standardisation of job satisfaction questionnaire, Behaviourometric, 1975.

21B5 TEACHER EFFECTIVENESS SCALE

Author : Pramod Kumar & D.N. Mutha.
Availability : Agra Psychological Research Cell, Belanganj, Agra.
Language : Hindi.
Uses : To assess the teachers effectiveness for the subject.
Level : Secondary teachers.
Main features : It is a Likert type 5-point scale consisting of 69 items on different teaching behaviour. All the

items are positively worded.

Reliability : Split-half reliability applying Spearman Brown formula (N = 100) = .67 with an index of reliability of .82, and test-retest reliability is found to be .75 (N = 60) with an index of reliability of .85.

Validity : Face-validity is fairly high. Content validity is ensured by Judges ratings. The scale is further validated against principal's ratings and found to be .77 (N = 50).

Time : No time limit.

Norms : Percentile norms are available in the Manual.

Reference : Kumar, P. & Mutha, D.N. Teacher effectiveness scale for secondary teachers : Its development and standardisation. Indian Journal of Psychometry & Education, 1974.

21B6 TEACHER EFFICIENCY SCALE

Authors : N.S. Chauhan & R. Jain.

Availability : Agra Psychological Research Cell, Belanganj, Agra.

Language : Hindi.

Uses : To measure teaching efficiency of teachers.

Level : Both the students and the teachers.

Main features : The scale has 100 items distributed in three categories A,B,C. Category °A' refers to personality characteristics with 83 items and °B' has class direction with 15 items. The judges in both the categories are students. Category °C' attempts to measure growth of students and has 12 items and teacher is required to make appraisal of this phenomenon.

Reliability : Test-retest reliability (N = 100) ranges from .57 to .78 for the three areas as well as for the scale as a whole.

Validity : Content validity is established.

Norms : Equivalent °Z' scores for raw scores of all the three areas are given in the Manual.

21B7 TEACHERS' MORALE SCALE (TMS)

Author : Prakash Chandra Shukla.

Availability : M/s Indian Psychological Corporation, santi-Sadan, Rai Behari Lal Road, Lucknow.

Language : Hindi.

Uses : To assess the morale of the teachers.

Level : Primary level teachers.

Main features : Likert type (5-point-scale) 50 items.

Reliability : Test-retest reliability = 85.

Validity : (1) Face validity, and (2) Criterion related validity = .68.
Time : No time limit.

21B8 JOB MOTIVATION ANALYSIS FORM (JMAF)

Author : M.P. Uniyal.
Availability : Author, Department of Education, Garhwal University, Srinagar, Garhwal.
Language : Hindi.
Uses : To explore the dimensions and differences between highly and low satisfied teachers in relation to their job images, job ambitions, job aspirations, job inspirations and job ideals.
Level : Teachers.
Main features : It is divided into two parts. Part one contains six subsections. Each subsection contains one semi-projective type open ended question. Part two contains two items.
Time : Twenty minutes.
Norms : Norms are available with the author.
Reference : Uniyal, M.P. "Job Motivation and Satisfaction of Teachers". D.Phil. (Edu.) thesis. Allahabad University, Allahabad.

21B9 JOB ANXIETY SCALE (JAS)

Author : M.P. Uniyal.
Availability : Author, Department of Education, Garhwal University, Srinagar, Garhwal.
Language : Hindi.
Uses : To measure the level of job anxiety.
Level : Teachers.
Main features : It contains 54 statements with yes/no response scheme.
Reliability : Test-retest and split-half reliability was found to be .76 and .63 respectively.
Validity : Validity coefficients ranges between .57 to .73.
Time : Twenty minutes.
Norms : Norms are available with the author.
Reference : Uniyal, M.P. "Job Motivation and Satisfaction of Teachers", D.Phil. (Edu.) thesis, Allahabad University, Allahabad.

21B10 TEACHER ADJUSTMENT INVENTORY

Author : S.K. Mangal.
Availability : Author, Department of Education, Kurukshetra

University, Kurukshetra.
Level : School teachers.
Main features : The inventory consists of 253 items on five factors of adjustment - (i) academic and general environment of the institution, (ii) socio-psycho-physical, (iii) professional relationship, (iv) personal life, and (v) financial and job satisfaction.
Reliability : Split-half and test-retest reliability for the five factors vary between .94 to .99.
Validity : Content, construct and criterion validity established.
Norms : Percentile norms are available for male and female teachers.

21B11 CLASS TEACHING - A CHECKLIST OF HELPFUL FACTORS

Author : R.P. Gupta.
Availability : M/s Indian Psychological Corporation, Shanti-Sadan, R.B.L. Road, Lucknow.
Language : English.
Uses : To assess the effectiveness of Teacher Training Programmes.
Level : Applicable to all teacher training students, regular teachers and principals.
Main features : Thirty-six main items plus an open ended section inviting fresh suggestions and a separate section for ranking the 5 most helpful factors.
Reliability : In the manual.
Validity : In the manual.
Time : Half an hour (there is no time limit).
Norms : Percentile norms available.
Reference : Gupta, R.P. Unpublished Ph.D thesis, Department of Education, Lucknow University, Lucknow, 1980.

21B12 SOCIAL CHARACTERISTIC DESCRIPTION

Authors . M.P. Uniyal and Beena Shah.
Availability : Authors, Department of Education, Garhwal University, Srinagar, Garhwal.
Language : Hindi.
Uses : To identify social characteristics of the students.
Level : College and graduate level students.
Main features : It contains 90 items distributed among 15 dimensions—Economic condition, Family educational background, Father's vocational status, Curricular preference, Co-curricular preference, Family reinforcement, Academic reinforcement, Hurdles, Age, Vocational aspiration of students, Vocational mobility, Motivation

for graduation, Determinants of courses of studies, Position among siblings and social belongingness.

Reliability : The tool was administered again after the gap of 15 days among the students and the percentage of identical returns was found to be 86.7. When the tool was administered among the parents, the percentage of identical returns from both the sources (student & parent) was found to be 87.8.

Validity : Validated on known groups of students and the judgement of 19 judges also supports the claim of its validity.

Time : No time limit, usually it takes about 45-50 minutes.

Norms : Norms are available with the authors.

Reference : Shah, Beena. "A Sociological Study of Educational Development of Graduate Students of Kumaun University with special reference to caste", Unpublished Ph.D. Dissertation, Kumaun University, 1981.

21B13 FAMILY CLIMATE SCALE (FCS)

Authors : M.P. Uniyal & Beena Shah.

Availability : Department of Education, Garhwal University, Srinagar, Garhwal.

Language : Hindi.

Uses : To assess the family climate of the students.

Level : Students of 13 plus age group.

Main features : It contains 82 items on a three point rating scale and cover 10 areas of family climate.

Reliability : Test-retest method was adopted to find out the reliability coefficients for each dimension. Its value were found to be between .69 & .83.

Validity : Factorial-analysis of FCS was carried out to know the value of its coefficient of validity. The correlation between two dimensions was found to be between .521 and .781.

Time : About 45 minutes.

Norms : Norms are available with the authors.

Reference : Sharma, A. "A study of family climate in relation to academic achievement of the students of Garhwal region, M.Ed. Dissertation, Garhwal University, 1982.

21B14 EDUCATIONAL LEADERSHIP BEHAVIOUR DESCRIPTION QUESTIONNAIRE (ELBDQ)

Author : Prakash Chandar Shukla.

Availability : M/s Indian Psychological Corporation, Shanti-Sadan, Rai Behari Lal Road, Lucknow.

Language : Hindi.

Uses : To study the leadership style of educational administrators .
Level : Primary level teachers.
Main features : Likert type five point scale, twenty-eight items (28).
Reliability : Dimension wise (test-retest reliability) initiating structure = +0.89, and consideration = .0.806.
Validity : (1) Face validity, (2) Criterian related validity (dimension wise) initiating structure = +0.652, and consideration = +0.573.
Time : No time required.

21B15 STUDENT ACTIVISM SCALE

Author : G.S. Aswal.
Availability : Education Department, Garhwal University, Srinagar, Garhwal.
Language : Hindi.
Uses : To identify activistic students on higher learning centres.
Level : College and University students.
Main features : It has 49 items but the test item has further been broken into nine items and has been given a scale of 5,4,3,2, and 1 at five positions i.e., strongly agree, agree, neutral, disagree and strongly disagree.
Reliability : The reliability of the test was identified by using K.R. formula which came out to be .694.
Validity : Two groups of high and low activists were compared on their personality needs. This reveals that the characteristics of each need variable has direct relevance with the activistic personality and split the high and low group into two distinct personalities.
Time : Six to seven minutes.
Norms : From the author.

21B16 ACTIVISM SCALE

Author : R.R. Sharma.
Availability : Author, Department of Education, Garhwal University, Srinagar, Garhwal.
Language : Hindi.
Uses : To determine activism students in order to facilitate the academic environment by proper method of guidance and counselling.
Level : College/University students.
Main features : It is a 50 situational item scale with three response alternatives. Weightages are given to the alternative chosen.

Reliability : The reliability coefficient was tested by test-retest method and K.R. method which came out to be sufficiently high.
Validity : Two groups of high and low activists were compared on Frustration test which reveals that these two groups of students have distinct factors of frustration related to their requisite behavioural tendencies.
Time : Twenty minutes.
Norms : Available with the author.

21B17 THE ENVIRONMENTAL AWARENESS TEST

Authors : A.B. Saxena, V.G. Jadhao and J.S. Rajpur.
Availability : Regional College of Education, Bhopal.
Language : Hindi.
Uses : III and IV class children (8+ to 10+).
Main features : The test consists of 57 items and measures physical environmental awareness of the children. There are three types of items - multiple choice, true-false and short answer.
Reliability : Split-half reliability = .80 (N = 100).
Times : Seventy-five minutes.
Reference : Saxena, A.B., Jadhao, V.G. & Rajpur, J.S. Development of an Environmental Awareness Test. Indian Educational Review, 1981, 16(3), 21-26.

21B18 A RATING SCALE

Author : R.C. Sharma
Availability : Author, Administrative Staff College of India, Hyderabad.
Level : Principals, Head of the Department of Education and Directors of Educational Institutions.
Main features : The scale records the judgement of the heads of the educational resource systems about the level of the adoption of the innovations which were developed in their institutions and communicated from them.
Reliability : Test-retest reliability = .78.
Validity : Validated against experts' ratings.
Reference : Sharma, R.C. A study of the characteristics of the resources system and the process of developing and communicating innovation and their impact on adoption process. Unpublished Ph.D. Dissertation, M.S. University, Baroda, 1979.

citations

C

21C1 CHANGE PRONENESS SCALE

Author : M. Mukhopadhyaya.
Reference : Mukhopadhyaya, M. Barriers to change in secondary education Unpublished Ph.D. Dissertation, M.S. University, Baroda, 1975.

2. Student Problems and Adjustment

complete instruments **A**

22A1 STUDY ORGANISATION INVENTORY (SOI)

Author : Jayalakshmi Indiresan.
Availability : Department of Educational Research, Technical Teachers' Training Institute, Adyar, Madras.
Language : English.
Uses : To identify and counsel the students regarding their study problems.
Level : Senior High School and University students.
Main features : This instrument contains 60 items with ten items to cover six dimensions of study organisation. They are (1) Planning, (2) Effective reading habits (3) note taking, preparation and revision (these three refer to the mechanical dimensions of study behaviour) (4) Motivation & interest (5) Concentration and clarity, (6) Academic neuroticism (these dimensions refer to the motivational and personality dimensions). These sixty items are in the Likert format with four response categories.
Reliability : Split-half reliability corrected by Spearman-Brown formula = .896.
Validity : Shows high significant correlation with University grades.
Time : About half hour.
Norms : Not available.
Reference : Indiresan, J. Relationship of certain background and behavioural characteristics to consistency of performance in continuous evaluation - Proceedings of the Fifth International Conference on Improving University Teaching, London, 1979.

22A1 STUDY ORGANISATION INVENTORY (SOI)

(The following statements have to be rated on 4-point scale Almost to never).

1. I plan my work before I begin to study.

2. I strictly observe my plan of study.
3. I distribute my study periods among various subjects.
4. I study regularly throughout the year.
5. I work harder in the subject I feel I am weak.
6. I plan my study even for holidays.
7. I get headache when I begin to study.
8. I cannot sit at a stretch and concentrate on my studies.
9. I take much time to get started to the task of study.
10. I look for main ideas while reading a lesson.
11. I question the material as it is being read.
12. I relate material learnt in one subject to that learnt in others.
13. I day dream when I study.
14. I understand the lesson while reading it, but I have trouble in remembering what I have read.
15. I find it difficult to decide what points are important in a lesson.
16. I note down the points as I read a passage.
17. I supplement my class notes with outside study.
18. I organise my notes so that the important points stand out.
19. I achieve little compared to the effort I put in.
20. I miss important points while taking down notes.
21. I go to the class well prepared.
22. I revise what is done in the class each day, when I get back home.
23. I spend a definite time each week in reviewing each course.
24. I find it difficult to take notes in the class.
25. I feel so tired that I cannot study efficiently.
26. I forget to do my homework.
27. I go on postponing what I should be studying today.
28. I plan in the morning how I will spend the day.
29. I study even in the midst of distractions like radio, people talking, children's play etc.
30. I plan my answer before I start writing in the examination.
31. I revise my answers in the examination.
32. I study hard only just before the examination.
33. I have difficulty in expressing myself in writing.
34. I cut classes under the slightest pretext.
35. I recall the important points after I read a lesson.
36. I have a regular place and time for studying.

37. My dislike towards certain subjects interferes with my studies.
38. I study the subjects that I enjoy regularly and put off studying those which I dislike to the last minute.
39. I spend too much of my time in reading fiction, going to movies etc. so that I cannot be efficient at my regular studies.
40. I have to wait for the °mood to read' before starting my studies.
41. I go back and test myself on what I have studied and check any doubtful points.
42. I find a new and unfamiliar approach to an already learned topic confusing and depressing.
43. When prescribed work seems unusually long or difficult, I easily become discouraged.
44. I work better when I am under constant supervision than when I am left alone.
45. I prefer much to to be given a specific assignment of work rather than a general direction that I can interpret myself.
46. Whether I like a course or not. I shall work hard to make a good grade.
47. I lose interest in my studies after the first few days and weeks.
48. Lack of interest in my studies makes it difficult for me to keep my attention focused on assigned learning.
49. Unless I really like a course, I believe in doing only enough to get a passing grade.
50. Even though an assignment is dull and boring, I stick to it until it is completed.
51. Some of my classes are so boring that I spend the class period drawing pictures, writing letters or day dreaming instead of listening to the teacher.
52. I lay aside returned examinations reports and homework assignments without bothering to correct errors noted by the teacher.
53. I strive to develop a sincere interest in every course I take.
54. Some of my courses are so uninteresting that I have to °force' myself to do the assignments.
55. Difficulty in assembling ideas with order and clearness within a brief amount of time results in my doing poorly on examinations.
56. I put off doing my assignments tutorials, term papers etc. until the last minute.
57. In preparing reports, assignments, term papers

etc., I make certain that I clearly understand what is wanted before I begin work.

58. I keep all the notes for each subject together, carefully arranging them in some logical order.
59. I keep my assignment upto date by doing my work regularly from day to day.
60. I study three or more hours per day outside of class.

22A2 D-I SCALE

Author : Ravi Wangu.
Availability : Faculty of Education, Kumaun University Campus, Almora.
Language : English.
Uses : To identify disciplined and indisciplined students.
Level : University students (both male and female).
Main features : Scale-Product Technique of Eysenck and Crown (1949) number of items : 82.
Reliability : Test-retest reliability (N = 138) varied from .69 to .89 for different sub-scales.
Validity : Has very high internal consistency. Factorial and cross-cultural validity has been established.
Time : Approximately 25 minutes.
Norms : Norms are under preparation.
Reference : Wangu, R. "Socio-psychological correlates of disciplined-indisciplined behaviour among university students". Unpublished Ph.D. thesis, Punjab University, Chandigarh, 1980.

22A2 D-I SCALE

(The following statements have to be checked on a 6-point scale of agreement).

1. To put teachers in embarrassing situation, an open display of emotions should be made.
2. If the students are expected to keep the class room clean and tidy, what for are the sweepers there!
3. It is not the concern of the students whether the course is progressing systematically or not.
4. It looks odd if one spends much time in studies.
5. Since the competition is increasing day by day, students should take their studies very seriously.
6. Hooting down a new teacher in the class provides lot of fun.
7. The courses in the University should be made easier to help students avoid worrying about attendance.

8. Late coming in the class should be discouraged as it disturbs the teaching-learning process.
9. Home assignments help in keeping students busy in a profitable way.
10. One derives fun by exploding a cracker in the class-room.
11. Enrollment in the University is meant more to select a life partner than for education.
12. There is no use taking tough courses as they take much of one's precious time and energy.
13. A systematic schedule should be followed for studies.
14. Students should not interrupt the work of faculty members.
15. The students have no responsibility towards the up-keep of the university campus.
16. Reading a novel or doing some other work when the teacher is teaching is shameful.
17. Students have nothing to do with the goals and purposes of the course.
18. Students need not use self control in their social behaviour.
19. University is a training ground for the responsibilities towards the community.
20. Courses requiring intensive study and preparation out of the class should be stopped.
21. Removing the parts of a teacher's vehicle is a bad gesture towards him/her.
22. Teachers need not plan their lectures because students don't attend classes very seriously.
23. Teachers should encourage livelier discussions in the class.
24. Keeping the library books at inappropriate places is justifiable as it helps in using those books extensively (In open shelf system).
25. There is no harm in removing a book from the library till your examinations are over.
26. Even if one has an artistic aptitude, modification of the pictures in the library magazines is not advisable.
27. Putting one's remarks on the magazines in the library spoils the magazines.
28. It is better to tear off the pages from the book drawn from the library than to take down notes.
29. There is no harm in talking in the library after spending some time in reading.
30. As the residents of the hostel are away from their parents/guardians, there is no harm in gambling.

31. Since student life is a carefree period, one should not care if the hostel room is messy.
32. When in a mood, there is no harm in rushing about noisily in the corridors of the hostel.
33. Drinking in the hostel shows how courageous one is.
34. It is adventurous to run away from the hostel after the night roll-call has been taken.
35. If the hostel entry time is restricted during nights, to enter the hostel by the backdoor after seeing the late night show is wrong.
36. Breaking the crockery as a protest helps in improving the quality of meals in the hostel mess.
37. Real friends are those who can help one in answering questions from outside the examination centre.
38. Because of competition in grades, students should be allowed to use unfair means in the examinations.
39. In the examinations, one should not write on the blotting papers to help a student who has not studied throughout the session.
40. One should make use of his strength and misbehave with the invigilator in the examination hall.
41. It is something odd to work for higher grades.
42. There is nothing wrong in writing answers and passing them into the examination hall for a candidate who is appearing in the examination.
43. The standards of academic achievement in the university should be very high.
44. Frequent tests should be given in all the courses.
45. It is wrong to get through the courses by personality pulls and bluffs.
46. The Campus problems can only be solved by heated discussions and display of anger.
47. Strikes prepare students for the struggle in future life.
48. Without knowing the cause, it is foolish to jump into rallies and demonstrations.
49. The hooliganism on the part of the students should not be taken a serious view of.
50. Politicians misguide the students to go on strike.
51. To show resentment to the authorities, damaging the things is the only way out.
52. When the things get tougher, bluffing is the only way out.
53. Students also have the responsibility towards the maintenance of social life on the campus.
54. Strikes lead students astray.
55. At the time of conflict with the authorities, settlement should be reached by finding out some

via media.

56. It is important to be with a particular political group in the campus.
57. In case of an argument, one must try to win it by all means (logical or illogical).
58. Strikes produce good patriots.
59. Educational standards have deteriorated due to strikes and demonstrations.
60. Going on strikes is wastage of time and energy.
61. Debates, declamations etc. are pretty pointless activities.
62. The lectures by big philosophers/educationists are of no use to the university students.
63. To be noisy and inattentive at lectures by dignitaries is not expected of the youth.
64. Seminars and student discussions are wastage of time as they don't lead students anywhere.
65. Trouble making at a gathering adds fun to otherwise lifeless lecturing.
66. When the opponents are strong, foul play is justified to win the match.
67. To exert leadership in the class, rebellions should be plotted.
68. Games should be played with an aim to win only (By fare or foul means).
69. Students should be encouraged to take an active part in social reforms.
70. Writing obscene language on the walls of the lavatory is a form of self expression, so it should not be objected to.
71. To short cut the path by jumping over a hedge or wall is not advisable.
72. There is no need for a student to be considerate of other students.
73. Students should not be stopped from getting drunk and disorderly.
74. It is the duty of the students to take care of the institutional property.
75. Puncturing the vehicle of the teacher gives pleasure.
76. Passing remarks on the opposite sex are the healthy signs of youth.
77. One should get tickets for a show through back door than wait in the queue.
78. Developing ideals at the university is a wastage of time.
79. It is the duty of the senior students to help freshers to adjust to the campus life.

80. Foreign students are our guests, they should be extended all possible help and sympathies.
81. Waiting in a queue is a wastage of time, if the person is strong enough to push people standing ahead of him.
82. The students should pay attention to rules and regulations.

22A3 ADJUSTMENT INVENTORY

Authors : D.N. Srivastava & Govind Tiwari.
Availability : Agra Psychological Research Cell, Agra.
Language : Hindi & English.
Levels : Graduate and Post-Graduate students.
Main features : The inventory consists of 80 °Yes' or °No' type of items and covers the four - home, educational, emotional and social areas of adjustment.
Reliability : The reliability coefficient have been found by three methods (i) split-half (ii) test-retest and (iii) Kuder Richardson formula 20. The coefficient varies between .87 to .89 for home, .87 to .96 for emotional, .83 to .89 for educational, .90 to .94 for social and .91 to .95 for the total inventory on the three methods.
Validity : The inventory was validated against the adjustment inventory by Sinha and Singh, r = .70 (N = 200) and the adjustment inventory by Mittal, r = .73 (N = 150).
Norms : Percentile norms were calculated for boys and girls separately. Five categories are provided on the basis of the scores.
Time : About twenty minutes.
Reference : Chauhan, N.S., Tiwari, G.P. and Khatter, I. Anxiety as a function of intelligence and adjustment. Indian Journal of Experimental Psychology, 1972.

22A3 ADJUSTMENT INVENTORY

(The following statements have to be checked on °yes' or °no' alternatives).

1. Usually old people in my family get angry.
2. I feel pleasure in giving respect to old people in the society.
3. Usually I remain unhappy.
4. I like the studies of college.
5. My brothers and sisters often quarrel with me.
6. People become friendly with me in no time.
7. Usually I am excited during by conversation with people.

8. I easily follow the topic taught in the class.
9. People at home give me little love.
10. Usually I feel the spell of loneliness.
11. I get nervous when I face some problems.
12. I feel difficult to concentrate in study.
13. My people at home little like my views.
14. Pessimists also feel pleasure to meet me.
15. My eye water at the sight of anyone in difficulties.
16. I do not know why I feel asleep in the class.
17. Usually I feel that I am a burden to my family.
18. I get pleasure in meeting with my friend.
19. I am envious of the progress of others.
20. I like to participate in the cultural activities.
21. Old people have great influence in my family.
22. There is great fun in cutting jokes with people during marriage festivals.
23. I feel great fear even at lightly ruined places.
24. I feel difficulty in expressing my views in writing.
25. I like to stay out instead of home.
26. I like to take part in co-operative activities.
27. I get angry when something is not done according to my wish.
28. I give correct answers to questions asked in class.
29. Often I feel that my home people are worried of me.
30. My friends do not like to meet me.
31. I am worried of my light responsibility.
32. After College studies I take interest at my studies at home.
33. People of home little like my views.
34. I immensely like to gossip in the company of my friends.
35. Often I think had I died at my birth, it would have been better.
36. I get nervous during examination days.
37. I am satisfied with my family members.
38. Often my acquainted people take advice from me.
39. I think it is better to die.
40. I am afraid of my teachers.
41. My family members pay attention to my health.
42. In every programme of my friends, they always invite me.
43. I am excited at light jokes of people.
44. Often my teachers encourage me.
45. My family members give threat to me.
46. I talk frankly infront of others.
47. Often I build castles in air.

48. Usually I feel that my colleagues do not care for me.
49. My family members criticise me without any cause.
50. I like to attend any interesting programme.
51. Often I feel restless.
52. Usually my colleagues abuse me.
53. Everyone loves me at home.
54. I like to talk with strangers.
55. I get easily provoked when people irritate me.
56. I have a few friends in my colleagues.
57. Often I desire to run away from home.
58. I get nervous when I see many people in a function.
59. Even ordinary things against me create disturbance.
60. I feel that the behaviour of my teachers are partial.
61. I am afraid of talking frankly with my relatives.
62. I like to talk with people in a friendly way.
63. Usually I get so disturbed that I get sleep very late.
64. Usually my colleagues make fun of me.
65. I like the atmosphere of my family.
66. I feel shy to talk with others.
67. My face blooms forth at a little joy.
68. Sometimes I think to leave the school.
69. My family people accuse me more than enough.
70. Often the passengers in a bus or train gossip with me.
71. Ordinary things of insult make me excited.
72. Usually I miss class due to my colleagues.
73. There is lack of family ties in my home.
74. I enjoy working with others than to work alone.
75. I am happy at a little praise.
76. I take part in Sports and Games along with my studies.
77. I have affectionate relations with my brothers and sisters.
78. My acquaintances like me very much.
79. I am surprized at ordinary events.
80. I get disturbed while sitting in class.

22A4 STUDENTS PERSONAL PROBLEMS INDEX

Authors : N.N. Wig & R.N. Nagpal.
Availability : Department of Psychiatry, PGI Medical Education and Research, Chandigarh.
Language : English.

Main features : It consists of 25 items yes-no type scale measuring sources of stress to young people.

22A4 STUDENT'S PERSONAL PROBLEMS INDEX

(The following items have to be checked on °yes' or °no').

1. Are you often bothered by repeated headaches or pressure in the head?
2. Are you frequently disturbed by thumping of the heart?
3. Do you often suffer from upset stomach?
4. Are your eyes often tired and painful while studying?
5. Do you often feel sleepy when you are trying to study?
6. Do you get easily tired while studying?
7. Do you sweat or tremble a lot during examinations or questioning?
8. Do you feel that you are not able to retain what you have read as well as you used to do?
9. Do you often find it difficult to concentrate while studying?
10. Do you get tense and nervous before examinations or other important events?
11. Do you often feel that you lack confidence?
12. Is it always hard for you to make up your mind when you have to take an important decision?
13. Do you often worry about your health?
14. Do you think your parents and friends do not care for you as much as you expect them to do?
15. Do you often wish you had some one at your side to advise you?
16. Do you often experience periods of loneliness?
17. Do you often wish you were dead and away from life?
18. Does worrying often keep you awake at night?
19. Do you have frequent ups and downs in mood either

with or without any apparent cause?
20. Do you frequently think about your past?
21. Are you often preoccupied with ideas about meaning and purpose of life?
22. Do you often think than you cannot do things which other can do easily?
23. Are you frequently distressed by silly pointless thoughts that keep coming into your mind against your will?
24. Are your feelings rather easily hurt?
25. Do you often day-dream about the things that can never come true?

instruments with technical information B

22B1 ADJUSTMENT INVENTORY

Author: Har Mohan Singh.
Availability: Agra Psychological Research Cell, Agra.
Language: Hindi.
Level: High School and College students.

Main features: The inventory consists of 64 'Yes' - 'No' type of items measuring home, health, social and emotional areas of adjustment.
Reliability: The coefficient of reliability (N = 258) determined by correlating the odd-even items, correlated by Spearman Brown prophecy formula, ranges between .80 to .93 for the four areas as well as the total scale.
Validity: The inventory is validated against Saxena's Adjustment Inventory and the coefficient varies between .72 to .92 for the four areas of adjustment.
Time: About twenty minutes.
Norms: Tentative norms on the basis of scores are given for men and women separately.

22B2 PROBLEM CHECK LIST

Author: Nirmal Bhagia.
Availability: Indian Psychological Corporation, R.B.L. Road, Lucknow.
Language: Hindi
Uses: To recognise the extent of school satisfaction of people, to spot out the more seriously disturbed children, to locate the areas of problems and difficulties of the individuals and to evaluate the schools

conditions.
Level: Secondary School students.

Main features: The check-list consists of 101 items covering five categories of problems related to academic, social, teacher, administration and personal. Each problem has a blank space before it where the subject is supposed to make a check-mark if he happened to recognise the problem as applicable to him.
Reliability: Split-half reliability (N = 176) = .76, and test-retest reliability (N = 150) = .92.
Validity: Validity is established by administering the check-list on the people of two groups highly satisfied and extremely dissatisfied and the two were found to differ significantly on 101 problems.
Time: About twenty minutes.
Norms: Tentative 5-grade norms are provided but it is suggested to prepare local norms.

22B3 SANTOSH - ASANTOSH MAPNI

Authors: R.P. Rastogi, L.P. Mehrotra and P.C. Saxena.
Availability: The first author, Colonelganj Inter College, Allahabad.
Language: Hindi.
Uses: To know which component(s) of the school/college generate satisfaction dissatisfaction among students individually or collectively.
Level: High School and Intermediate students but can be used for Junior H.S. boys also.

Main features: Likert's five point scale, 60 items, measures five dimensionwise as well as total S-D with school.
Reliability:

1. Split-half reliability (N = 100) = .919.
2. Inter item correlation - out of 1770 obtained correlation, 1657 were significant at or beyond .01 level and 70 were significant at or beyond .05 level.
3. Correlation coefficients between different subtests ranged from .577 to .730 (N = 900).
4. Dependability coefficient: at 15 days interval (N = 90) = .7807. Dimensionwise: A (.6912), B (.7191), C (.6617), D (.6389), E (.7807).

Validity: A - Intrinsic validity (N = 900)

1. Centroid Factors - Only one 'G' factor was found.

Factor loadings for the five dimensions: .840; .766; .866; .832 and .848.

Factorwise percentage variance - 97.028% sub-testwise contribution towards the scale in factor I - 20.43%, 16.99%, 21.71%, 20.04% and 20.82%.

2. Orthogonal Factors (Rotated): Only one significant factor evolved with eigen value 4.227. Communalities for five subjects : .722, .995, 1.004, .915 and .989.
3. Factorial validity coefficients for five subject: .816, .617, .850, .834 and .989.

B - Relevant validity: (N = 900).
'h' values for the five subjects: .842, .799, .869, .849 and .858.
C - External validity:
1. Against students' expression = .759 (N = 00).
2. Against teachers' ratings = .63 (N = 50).

Time: Twenty minutes.
Norms: Available with author.
Reference: Rastogi, R.P. School climate, psychological health, and class room functioning of students in relation to students' satisfaction-dissatisfaction with school - unpublished Ph.D. thesis, Kanpur University, 1981.

citations C

22C1 A SMOKING PROBLEM CHECK-LIST

Authors: L.N.K. Sinha & K.P. Krishna.
Reference: Sinha, L.N.K. & Krishna, K.P. A smoking problem check-list for college students, psychological studies, 1970, 15(1), 50-54.

3. Interests and Preferences

complete instruments A

23A1 STUDY INVOLVEMENT INVENTORY (SII)

Author: Jayalakshmi Indiresan.
Availability: Department of Educational Research, Technical Teachers' Training Institute, Adyar, Madras.
Language: English.
Uses: In the identification and counselling of students especially those who exhibit apathy and under-

achievement.

Level: Senior high school and University students.

Main features: The inventory consists of 25 items representing five dimensions of study instrument as organisational identification, self confidence, involvement, feed back and peer relations. The items are in the Likert format.

Reliability: The split-half reliability of the scale corrected by Spearman-Brown formula was calculated to be .923.

Validity: Factor analysis of the data yielded five psychologically meaningful dimensions which closely reflect the dimensions in the theoretical construct, thus, substantiating the content and construct validity of the test.

Time: About thirty minutes.

Norms: Not available.

References:

1. Indiresan, J. A theoretical model of the relationship between motivation, identification and involvement affecting performance - Proceedings of the Fourth International Conference on Improving University Teaching - Aachen, 1978.
2. Indiresan, J. Construction and development of a study involvement inventory - A factor analysis report. Indian Educational Review (under publication).

23A1 STUDY INVOLVEMENT INVENTORY

(The following statements have to be checked on a 4-point scale of agreement).

1. This school has a fine tradition of public service.
2. I feel this school is doing an important job in showing how schools should be managed.
3. I get the 'what is the use' feeling when I do not succeed in my studies.
4. Most things in life are more important than my studies.
5. My teachers correct and check my work.
6. I feel close to my classmates.
7. I feel a sense of pride in studying in this school.
8. Generally speaking my stay in this school has not been satisfactory.
9. I am very clear about my future career.
10. The major satisfaction in my life comes from my

studies.

11. The teachers compliment when my work is outstanding.
12. My classmates help each other when we need it.
13. I would advise any youngster to join this school.
14. The record of this school is an example of what a good school can achieve.
15. I am confident of my success in my studies.
16. I have other activities more important than my studies.
17. If I make any mistake, I am corrected.
18. I am satisfied with my relationship with my fellow students.
19. If I had my life to live over again, I would still choose to study in this school.
20. If I hear (or read) any criticism about my school I would get very angry.
21. When I fail in some study, I stop making further efforts.
22. To me, my studies are only part of who I am.
23. This school has a fine set of teachers.
24. I feel that I am unfit for studies.
25. I used to care about my studies, but now other things are more important to me.

23A2 THE STUDY INVOLVEMENT INVENTORY

Author: Asha Bhatnagar.
Availability: M/s National Psychological Corporation, 4/230, Karcheri Ghat, Agra.
Languages: English & Hindi.
Uses: To measure the involvement of students in their scholastic pursuits (studies).
Level: Secondary School students.

Main features: The inventory has 40 items in Likert type format with their overall point response namely yes, undecided and no. It also has two filler items.
Reliability: Test-retest reliability of the inventory is .87 (N = 150). The split-half reliability applying the Spearman-Brown formula was found to be .67 (N = 150) with index of reliability of .70.
Validity: The inventory has a high content and construct validity.
Time: There is no fixed time limit, but it take about 10 to 15 minutes.

Norms: The percentile norms have been prepared on 600 students.

23A2 THE STUDY INVOLVEMENT INVENTORY

1. One has to work very hard to achieve success.
2. I study because my parents want me to study.
3. Teachers should consult students about homework.
4. I like teachers very much.
5. I am proud of my marks.
6. I always like to be tidy in the school.
7. Teachers seem to be very arrogant.
8. I often dream that I have failed.
9. I feel pity on boys who are weak in studies.
10. If I do not understand lesson, I ask somebody.
11. I can do anything for studies.
12. I like those students who study.
13. Inspite of my parents' insistence I do not study.
14. Teachers know a great deal about home work.
15. It is my strong desire to get prizes for studies.
16. My books are always arranged properly at one place.
17. I enjoy very much when some students imitate teachers.
18. I find arithmetic sums very difficult.
19. I should pay attention to boys who are weak in studies.
20. Most of my friends help me in studies.
21. I hope to be a great man when I grow up.
22. I am proud of my school.
23. One feels happy without studies.
24. Teachers in my school have good character.
25. Success begets praise from all.
26. One should finish work on time.
27. It is foolish to solve mathematical problems.
28. I feel ashamed if I am not able to answer a question in my class.
29. Most of my friends are weak in studies.
30. My brothers and sisters help me in studies.
31. Goal of life is to study.
32. I like all my class fellows.
33. Homework should not be given.
34. Teachers' work is full of responsibility.
35. Only educated persons get respect in the society.
36. Homework should be finished on time.
37. No student can be happy in school.
38. I feel ashamed when I lag behind in the class.
39. I help my friends in solving mathematical problems.

40. I like those teachers who help us.

23A3 RAO'S STUDY HABITS INVENTORY

Author : D. Gopal Rao.
Availability : Agra Psychological Research Cell, Agra.
Language : English.

Main features : The inventory consists of 40 items representing various study techniques. The inventory is a 5-point scale having five category of responses. Both positive and negative items have bean included in the scale.
Reliability : The reliability was determined by the split-half method. The product moment coefficient of correlation was calculated between the scores on odd and even number of items.
Time : fifteen to twenty minutes.

23A3 RAO'S STUDY HABITS INVENTORY

(The following statements have to be checked on a 5-point scale).

1. I plan my work before I begin to study.
2. I strictly observe my plan of study.
3. I distribute my study periods among various subjects.
4. I study regularly throughout the year.
5. I work harder in the subject I feel I am weak.
6. I plan my study even for holidays.
7. I get headache when I begin to study.
8. I cannot sit at a stretch and concentrate on my studies.
9. I take much time to get started to the task of study.
10. I look for main ideas while reading a lesson.
11. I question the material as it is being read.
12. I collect new words and phrases as I read a passage.
13. I look up the meaning of an unfamiliar work in the dictionary.
14. While reading, I try to understand the authors view point by relating it to my own experience.
15. I relate material learnt in one subject to that learnt in others.
16. I day-dream when I study.
17. I understand the lesson while reading it, but I

have trouble in remembering what I have read.

18. I find it difficult to decide what points are important in a lesson.
19. I note down the points as I read a passage.
20. I supplement my class notes with outside study.
21. I organise my notes so that the important points stand out.
22. I find it difficult to take notes in the class.
23. I miss important points while taking down notes.
24. I go to the class well prepared.
25. I revise what is done in the class each day. when I get back home.
26. I spend some time each week, in revising the lesson.
27. I feel I spend more time in my studies but achieve little.
28. I feel so tired that I cannot study efficiently.
29. I find my studies interesting.
30. I feel I should keep on studying throughout my life.
31. I take pride in doing well in my studies.
32. I forget to do my homework.
33. I go on postponing what I should be studying today.
34. I plan in the morning how I spend the day.
35. I study even in the midst of distractions like radio, people talking, children's play etc.
36. I plan my answer before I start writing in the examination.
37. I revise my answers in the examination.
38. I study hard only a few months before the examination.
39. I have difficulty in expressing myself in writing.
40. I get nervous during the examination.

23A4 STUDY HABIT INVENTORY

Author : B.V. Patel.
Availability : Agra Psychological Research Cell, Belanganj, Agra.
Languages : English & Hindi.
Uses : To find out types of study habits of students.
Level : Secondary School students.
Main features : The inventory consists of 45 statements covering seven areas as (i) home environment and planning of work (ii) reading and note taking (iii) planning of subjects (iv) habits of concentration (v) preparation

for examination, (vi) general habits and attitudes, and (vii) school environment. Each is rated on a 5-point scale.

Reliability : Split-half reliability = .82, test-retest = .79.

Validity : Validity was established by correlating the scores on this scale with the teacher's opinion and examination marks and found to be .50 and .40 respectively.

Norms : Five letter grade norms are available.

23A4 STUDY HABITS INVENTORY

(The following statements have to be checked on a 5-point scale).

1. I frame my own time-table to study at home.
2. I work according to my time-table.
3. I study regularly in my study-room.
4. I prepare almost all my subjects before going to school and read them again at home, whatever is done in the class.
5. I join tuition classes.
6. I read at place where I get disturbed by radio, people's talk, children's play, relatives, guests etc.
7. I cannot study well as I keep myself engaged in the domestic work.
8. I make note of important points during reading.
9. I use dictionary to look up meanings of new words.
10. I pay more attention to new words while studying.
11. I take down detailed notes of what is being taught in the class room.
12. The doubtful points which arise during reading are referred to the subject teacher of clarity.
13. I try to solve at once, the difficulties met with while reading.
14. I miss important points while taking notes in the class room.
15. I read annotations (guides) rather than text books.
16. I underline the important points in my text-books while reading.
17. I pay more attention to the subjects I find difficult.
18. I devote more time to study subjects in which I am weak.
19. I give priority to studying the difficult subjects.

20. I read the same subject for a long time.
21. I study only that subject I am interested in and leave out the subject which I find uninteresting.
22. I study with concentration.
23. I feel I don't study at all.
24. My mind goes astray when I read.
25. I understand that I read, but I don't remember it.
26. In examination I think of the answers of the questions before.
27. I get nervous at the time of examination.
28. I read till late at night at the time of examination.
29. I read class-notes at the time of examination.
30. I do not study regularly for I get important questions and suggestions at the time of examination.
31. I do not prepare questions occurred (asked) at previous examination thinking that they would not be set again.
32. I memorize definitions, maxims, formulas etc. after understanding them.
33. I discuss the subjects read, with my friends.
34. I read while reclining on a bed.
35. I read aloud (loudly).
36. I try to compare things learnt in one subject with those in another.
37. I ruminate over all things I read.
38. Before I start reading new lessons I briefly revise the lesson read.
39. After reading one paragraph, I at once review it mentally.
40. I spend my leisure time at school in reading.
41. I use books from the library.
42. I read news papers and other books too.
43. I participate in the class room discussion.
44. I answer the questions asked by the teacher while teaching.
45. I can not progress in my study due to my dislikes for certain teachers and subjects.

instruments with technical information B

23B1 STUDENTS LIKING SCALE

Authors : S.P. Malhotra and B.K. Passi.
Availability : National Psychological Corporation, Kacheri Ghat, Agra.

Languages : English & Hindi.
Uses : To measure the liking of the students towards their teachers.
Level : Secondary school and college students upto graduation level.

Main features : It is a Likert type scale with 30 items covering four aspects of teacher behaviour - (i) Teacher behaviour with students inside the class room, (ii) Teacher behaviour with students out side the class (iii) Teacher behaviour with colleagues (iv) Teacher behaviour with principal.
Reliability : The test-retest reliability of the scale came out to be .92.
Validity : Face validity and concurrent validity were established. Concurrent validity against colleague rating and principal's rating came out to be .89 and .79 respectively.
Time : There is no time limit but it takes about 30 minutes.
Norms : Based on the sample of 250 teachers, the norms have been established for the population of Punjab, Haryana and Gujarat.

23B2 INTEREST SCHEDULE

Authors : Q.G. Alam & Ramji Srivastava.
Availability : Prasad Trading Corporation, J1/53, Dara Nagar, Varanasi.
Language : Hindi.
Uses : Providing vocational guidance to students.
Level : College and Senior High School students.

Main features : Fifty items comprises of ten areas viz., literacy, scientific, science, recreational, aesthetic, polit-cal, social, commercial.
Reliability : Spearman Brown and K.R. 20 coefficients for ten occupational interest areas ranging from .70 to .85 and .70 to .84 respectively.
Validity : Construct and content validities have been ensured.
Time : Forty to fifty minutes.
Norms : Norms based on t-scores are available from publisher/author.

23B3 MATHEMATICAL INTEREST INVENTORY

Author : L.N. Dubey.

179 Education

Availability : Agra Psychological Research Cell, Agra.
Language : Hindi.
Uses : To measure the interest of boys and girls in mathematics.
Level : Higher Secondary students (13 - 15 years).

Main features : The inventory consists of 40 °yes' or °no' type of items.
Reliability : Rational equivalence method (K.R. formula) = .89, and split-half (S.B. formula) = .91.
Validity : Predictive validity is established.
Time : No time limit.
Norms : Percentile norms are available.

23B4 VOCATIONAL INTEREST RECORD

Authors : V.P. Bansal & D.N. Srivastava.
Availability : Agra Psychological Research Cell, Agra.
Languages : English & Hindi.
Level : School and College students.

Main features : There are 128 vocational subjects and activities of different faculties and are distributed in eight vocational fields i.e., agriculture, artistic, commercial, executive, household, literary, scientific and social.
Reliability ; (1) Split-half reliability varies from .73 to .83 for different areas.
(2) Test-retest reliability (N = 175) varies between .74 to .86 for different areas of interest.
Validity : The validation criteria used was to correlate the scores of this vocational interest record with the teacher's ratings. The coefficient of correlation varies between .56 to .70.
Norms : Stanine grades norms are available for boys and girls.
Time : About 10 - 15 minutes.

23B5 VOCATIONAL INTEREST RECORD

Author : Kamal Dwivedi.
Availability : Agra Psychological Research Cell, Agra.
Language : Hindi.
Level : College students.

Main features : There are twenty groups of items representing different activities. Each group consists of ten items.

Reliability : Test-retest reliability varies between .62 to .99 for different areas of interests. Split-half reliability and internal consistency of the test are also determined.

Validity : Validated against self-criterion. Average correlation = .68 and its median value is .71.

Norms : Percentile rank norms available for girls.

23B6 EDUCATIONAL INTEREST RECORD

Authors : V.P. Bansal & D.N. Srivastava.
Availability : Agra Psychological Research Cell, Agra.
Languages : English & Hindi.
Level : School & College students.

Main features : There are 128 educational subjects and activities of different faculties and are distributed in eight educational fields - Science, Engineering, Medical, Agriculture, Humanities, & Arts, Home Science, Fine Arts and Commerce.

Reliability : Split-half reliability ranges between .74 to .86 and the test-retest reliability ranges between .76 to .88 for the different areas.

Validity · Validated against teacher's rating; correlation varies between .58 to .73.

Time : About 10 - 15 minutes.

Norms : Stanine grades norms are available for boys and girls.

23B7 INTEREST INVENTORY

Author : M.N. Palsane.
Availability : M/s Anand Agencies, 1433-A, Shukrawar Peth, Pune.
Language : Marathi.
Level : Higher Secondary students.

Main features : The inventory includes thirteen areas of interests covering almost all common occupations available to the people.

Reliability : The test-retest reliability coefficient for all the thirteen areas ranges from .68 to .91 (N = 200).

Validity : The content and face validity has been ascertained by judges opinions.

Time : Nor time limit.
Norms : Norms are available separately for boys and girls on the basis of mean scores.

23B8 STUDY HABIT INVENTORY

Author : M.N. Palsane.
Availability : M/s Anand Agencies, 1433-A, Shukrawar Peth, Pune.
Language : Marathi.
Level : School & College students.

Main features : The inventory consists of 45 items on 3-point scale. The items belong to the areas of budgeting time, physical conditions for study, reading ability, note taking, motivation, memory, examinations and health.
Reliability : Test-retest (N = 200) = .88.
Validity : Face validity.
Time : No time limit.
Norms : Norms on the basis of raw scores.
Reference : Palsane, M.N. A guide to study habits, Baroda : Good Companions (Raopura).

citations C

23C1 INTEREST INVENTORY (INTEREST IN TEACHING)

Author : G.P. Sherry.
Availability ; Author, Department of Education, D.E.I. Women's Training College, Dayalbagh, Agra.

23C2 OCCUPATIONAL ASPIRATION SCALE

Author : J.S. Grewal.
Availability : National Psychological Corporation, 4/230, Kacheri Ghat, Agra.

23C3 EDUCATION & VOCATIONAL ASPIRATION SCALE

Authors : B.G. Sudha & Satyanarayanan.
Availability : Department of Education, University of Bangalore, Bangalore.

adaptations **D**

23D1 INDIAN ADAPTATION OF GEIST PICTURE INTEREST INVENTORY

Author : N.S. Chauhan & Govind Tiwari.
Availability : National Psychological Corporation, Kacheri Ghat, Agra.

4. Attitudes

complete instruments **A**

24A1 AN ATTITUDE SCALE FOR MATHEMATICS

Author : H.G. Desai.
Availability : Department of Education, Saurashtra University, Rajkot.
Language : Gujarati.
Uses : To measure attitude towards mathematics.
Level : High School students.

Main features. Thurstone type attitude scale : twenty items.
Reliability : Split-half reliability = 0.86, and test-retest = 0.74.
Validity : Validated against teachers' ratings; r = 0.66.
Time : Fifteen minutes.
Norms : Norms - sex, grades, areas (districts) available for entire Saurashtra. Standardization sample (N) = 3,505.
Reference : Desai, H.G. "The attitudes to mathematics of high school students of Saurashtra - A field study". Journal of Education & Psychology, April 1975.

24A1 AN ATTITUDE SCALE FOR MATHEMATICS

1. Mathematics should be made a compulsory subject.
2. Mathematics is a very interesting subject.
3. In the age of science one has to study mathematics.
4. Though mathematics is a hard subject, it is very useful.
5. For a student paying attention mathematics is easy.
6. Mathematics is a subject which is both interesting and informative.

7. If one makes an effort, one can learn mathematics.
8. Mathematics is a laborious subject.
9. Life without mathematics is incomplete.
10. Mathematics is not that easy as other subjects are.
11. Mathematics is a subject for the smart pupils.
12. One does not necessarily have to study mathematics in order to be successful in life.
13. You can learn mathematics only if you work very hard.
14. I don't understand why one should study mathematics.
15. Nobody would study mathematics, if it were not compulsory for college entrance.
16. Mathematics means nothing but computing examples.
17. I don't see any special use of mathematics in life.
18. Mathematics has made education uninteresting.
19. God save from mathematics.
20. Mathematics is taught in schools so that teachers can get tuitions.

24A2 MATHEMATICS ATTITUDE SCALE (MAS)

Author : Mulkh Raj Tuli.
Availability : Faculty of Education, Kumaun University, Almora.
Languages : English & Hindi.
Uses : To measure attitude towards mathematics.
Level : High/Higher Secondary Schools pupils.

Main features : Scale product method; 32 items on nature of mathematics, utility of mathematics and experience.
Reliability : Test-retest = .85, and split-half = .89.
Validity : Factorial validity & cross-cultural.
Time : Fifteen minutes.
Norms : From the author.

24A2 MATHEMATICS ATTITUDE SCALE

(The following statements have to be checked on a 6-point scale of agreement).

1. Mathematics is a search for truth.
2. Mathematics is a fascinating subject.
3. Mathematics is an embodiment of logic.
4. Mathematics is an exact science.
5. Mathematics is useful for the study of all disciplines of knowledge.
6. Mathematics has a harmony.

7. Mathematics has a symmetry.
8. Mathematics has a sequence.
9. Mathematics develops initiative.
10. Mathematics develops drive.
11. Mathematics develops inventiveness.
12. Mathematics develops scientific attitude.
13. Mathematics develops patience.
14. Mathematics develops competence in qualitative reasoning.
15. Mathematics develops problem solving ability.
16. Mathematics helps in development of confidence.
17. Mathematics helps in development of courage of conviction.
18. Mathematics helps in concentration of attention.
19. Mathematics inculcates habits of hard work.
20. Mathematics inculcates habits of verification.
21. Mathematics inculcates habits of original thinking.
22. Mathematics contributes to economic growth.
23. Mathematics should not be taught in schools.
24. Mathematical reasoning contributes to the fulfilment of sense of achievement.
25. Mathematical reasoning is more precise than the reasoning involved in the study of other subjects.
26. Mathematical truth has validity independent of place and human authority.
27. One enjoys adventure with mathematical games.
28. One feels a definite and positive reaction towards mathematics.
29. One thinks about mathematical problems even out side school and likes to work them out.
30. The domain of mathematics is characterised by certainty.
31. The lessons in mathematics are meaningful.
32. To work out mathematical problem is a gratifying experience.

24A3 ATTITUDE SCALE TOWARD INTERNATIONAL EVALUATION

Author : B.A. Parikh.
Availability : Agra Psychological Research Cell, Tiwari Kothi, Belanganj, Agra.
Languages : English, Hindi and Gujarati.
Uses : To measure attitudes towards internal evaluation system in colleges.
Level : College students and adults.

Main features : Gutman type scale; forty items.
Reliability : Split-half correlated with S-B formula = .510,

Kuder Richardson formula = .610, and Coefficient of reproducibility cornell techniques = .843.

Validity : Validated against marks obtained in internal test examination : r = .735.

Time : Ten to fifteen minutes.

Norms : Available with authors.

Reference : Parikh, B.A. Development of a scale for measurement of attitudes towards internal evaluation. Journal of @South Gujarat University, 1977, vi, 19-28.

24A3 MEASUREMENT OF ATTITUDES TOWARD INTERNAL EVALUATION

(The following statements have to be checked on 3-point scale of agreement).

1. Internal evaluation is a continuous process, and so it makes a true evaluation of the student.
2. Through the results of the internal assessment the student can get a correct estimate of his abilities.
3. Internal evaluation system has turned the colleges into schools.
4. The number of examinations in the internal evaluation are an unnecessary burden.
5. Internal assessment result's motivates the student to remedy the deficiencies in his study.
6. The internal test examinations are wrong to the student and hence he has to suppress his desire for other types of knowledge.
7. From the results of the internal test the student can know about his progress even while he is studying.
8. Internal evaluation system removes the limitations defects of the external examination conducted at the end of the year.
9. Internal tests consume a lot of teaching days and hence the course remain unfinished.
10. Too many intermittent tests in the internal evaluation is an hindrance for the development of a serious attitude towards annual University examination.
11. Internal evaluation system provides an incentive for regular study.
12. In the internal evaluation system the teachers and students can plan the work of their study.
13. In the internal evaluation tests there is lesser strain on memory, hence it gives better estimate of the students ability for understanding.

14. Some teachers assess the answerbooks of the internal tests with a prejudiced mind.
15. Some teachers are revengeful and give less marks to the students who are generally absent in the class.
16. Some teachers give marks in the internal examinations only if the answers by the students are written from the notes dictated by them.
17. Internal evaluation system improves the study habits.
18. Internal evaluation system enables the teacher to improve and adjust the teaching schedule according to the needs of the students.
19. Internal evaluation system has encouraged teaching restricted to only the questions important in examination.
20. Internal evaluation system has encouraged the malpractice of private tuitions.
21. The results of the students in the internal tests enable their parents to know about the progress of their children.
22. Some teachers threaten the students to fail them in the internal examinations.
23. Some teachers reveal the questions asked in the internal tests and hence the marks obtained by the students in the internal tests have no value.
24. Internal evaluation has encouraged healthy competition of study among the students.
25. In the internal evaluation system the student has to study regularly hence the annual examinations become easier.
26. Some teachers instead of teaching the subject according to the syllabus, dictate notes in the class-about important questions.
27. Some teachers are not so careful and vigilant in assessing the answer-books of the internal examinations.
28. Because of internal tests the students are inclined to be regular in attendance in the class.
29. In the internal examinations the courses are divided into units, hence it is easy to score high marks.
30. Some students maintain cordial relations with the teachers, so that they are favoured in the examinations.
31. In the internal evaluation system the teachers also have to be constantly active and vigilant.
32. The experience of appearing at the examination in the internal test prepares the students in a better

manner for the annual examination.

33. Because of the internal examinations the students are afraid of committing mischief in the class.
34. From the performance in the internal tests the teachers can know the defects of the students, hence can take measures to remedy them.
35. Because of intermittent tests the students have no time for extra curricular activities.
36. Because of the internal tests the student is constantly worried.
37. Tutorial system which is an integral part of the internal evaluation system helps a lot to the students in their studies.
38. Only the book-worm students favour internal evaluation.
39. The marks obtained in the internal tests should not be given much weightage in awarding class in the final examination.
40. Most of the teachers are considerate and honest in the assessment in the internal examinations.

24A4 SCALE FOR MEASUREMENT OF ATTITUDES TOWARDS NCC

Author : B.A. Parikh.
Availability : Agra Psychological Research Cell, Tiwari Kothi, Belangunj, Agra.
Languages : English, Hindi and Gujarati.
Uses : To measure attitudes of students towards NCC.
Level : School and College students.

Main features : Thurstone scale, 22 items.
Reliability : .85 (Flanagan formula), .82 (split.half), and .83 (alternate form Rulon formula).
Validity : Group joining NCC was compared with group joining NSS or group joining no activity. ANOVA, F significant at .01.
Time : Ten minutes.
Norms : Available with author.
Reference : Parikh, B.A. Development of a scale for measurement of attitudes towards NCC activities. Indian Psy. Review, 1977, 15(2), 46-48.

24A4 MEASUREMENT OF ATTITUDES TOWARD NCC ACTIVITIES

1. NCC training is a waste of time.
2. NCC activity is a waste of nation's money.
3. NCC training is merely an activity for giving

strain to legs.

4. It seems there is no specific advantage of NCC training.
5. NCC organisation is an organisation to provide employment for retired and low categoried officers and soldiers.
6. NCC training serves no useful purpose.
7. Discipline attained through NCC training is merely an external discipline.
8. Looking from the behaviour of the NCC cadets to-day it cannot be felt that the aims of NCC °Duty and Discipline' have been achieved.'
9. There is no return of the money spent on NCC in terms of the development of the students.
10. Most of the students taking NCC training do not seem to feel pride and dignity for it.
11. It is not always so that those who take NCC training become self-dependent.
12. NCC activity should be a voluntary activity for students.
13. Through NCC training the student atleast learns how to walk like a young man.
14. NCC training camps provide an experience of community life.
15. The student who has taken NCC training does not feel shame in physical labour and such other tasks.
16. NCC training provides a good outlet for the energy of aggressive and dominant students.
17. NCC training develops positive attitudes towards defense and defense-forces of the country.
18. Training in NCC should be considered a qualification for recruitment in Government and public sector, corporate jobs.
19. Cadets are very much useful in civil-defense.
20. If the discipline coming from NCC training is imbibed fully, the life of the man also becomes disciplined.
21. Every able bodied students should take NCC training.
22. NCC training is a purposeful youth activity.

24A5 ATTITUDE SCALE TOWARDS STRIKE

Authors : B.S. Siddaramaiah, B.K. Murthy, V.Venkataramaiah, and M.K. Sethu Rao.

Availability : Authors, College of Agriculture, Dharwar (Karnataka).

Language : English.
Level : College students.

Main features : The scale consists of 14 statements related to strike. Scale values for each statement is given.
Reliability : Split-half reliability (N = 40) = .94.
Validity : Content validity is established.
Reference : Siddaramaiah, B.S., Murthy, B.K., Venkataramaiah, P. and Sethu Rao, M.K. A scale to measure the attitude of College students towards strike. Journal of Education and Psychology, 1979, XXXVI(4), 200-203.

24A5 ATTITUDE SCALE TOWARDS STRIKE

(The respondents have to check the following statements with which they agree).

1. Strike is the only way to show our unity.
2. Strike sets right the mal-administration.
3. Strike to youth is a means to escape from regular classes.
4. Now-a-days students' strike is becoming a fashion.
5. Strike is the right means of satisfying our demands.
6. Students on strike are the best weapons in the hands of politicians.
7. There is more loss than gain to the nation by going on strike.
8. Strike retards the developmental activities of the nation.
9. It is most enjoyable to participate in procession of the strike.
10. Students spoil their career by going on strike.
11. Strike indicates students' indiscipline.
12. To go on strike is simply a waste of time and energy.
13. Strike should be the last instrument to fight for justice.
14. Strike is a means of destruction.

instruments with technical information B

24B1 TEACHERS' ATTITUDE SCALE (TAS)

Author : Prakash Chandra Shukala.

Availability : M/s Indian Psychological Corporation, Shanti-Sadan, Rai Behari Lal Road, Lucknow.
Language : Hindi.
Uses : To evaluate teachers attitude towards their job.
Level : Primary level teachers.

Main features : Likert type scale (5-point); Fifty items.
Reliability : Test-retest method = .89.
Validity : (1) Face validity, (2) Criterion related validity +0.69.
Time : No time limit.

24B1 JOB ATTITUDE SCALE (JAS)

Author : M.P. Uniyal.
Availability : Author, Department of Education, Garhwal University, Srinagar, Garhwal.
Language : Hindi.
Uses : To identify the teachers' attitude towards their job.
Level : Teachers.

Main features : It contains 58 items to be answered on a 5-point rating scale ranging between strongly agree to strongly disagree. It has nine areas.
Reliability : Test-retest and split-half reliability was found to be .62 and .73 respectively.
Validity : Values of inter-area correlations were found to be between .131 and .472. Coefficient of validity against Millers and Roy's attitude scales was found to be .513 and .682 respectively.
Time : Twenty-five minutes.
Norms : Norms are available with the author.
Reference : Uniyal, M.P. "Job Motivation and Satisfaction of Teachers". D.Phil. Dissertation, Allahabad University, Allahabad.

24B3 A SCALE TO MEASURE TEACHERS' ATTITUDE TOWARDS POPULATION EDUCATION IN SECONDARY SCHOOLS

Author : Neelam Srivastava.
Availability : Devki Tewari Faculty of Education, University of Lucknow, Lucknow..
Language : English.
Uses : To measure teachers' attitude towards introducing population education in secondary schools.
Level : Secondary school teachers.

191 Education

Main features : It is a Likert type 40 items; 5-point rating scale.
Reliability : Split-half reliability = .62 (N = 100), test-retest reliability = .65 (N = 100), and parallel form reliability = .65 (N = 100).
Validity : Predictive validity established.
Reference : Srivastava, Neelma : A scale to measure teachers' attitudes towards population education in secondary schools. Indian Educational Review, 1981, 16(4), 101-107.

24B4 VIOLENCE-NON-VIOLENCE REACTION STUDY

Author : V.K. Mittal.
Availability : Author, Department of Psychology, Meerut College, Meerut.
Uses : To measure the attitude of students violence, non-violence etc.
Level : College going population.

Main features : It is a Guttman type scale consisting of 18 items with 4 alternative statements in each. The items are related to (a) attitude towards self and society, (b) attitude towards evils, (c) attitude towards violence and non-violence, (d) attitude towards opponents and (e) implementation of approach and mechanism of social change.
Reliability : Split-half reliability = .80, and coefficient of reproducibility = .82.
Validity : Besides content validity College teacher's rating is used as criterion for validity, $r_{bis} = .73$.
Norms : Percentile norms are available.

citations C

24C1 LEADERSHIP ATTITUDE INVENTORY

Author : Bhagwat Singh.
Availability : Author, Department of Education, Banaras Hindu University, Varanasi.

24C2 ATTITUDE TOWARDS LEARNING OF SCIENCE

Author : Rup Prakash.
Availability : Rupa Psychological Centre, B-19/60,

Deoriabir, Bhelupur, Varanasi.

24C3 A SCALE OF ATTITUDE OF SECONDARY SCHOOL TEACHERS TOWARDS TEACHING

Author : Santi Datt.
Availability : Institute of Education of Women, Hastings House, Alipore, Calcutta.

24C4 MYSORE TEACHER ATTITUDE

Author : P.R. Nayar.
Availability : Author, Department of Education, University of Mysore, Mysore.

24C5 TEACHERS' ATTITUDE INVENTORY

Author : R.C. Gupta.
Availability : Author, Department of Education, Banaras Hindu University, Varanasi.

24C6 MEASUREMENT OF ATTITUDE TOWARDS PROFESSIONAL TRAINING (TEACHERS)

Author : Malti Shukla.
Availability : Author, Teachers Training College, Banaras Hindu University, Varanasi.

24C7 ATTITUDE SCALE FOR TEACHING

Author : G.P. Sherry.
Availability : Author, P.G. Department of Education, DEI Women's Training College, Dayalbagh, Agra.

24C8 SCIENCE ATTITUDE SCALE

Author : Avinash Grewal.
Availability : National Psychological Corporation, Agra.

5. Institutional Characteristics

complete instruments A

25A1 AGRICULTURAL UNIVERSITY ENVIRONMENT INDEX (AUEI)

Authors : S.Y. Kulkarni & Y.P. Singh.
Availability : Senior Author, Department of Agricultural Extension, Punjabrao Krishi Vidyapeeth, Ajika.
Language : English.
Uses : To assess organisational climate of Agricultural Universities.
Level : For Post-Graduate students and faculty members of Agricultural Universities.

Main features : Instrument has been used to measure organisational climate of two Agricultural Universities, one having High Academic Excellence score but matching on budget as a surface variable. (i) Number of items - 73, (ii) Dimensions - 8, (iii) Technique - five points scale.
Reliability : The instrument has a test-retest reliability of .812 and split-half reliability of .974. Areawise reliability coefficient varies between .342 to .812 by test-retest method and between .641 to .861 by split-half method.
Validity : Content validity assured.
Norms : Not yet available.
Reference : Kulkarni, S.Y. "Organisational Climate as a Discriminator in Academic Excellence," Ph.D. thesis, Division of Agricultural Extension, I.A.R.I., New Delhi, 1981.

25A1 AGRICULTURAL UNIVERSITY ENVIRONMENT INDEX

(The following items have to be checked on a 5-point scale).

1. Courses, examinations and readings are frequently revised.
2. Most of the courses are real intellectual challenges.
3. Impartial and justified assessment is the speciality of evaluation here.
4. Teachers give sufficient illustrations with the help of field problems while teaching.
5. Excellence in scholarship is the dominant feature of this university.
6. Teachers here keep the students informed of the uptodate knowledge of the subject.
7. Because of the pressure of other commitments, many

instructors are unable to prepare adequately for their course.

8. Most of the instructors here are dedicated scholars in their fields of specialization.
9. Persons without having adequate teaching experience or skills are permitted to teach in this university.
10. Suggestions for improvement from lower cadre are accepted and appreciated here.
11. Lectures by an outstanding scientists are poorly attended.
12. Students and faculty in this university voluntarily opt to do rural social service as an optional activity.
13. Close teacher-pupil contact can easily be brought out to the notice here.
14. Seniors often talk high about their junior colleagues.
15. Freedom to scientists for selection of research projects of their own choices.
16. Students set high standards of achievement for themselves.
17. Library is one of the outstanding facility of the campus.
18. Students have many opportunities to develop skills in organising and directing the work of others.
19. The university is outstanding for the emphasis and support it gives to research.
20. Farmers regard this university as their second home.
21. Students here are encouraged to appear for competitive examinations.
22. Persons in this university are not tense with personal problems.
23. Many research schemes had to be dropped due to procedural delays and other constraints in this university.
24. Prestige of the Department here is judged by the number of its students qualifying in competitive examinations.
25. Special lectures by those who have done rural social service with great dedication are frequently arranged.
26. Mutual respect is the speciality of relations among the members of faculty in this university.
27. On the important issues faculty and Administrators arrive at decisions jointly.
28. Research accomplishments of this university are of

high order.

29. Many opportunities exist outside the class room for intellectual and aesthetic self expression on the part of students.
30. There are good facilities for the students to learn vocationally useful skills and techniques.
31. There is too much of delay between the time of submission of research proposals and the time they are sanctioned.
32. Extension is most valued activity in this university.
33. Heads of the Departments and other administrators take special care that the work of individual scientist do not suffer for want of materials and technical services.
34. Faculty members are not encouraged to go for higher studies.
35. Research projects are need based.
36. None is criticised publicly here.
37. There are no good opportunities for professional growth here for interested scientists.
38. Most of the research problems here are based on the problems posed by extension.
39. Students put a lot of energy into everything they do in and outside the class.
40. Variety of training programmes for farmers and different groups in response to their needs and requests are organised.
41. Faculty members are not encouraged to participate in seminars and conferences to their professional benefits.
42. Adequate guidance is available to those who want to prepare for competitive examinations.
43. University lays emphasis on publication of papers in quality journals.
44. University's recommendations are considered highly credible by the farmers.
45. There are many excellent facilities for research on this campus.
46. There is often informative and stimulating discussion in the seminar.
47. Issues, problems and plan of rural development are invariably discussed here.
48. There is close cooperation between this university and the State Department of Agriculture in developing an effective extension programme.
49. Emphasis here on teaching is inadequate.
50. Scientists in this university welcome problems for

extension.

51. Careful reasoning and clear logic are valued most highly in grading students papers, reports or discussions.
52. Data cooking is considered as a sin of high order in this campus.
53. Researchers freely share rare equipments with each others.
54. There is high degree of sensitivity to the rural needs here.
55. This university has a reputation for being very friendly with farmers.
56. Alumni who have competed examinations (ARS, fellowships etc.) are sought for guidance.
57. Most of the students are interested in joining N.S.S.
58. Here delegation of authority commensurates with responsibility.
59. Students here plan a career involving work and stay with rural people.
60. Most scientists work off-time in experimental plots and laboratories.
61. Men readily cooperate with each other.
62. No signs of bossism or authority projected here in this university.
63. Farmers of this locality owe a lot to this university.
64. Atmosphere on the campus is very friendly.
65. Scientists are meticulous in planning their projects.
66. Authority take quick decisions communicating the same to the persons concerned.
67. Scientists here consider extension experience a must for doing a good job in teaching and research.
68. Education here tends to make students more practical and realistic.
69. Here senior scientists encourage junior scientists to develop autonomy rather than only receiving their technical assistance.
70. Inter-disciplinary help from the allied fields are easily available here.
71. Unconventional ideas for researches are encouraged in this university.
72. There are many opportunities for individual creative thinking activity.
73. Scientists willingly participate in Extension activities.

citations C

25C1 SCHOOL CLIMATE SCALE

Authors : M.P. Uniyal and A.R. Bisht.
Availability : Faculty of Education, Kumaun University, Almora.
Reference : Uniyal, M.P. & Bisht, A.R. School climate and reactions to frustration. Indian Educational Review, 1980, 15(2), 95-101.

adaptations D

25D1 SCHOOL ORGANISATIONAL CLIMATE DESCRIPTION QUESTIONNAIRE

Author : Motilal Sharma.
Availability : Author, 8-Shri Ganesh Shiv Kripa, Ichhanath, Surat.
Languages : English & Hindi.
Uses : To study institutional climate of schools as well as other organisations.

Main features : This is an Indian adaptation of organisational climate description questionnaire (Halpin & Crofts, 1963). The instrument consists of 64-Likert type items distributed over eight dimensions. These dimensions have been grouped under two categories (a) Group behaviour characteristics disengagement, alienation, esprit intimacy and (b) Leader behaviour characteristics - psycho-physical hindrance, controls, production emphasis and humanised thrust. Six types of climate have been described as open, autonomous familiar, controlled, paternal and closed climate. For each statement four categories of responses are assigned as rarely occurs, sometimes occurs, often occurs and very frequently occurs. Further details are given in the Manual.
Reliability : K.R.-20 was used for calculating the coefficients of reliability (internal consistency) for each of the subtests. Coefficient of internal consistency ranged between .34 to .81 (N = 115) for the eight subjects. Communalities estimates also ranged between .28 to .61 and .10 to .70 for individual and school scores separately.
Validity : Validity is established by experts ratings and by correlating the scale with that of Halpin and Crofts study. Details are given in the Manual.

References : (1) Sharma, Motilal, Buch, P.M., & Rai, K. Organisational Climate of Secondary Schools of Rajasthan and Gujarat : A comparative study. In Sharma, et al. (Eds.) Diagnosing the school personality, Baroda, CASE, 1971.

(2) Sharma, Motilal, An investigation into organisational climate of secondary schools of Rajasthan ; Unpublished Ph.D. thesis, M.S. University, Baroda, 1973.

(3) Sharma, Motilal, Organisational climate and academic achievement, Indian Jr. Psychometry and Education, 11, 1-2, 1971.

(4) Sharma, Motilal & Santhanam, M.R. Percolation of school climate into the class room. Education and Psychology Review, Oct., 1973.

(5) Sharma, Motilal & Qureshi, Z.M. Teacher morale and organisational climate : An exploratory study. The progress of education, Dec., 1972.

PART THREE

ORGANISATIONAL BEHAVIOUR

Organisational Behaviour

In this part of the Handbook the instruments dealing with organisational behaviour have been reported. These instruments are reported under two sections :

i industrial organisations,
ii health organisations.

The instruments dealing with educational organisations have been reported in the earlier part. The instruments dealing with agricultural practices etc. have been reported in the next part under the section of modernisation and social change. The instruments in this part deal with various dimensions of organisational behaviour like job satisfaction, job motivation, organisational effectiveness, occupational and role stress, participation, role conflicts and attitudes etc. The detailed break-up of instruments is given in Table 3, below.

TABLE 3

Classification	Original reproduced	Only information provided	Citations	Adaptations	Total
1. Industrial Organisations	41	7	5	2	55
2. Health Organisations	3	-	-	-	3
Total	44	7	5	2	58

Industrial Organisations :

There are in all 55 instruments listed under this. Of these 41 have been reproduced here. Only technical information for other seven instruments is provided. Five instruments have been cited and two are adaptations. The areas covered by the instruments reproduced here include managerial styles, interpersonal needs, motivational aspects in organisations, organisational effectiveness, job satisfaction, managerial behaviour, job anxiety, occupational and role stress, participation, performance rating, general personality of workers, and role-conflict etc. The instruments are meant for industrial workers, managers, working women and others who are engaged in some organisations.

Most of the instruments have reported either split-half or test-retest reliability. A few have reported both the reliabilities. For some instruments, only reliability coefficients are reported. A number of instruments have also reported Cronbach's alpha reliability. The values wherever reported are fairly high. Validity has been reported for 18 of the instruments. Face, construct and factorial validities are reported for some of the instruments. A few have reported only factorial validity. Ratings and biserial coefficient of correlation have also been used to validate some of these instruments.

Norms are not available for most of these instruments. As the norms of the kind of industrial population are subject to be changing according to geography, size of industry and type of industry these are generally of restricted utility.

Among the instruments reproduced here, 10 are developed by Udai Pareek. Detailed information regarding reliability, validity, norms etc. are not provided for most of these instruments which are available with author. These instruments deal with various aspects of organisational behaviour and are very useful for researchers, managers and executives to understand various aspects of organisational behaviour like managerial style, values, preferences, general belief, locus of control, interpersonal need, and different motivational aspects in organisations. The instruments are reproduced here for references and the details can be had from the authors.

There are three instruments by T.V. Rao. The details about these instruments are not given which are available with author. These instruments are reproduced here for references. These instruments are also very useful for industrial organisations to study supervisory styles, sales styles and motivational orientations.

There are a series of instruments by C.N. Daftuar. One is a Likert-type scale and measures nine dimensions of organisational effectiveness. The other one is meant for supervisors and executives and measures six managerial or leadership styles in organisations. There are other instruments which measure job satisfaction of employees, dysfunctional consequences of control system, employees' attitude towards delegation of authority and power strategy of employees in organisations. Reliability in terms of Cronbach's alpha is reported for all the instruments. Other informations are available with author. There is a very useful organisational behaviour questionnaire by R.P. Singh and Janak Pandey which measures organisational power, climate, control and personal consequences.

There are three instruments by Prayag Mehta and Mahaveer Jain; two measure the level of satisfaction with work. One is meant for workers and the other one is for managers. These instruments are well standardised and good references are available on them. The other one is a general opinion questionnaire and measures the level of authoritarian tendency among industrial workers. The role-conflict inventory by B.A. Parikh is meant for married working women and measures the level of adjustment and degree of conflict. This instrument also reports fairly high reliability and validity.

There are two motivation instruments reproduced here. The employees' motivation schedule by A.K. Srivastava is available in Hindi and English and reports highly significant standardisation data. It assesses the level of various needs of the employees which motivate them to work efficiently. The other one is a job motivation scale by Akhtar and Bhargava. Standardisation data are not available for this scale but it seems to be useful for comparing the job motivation of various professional groups. The job anxiety scale by Srivastava and Sinha reports will standardization data and is a good instrument for assessing the level of job anxiety of employees.

There is another instrument by Srivastava and Singh

which seems to be good to assess the degree of perceive stress arising from various aspects of the job of th employees.

There is one well used instrument developed by Pestonje which is meant for industrial workers and supervisors an measures organisational change. The other one an inventor is for evaluating the job satisfaction of white colla workers. It is the modification of the earlier S-I Employees' Inventory which was standardized for blue colla workers.

Two other instruments by Singh and Pestonjee ar reproduced here and good references are available on them One ascertains the level of efficiency and the other one as sesses the level of participation in decision making. A fe inventories are reproduced here which measure workmen per sonality, fatigue, business ethics, and off-the-job ac tivities. There is one attitude scale which locates pro-an anti-management industrial employees. A scale by Sinha an Sharma measures the happiness of industrial workers. Ther is one job satisfaction instrument by Mishra and other which assesses the efficiency of a worker in relation to jo satisfaction and reports high reliability and validity. Tw Instruments by Babu Thomas are also reproduced here. O these one assesses the afflation of trade unions and th other one assesses motivation of workers.

A few other instruments which are not reproduced here seem to have better standardization data than some of thos reproduced here. Two instruments, Role Pics (oh) and OR Scale by Udai Pareek are unique, well standardized and wel used instruments. The first one is semi-projective in natur and measures eight styles of coping with stress. The othe one is a scale and measures 10 types of organisational rol stresses. These instruments along with the manual are com mercially available. The other instruments for which th technical information only is provided are Supervisors Rating Scale, Supervisors' Orientation Schedule, Aspiratio Inventory for Industrial Workers and Union Scale. Five in struments have been cited and two are adaptations. The firs one is a stress questionnaire and measures job stress. Th other one is a job involvement scale and assesses the leve of job involvement of workers.

Health Organisations :

Only three instruments are available which have bee

reproduced here under this section. The first one is a hospital climate questionnaire by C.N. Daftuar and covers eight dimensions of organisational climate. It is available in English and can be used with literate English knowing employees. Cronbach's alpha coefficient is reported which is fairly high. Other details cán be had from the author. The scale is reproduced here for reference.

The other one is a job satisfaction scale. Reliability and validity is established. The reliability value is fairly high. The scale measures job satisfaction of family welfare personnel. There is one S-D Inventory by Pestonjee which measures job satisfaction of Medical Professionals.

ORGANISATIONAL BEHAVIOUR

1. Industrial Organisations

complete instruments A

31A1 MANAGERIAL STYLE QUESTIONNAIRE

Author : Udai Pareek.
Availability : Indian Institute of Management, Ahmedabad.
Language : English.
Uses : To understand influencing style of managers.
Level : Managers, and trainers.
Main features : Self-rating 5-point scale. Number of items 30.
Reliability & Validity : Established, available with author.
Time : Twenty minutes.
Norms : Available with author.
References :

(1) Pareek, Udai; SPIRO : Measuring influence styles. Navin Publications, Ahmedabad.
(2) Bose, K. & Pareek, Udai : The dynamics of conflict management style of the bankers (unpublished manuscript).

31A1 MANAGERIAL STYLE QUESTIONNAIRE

1. Assure your subordinates of your availability to them.
2. Communicate strong feelings and resentment to the senior managers, without caring whether this will affect your relationships with them.

3. Encourage your subordinates raise questions with you about what should or should not be done.
4. Discuss new ideas with the participants even without working out their details.
5. Collect all the necessary information needed to work a problem.
6. Give your subordinates the needed solutions to their problems.
7. Think out unusual and new solutions.
8. Admonish the subordinates for not acting according to your instruments.
9. Take up your subordinates' cause and fight for them.
10. Collect all the information and data, even when those are not immediately needed or used.
11. Help your subordinates know some of their own strengths.
12. Champion the subordinates' cause even at the cost of effectiveness.
13. Help your subordinates see ethical or normative dimensions of some of their behaviour or actions.
14. Overwhelm your subordinates with new ideas.
15. Think out (generate) many alternatives before adopting one for action.
16. Guide your subordinates in detail about the problems and their solutions.
17. Try out new things.
18. Give clear instructions to your subordinates on what should not be done.
19. Zealously argue your case (point of view) in organisational meeting.
20. Spend most of the time in specific tasks to be performed.
21. Reassure your subordinates of your continued help.
22. Express resentment to the concerned authorities about what has not been done as promised.
23. Help your subordinates examine the appropriateness of the proposed action.
24. Try out new ideas/ways even without waiting to consolidate the previous ones.
25. Continuously search various resources from which needed information can be obtained to work out solutions to problems.
26. Encourage subordinates to come frequently to you to seek your advice and help.
27. Feel excited in trying out new ways and take a problem as a challenge.
28. Clearly prescribe standards of behaviour to be fol-

lowed in your department/section.

29. Express frankly your feelings and reactions in the meetings and to your senior managers.
30. Primarily work on organisational tasks, even at the cost of sensitivity and attention of feelings of people.

31A2 VALUE PREFERENCE SURVEY

Author : Udai Pareek.
Availability : Indian Institute of Management, Ahmedabad.
Language : English.
Uses : To measure the value of the various outcomes (various aspects of achievement).
Level : Managers and entrepreneurs.
Main features : It is a 12 items questionnaire rated on a 4-point scale. Seven items are scored and the five are the filler items.
Reliability : Split-half reliability (N = 20) = .43.
Validity : Established.
Time : Ten minutes.
Norms : Available with author.
References :

(1) Pareek, Udai : Value preference survey. In motivational dimensions of entrepreneurship : A book of readings for trainers. Malaysian Industrial Development Finance, Berhad, Malaysia, 1979.
(2) Sarupria, D. A study of psychological factors in entrepreneurship and managerial effectiveness. Unpublished Doctoral Dissertation, Gujarat University, Ahmedabad, 1981.

31A2 VALUE PREFERENCE SURVEY

1. Earning profit
2. Determining or shaping things according to one's ideas
3. Progressing in life
4. Achievement in life
5. Achievement of a goal
6. Meeting a challenge
7. Satisfaction of the conscience
8. Independence
9. Getting others' help
10. Accomplishing things through one's own efforts
11. Getting tasks done by others
12. Continuously things about a task.

31A3 GENERAL BELIEF INVENTORY

Author : Udai Pareek.
Availability : Indian Institute of Management, Ahmedabad.
Language : English.
Uses : To measure the perceived instrumentality.
Level : Managers and entrepreneurs.
Main features : Twelve items questionnaire rated on 0-4 point scale. Seven items are scored and 5-filler items are ignored.
Reliability : Split-half reliability (N = 20) = .43.
Validity : Established.
Time : Ten minutes.
References :

(1) Sarupria, D. A study of psychological factors in entrepreneurship and managerial effectiveness. Unpublished Ph.D. Thesis, University of Gujarat, Ahmedabad, 1981.
(2) Rao, T.V. & Moulim T.K. (Eds.) Identification and selection of small scale entrepreneurs. Indian Institute of Management, Ahmedabad, 1979.

31A3 GENERAL BELIEFS INVENTORY

1. You can achieve your goal if you pursue it, and do not give it up in spite of many difficulties.
2. If you try different ways of solving a problem, when your original ways do not work, you achieve real independence.
3. Doing something for the society satisfies your conscience.
4. The harder you work, the more profit you earn.
5. You may be able to shape things according to your ideas, if you work on a task until it is finished.
6. Your progress in life is in proportion to your ability to impress people.
7. Your achievement is greatly related to your good behaviour with people.
8. The challenge can be met if you work out details of what you want to do, including how to go about doing it.
9. One who is bothered about incomplete tasks is likely to succeed in achieving them.
10. People help a person in the achievement of his goals if he is helpful to them.

11. One who asserts himself in meetings get task done by others.
12. One who has to do things by himself should spend a lot of time on the task in hand.

31A4 ASFI

Author : Udai Pareek.
Availability : Indian Institute of Management, Ahmedabad.
Language : English.
Uses : To measure the locus of control and attributional competence.
Level : Managers and entrepreneurs.
Main features : Paired comparison technique used. Number of items = 24 , 12 for success and 12 for failure of persons.
Time : 15 - 20 minutes.

31A4 ASFI

A. In your opinion which of the two factors in each pair contributes more towards the success of a manager? Tick one in each pair.

1. (a) Competence
   (b) Hard work
2. (a) Availability of opportunity
   (b) Chance of getting a break
3. (a) His/her effort
   (b) Contacts with proper persons or source
4. (a) Good luck
   (b) His/her involvement in the goal
5. (a) Favourable opportunities
   (b) Basic ability of the person
6. (a) Ability to succeed
   (b) Good luck
7. (a) Technical knowledge
   (b) Involvement in the task in hand.
8. (a) Favourable opportunities
   (b) Chance of getting a break
9. (a) His/her effort
   (b) Favourable opportunities.
10. (a) Sudden favourable conditions like inheritance of money
    (b) Hard work.
11. (a) Special government schemes
    (b) His/her competence.

12. (a) Ability to take advantage of the opportunity
    (b) Chance of getting a break.

B. In your opinion which of the factors in each pair contributes more towards the failure of a person?

Tick mark one in each pair.

1. (a) Lack of competence
   (b) Lack of effort
2. (a) Lack of proper contacts
   (b) Unfortunate circumstances.
3. (a) Lack of involvement in the goal
   (b) Lack of availability of resources.
4. (a) Bad luck
   (b) Neglecting the task.
5. (a) Unfavourable conditions
   (b) Lack of ability.
6. (a) Lack of ability to calculate and act
   (b) Not getting a break
7. (a) Lack of technical knowledge
   (b) Not giving enough time to the task
8. (a) Unfovourable conditions
   (b) Bad luck
9. (a) Lack of effort
   (b) Lack pf/rp/er contacts
10. (a) Not getting a break
    (b) Lack of effort
11. (a) Lack of availability of resources
    (b) Lack of ability to calculate and act
12. (a) Lack of competence
    (b) Bad luck.

31A5 O-P SCALE

Author : Udai Pareek.
Availability : Indian Institute of Management, Ahmedabad.
Language : English.
Uses : To measure perceived openness and perceptiveness.
Level : Managers and trainers.
Main features : It is a ten items scale rated on a 5-point scale.
Time : Ten minutes.

31A O-P SCALE

(Answer the following questions for your department/organisation by using the following key ; some, several, quite a large number, and almost all).

1. How many persons in your department/organisation give positive feedback or express positive feelings to

   (a) their seniors?
   (b) their juniors?
   (c) their peers?

2. How many persons give negative feedback or express hard feeling to

   (a) their seniors?
   (b) their juniors?
   (c) their peers?

3. How many persons share their personal problems with

   (a) their seniors?
   (b) their juniors?
   (c) their peers?

4. How many persons freely express their disagreements with

   (a) seniors?
   (b) juniors?
   (c) peers?

5. How many freely share their opinions on critical and sensitive organisational issues with

   (a) seniors?
   (b) juniors?
   (c) peers?

6. How many persons are perceptive of the positive feelings of the following about them (even when such feelings are not expressed

   (a) seniors?
   (b) juniors?
   (c) peers?

7. How many persons are perceptive of the critical and hard feelings of the following about themselves

(a) seniors?
(b) juniors?
(c) peers?

8. How many persons are perceptive of the personal problems of the following (even when they do not share them)

(a) seniors?
(b) juniors?
(c) peers?

9. How many persons are perceptive of the disagreements of the following even when the latter do not express these to the former

(a) seniors?
(b) juniors?
(c) peers?

10. How many are perceptive of the opinions of the following on sensitive and critical organisational issues even when the latter do not express their opinions

(a) seniors?
(b) juniors?
(c) peers?

31A6 IPNI

Author : Udai Pareek.
Availability : Indian Institute of Management, Ahmedabad.
Language : English.
Uses : To measure interpersonal needs.
Level : Managers, entrepreneurs and students.
Main features : It consists of 60 items checked on 1-6 point scale.
Reliability & Validity : Available with author.
Time : Twenty minutes.
Reference : Pareek, Udai : Motivational dimensions of entrepreneurship : A book of readings for trainers. Malaysian Industrial Development Finance, Berhad, Malaysia, 1979.

31A6 IPNI

1. I join groups and organisations when I get an opportunity.
2. I like to be made a member of committees.

3. I try to develop personal relations with others.
4. I like people to be close to me.
5. I tend to help people resolve their conflicts.
6. I like people to empathise with me (try to feel as I do).
7. I appreciate other people's accomplishments.
8. I like people to appreciate my work.
9. I tend to dominate the group I work with.
10. I dislike taking independent decisions.
11. I try to maintain my reputation in a group.
12. I enjoy trying a new thing after having read about it.
13. I do not like to join committees and other groups.
14. I like people to include me in their groups.
15. I tend to share emotions with people.
16. I like people to express their emotions to me.
17. I enjoy working for myself rather than for a group or a community.
18. I do not like people to share my grief and distress.
19. I like to compliment people for their experience and expertise.
20. I like people to compliment me for my accomplishments.
21. If people ignore my views in a group I tend to keep quiet.
22. I like my seniors to solve the problems for me, or guide me to find solutions.
23. I try to influence other people.
24. I like to get more ideas from books.
25. I try to participate in group activities.
26. I do not want people to invite me to parties.
27. I like to be close to people.
28. I like people to keep a distance with me.
29. I tend to empathise with people (feel as they do).
30. I like people to collaborate with me in achieving a goal.
31. I give attention to people.
32. I do not care whether people give me credit for my contribution or not.
33. I enjoy competing for power in a group or an organisation.
34. I don't like others to try to get me do things their way.
35. I enjoy seeing people accept my point of view, even without expressedly acknowledging so.
36. I do not like others giving me suggestions.
37. I invite people for visits.

38. I like people to consult me.
39. I am cool and distant to people.
40. I like people to share their emotions with me.
41. I tend to tolerate discomfort for the sake of others.
42. I like people to help me when I need some help.
43. I am impatient with people when I am busy.
44. I like people to use my skills and expertise.
45. I like others to do things my way.
46. I like it if others tell me what I am supposed to do.
47. I try to leave an impression on people.
48. I take a decision after consulting people.
49. I like to do with people.
50. I like to be invited for visits.
51. I enjoy having close relationships.
52. I like people to be warm and personal to me.
53. I tend to collaborate with others in achieving a goal.
54. I like people to support me in crises.
55. I applaud people for their achievements.
56. I like people to quote me.
57. I like to tell others what is to be done.
58. I like others to guide me.
59. It makes no difference to me if people agree with me or not.
60. I like people to give new ideas and suggestions.

31A7 MAO (B)

Author : Udai Pareek.
Availability : Indian Institute of Management, Ahmedabad.
Language : English.
Uses : To measure motivational aspects of behaviour in organisations.
Level : Students, Banks and Institutions.
Main features : Sixty statements questionnaire measuring 5 motivational aspects of behaviour. 60 items are divided into 12 task dimensions of 5 items each. Items are rated on a 5-point scale.
Reliability : Available with author.
Time : Thirty minutes.
Reference : Sen, P.C. Personal and organisational correlates of role stress and coping strategies in some public sector banks. Unpublished Doctoral Dissertation, Gujarat University, Ahmedabad, 1982.

31A7 MAO (B)

1. I enjoy working on moderately difficult (challenging) goals.
2. I am overemotional.
3. I am forceful in my arguments.
4. I refer matters to superiors.
5. I keep close track of things (monitors the action).
6. I make contributions to charity, etc.
7. I set easy goals and achieve them.
8. I relate very well to people.
9. I am preoccupied with my own ideas, and am a poor listener.
10. I follow an ideal.
11. I demand conformity from my people.
12. I take steps to develop my people.
13. I strive to excel performance/targets.
14. I give more importance to personal relationship than to organisational matters.
15. I build on the ideas of my subordinates.
16. I seek approval of superiors.
17. I ensure that things are done according to the plan.
18. I consider difficulties of others even at the cost of the task.
19. I am afraid of making mistakes.
20. I share feelings with others.
21. I enjoy arguing and winning in my arguments.
22. I have genuine respect for seniors.
23. I admonish people for not completing the tasks.
24. I go out of way to help my people.
25. I search new ways of overcoming difficulties.
26. I have difficulty in expressing negative feelings to others.
27. I set examples and models before others.
28. I hesitate to take hard decisions.
29. I clearly define the roles and procedures for my people.
30. I undergo personal inconvenience for others.
31. I am conscious of my limitations or weaknesses than of my strengths.
32. I like interest in personal matters of my people.
33. I am laissez faire (do not care about how things happen).
34. I learn from my seniors.
35. I centralise most tasks to ensure that things are properly done.
36. I have empathy for and understanding of my people.
37. I want to know how well I have been working, and I

use the feedback to improve myself.

38. I avoid conflict in the interest of group feelings.
39. I give new suggestions and ideas.
40. I tend to please others.
41. I lay down systems clearly for my people.
42. I am willing to take the responsibility for others' work to help them.
43. I show low self-confidence.
44. I recognise and respond to feelings.
45. I am given the credit for work done in a team.
46. I seek help from those who know the matter.
47. In case of difficulties, I rush to put things right myself.
48. I develop team work amongst my people.
49. I work effectively under pressure of deadlines.
50. I am uneasy and less productive when working alone.
51. I give credit and recognition to others.
52. I look for support for my action and proposals.
53. I seek positions of authority.
54. I hesitate to take strong action because of human considerations.
55. I complain about difficulties and problems.
56. I take initiative in making friends with other colleagues.
57. I am more conscious of status symbols like furniture, size of room, etc.
58. I like to get ideas from others.
59. I tend to form small groups to effectively influence decisions.
60. I like to take responsibility for group work.

31A8 MAO (C)

Author : Udai Pareek.
Availability : Indian Institute of Management, Ahmedabad.
Language : English.
Uses : To measure motivational climate of organisation.
Level : Students, entrepreneurs and institutions.
Main features : The questionnaire consists of 72 items measuring six motives like achievement, power, extension, affiliation, dependency and control. The items are divided into 12 task dimensions of six items each. The items are ranked from 1 to 6.
Reliability : Test-retest reliability established.
Validity : Validity established by factor analysis.
Time : Thirty minutes.
Norms : Available with the author.
References :

217 Organisational Behaviour

1. Pareek, Udai : Motivational climate questionnaire : Mimeographed report. Indian Institute of Management, Ahmedabad, 1975.
2. Sen, P.C. Personal and organisational correlates of role stress and coping strategies in some public sector banks. Unpublished Doctoral Dissertation, Gujarat University, Ahmedabad, 1982.
3. Surti, K. Some psychological correlates of role stress and coping styles in working women. Unpublished Doctoral Dissertation in psychology, Gujarat University, Ahmedabad, 1982.

31A8 MAO (C)

1. Orientation

a. People here are mainly concerned about following laid down rules and procedures.
b. The main concern of people here is to help each other develop greater skills, and so, advance in the organisation.
c. Achieving goals or targets set, or excelling them, seems to be the main concern.
d. Consolidating one's own personal position and influence seems to be the main concern.
e. The dominant concern here is to maintain friendly relations with others.
f. The main concern of the people here is to develop their competence and expertise.

2. Interpersonal relationship

a. In this organisation most informal groups are formed around experts.
b. The atmosphere here is very friendly and people spend enough time in informal social relations.
c. There are strong cliques in the organisation to protect their interests.
d. Business-like relationship prevails here-people are warm, but get together mostly for ensuring excellence in performance.
e. People have strong associations mostly with their supervisors and look for suggestions and guidance from them.
f. People have high concern for one another and help each other spontaneously when such help is needed.

3. Supervision

a. Supervision here is usually to check mistakes and 'catch' the person.
b. Supervisor here strongly prefer that their subordinates ask them for instructions and suggestions.
c. Supervisors here take pains to see that their subordinates improve personal skills and chances of advancement.
d. Supervisors reward outstanding achievement.
e. Supervisors try to use their expertise and competence rather than their formal authority in influencing their subordinates.
f. Supervisors here are more concerned with maintaining good relations with their subordinates than stressing duties and performance.

4. Managing Problems

a. People here take problems as challenges and try to find better solutions than anybody else.
b. Experts are consulted, and they play an important role in solving problems.
c. People mostly consult their friends while dealing with problems.
d. Problems are solved keeping in mind the needs and benefit of the people in the organisation and the society at large.
e. People usually refer the problems to and look for solutions from their seniors.
f. Usually problems are solved by supervisors without involving their subordinates.

5. Managing Mistakes

a. The person making a mistake is not rejected he is shown much warmth by his friends.
b. Here the philosophy is that the supervisor can commit no mistake and the subordinate dare not make one.
c. Usually people are able to acknowledge and analyse their mistakes because they can expect to receive help and support from others.
d. A mistake by a subordinate is treated as an experience (by the boss) from which lessons are learnt to prevent failure and improve performance in the future.
e. Subordinates expect guidance from their supervisors

to correct or prevent making mistakes.
f. Help of experts is sought in analysing and preventing mistakes.

6. Managing Conflicts

a. Most interpersonal and interdepartmental conflicts arise out of striving for higher performance and these are analysed and resolved with the overriding consideration being high productivity.
b. Conflicts are usually avoided or smoothed over to retain the friendly atmosphere.
c. Arbitration or third-party intervention (usually by experienced persons or seniors) is sought and used.
d. In a conflict situation those who are stronger force their point of view.
e. In resolving conflicts an appeal is made to principles and organisational ideals and the larger good of the organisation.
f. Relevant experts are consulted and used in resolving conflicts.

7. Communication

a. Instructions are issued after due consideration by the authorities and are expected to be carried out.
b. Most communication is informal and friendly and arises from as well as contributes to warm relations at work.
c. People ask for information from those who are experts on the subject.
d. Relevant information is made available to all who need and can use such information for achieving high performance.
e. People communicate information, suggestions and even criticisms to others out of concern for them.
f. Communication if often selective-people usually give or hold back crucial information as a way of control.

8. Decision Making

a. While taking decisions, people make special attempts to maintain cordial relations with all concerned.
b. Decisions are made at the top and communicated downward, and people here generally prefer this.
c. People who have demonstrated high achievement have

a great say in the decisions made here.

d. Decisions here are generally made without involving subordinates or colleagues.

e. Decisions are made and influenced by specialists and knowledgeable persons.

f. Decisions are made by keeping in view the good of the employees and of society.

31A9 MAO (R)

Author : Udai Pareek.
Availability : Indian Institute of Management, Ahmedabad.
Language : English.
Uses : To measure motivational aspects of roles in organisations.
Level : Students, Institutions and Banks.
Main features : Twenty-five items questionnaire consisting of five motivational dimensions. It is rated on a five point scale.
Reliability & Validity : Available with author.
Reference : Sen, P.C. Personal and organisational correlates of role stress and coping strategies in some public sector banks. Unpublished Doctoral Dissertation, Gujarat University, Ahmedabad, 1982.

31A9 MAO (R)

1. Do something challenging and worthwhile.
2. Influence or make an impact on others.
3. Admonish (punish) those who do not conform.
4. Work with friendly people.
5. Do something useful for others.
6. Get immediate feedback on your performance.
7. Have autonomy and do work independently.
8. Direct and instruct people below you.
9. Develop close personal relations.
10. Develop your junior colleagues or subordinates.
11. Set standards of excellence.
12. Give ideas or suggestions to your superiors.
13. Control the people below you.
14. Share feelings and emotions with others.
15. Help others.
16. Show efficiency can be rewarded for it.
17. Make contributions to significant decisions.
18. Admonish (punish) those who do not perform.
19. Interact with colleagues.
20. Cooperate with others in a common task.
21. Stretch your abilities and skills.

22. Get recognition for the work done.
23. Get regular reports from other sections or subordinates.
24. Interact with others on non-task matters.
25. Work in teams.

31A10 MAO (S)

Author : Udai Pareek.
Availability : Indian Institute of Management, Ahmedabad.
Language : English.
Uses : To measure managerial style of respondents in organisations.
Level : Students, Institutions and Entrepreneurs.
Main features : 48 items questionnaire consisting of 8 different aspects of managerial work. Items are rated on a 6-point scale.
Reliability & Validity : Available with author.
Time : Twenty to thirty minutes.

31A10 MAO (S)

1. What is your main concern in the department?

a. to ensure that laid down rules and regulations are properly followed.
b. to encourage the employees to help each other develop greater skills, so that they can advance in the organisation.
c. to achieve the goals or targets set.
d. to control the staff and maintain good discipline.
e. to maintain good friendly climate amongst my employees.
f. to develop competence and expertise amongst the people working with me.

2. What is your characteristic way of working with people?

a. I interact mostly with people on the basis of their expertise.
b. I have informal social interaction with most of my people.
c. I interact with a few trusted and competent people.
d. I interact with others mainly in relation to the achievement of the targets or goals.
e. I meet people to give instructions and provide

guidance.

f. I interact with my people to help them develop and advance in the organisation.

3. How would you like to characterise your supervisory style?

a. Check people so that they do not make mistakes.
b. I give them instructions and suggestions.
c. I improve their personal skills and chances of advancement.
d. I reward (and/or appreciate) outstanding performance.
e. I use my own expertise to make an impact on my people.
f. I ensure development of good friendly relations and team spirit.

4. How do you usually deal with a problem in your department?

a. I pose it as a challenge to my people to find an innovative solution.
b. I discuss it with someone in my department who is an expert or is knowledgeable.
c. I discuss it with those who are close to me.
d. I work out a solution which will benefit my people or the organisation.
e. I discuss with or refer it to a senior person for solution.
f. I solve it on my own.

5. How do you usually deal with mistakes?

a. I do not reject the person making a mistake, and show warmth to him.
b. I follow the philosophy that the supervisor can commit no mistakes, and the subordinates dare not commit one.
c. I encourage people to own up and analyse their mistakes and receive help and support from others.
d. I treat the mistake of my people as an experience from which they can learn to prevent failure and improve performance in the future.
e. I correct the mistakes and guide my subordinates to prevent mistakes in the future.
f. I encourage people to seek help of experts or knowledgeable persons in understanding the mistake

and preventing it in the future.

6. How do you usually deal with conflicts?

a. I analyse the causes and resolve the conflict with the overriding consideration for productivity.
b. I tend of avoid or smooth over the conflicts to retain cordial atmosphere.
c. I seek the arbitration of the senior persons.
d. I decide myself and tell people what to do or not to do.
e. I appeal to people to keep the ideals and larger good of the organisation in mind.
f. I accept the experts' opinions.

7. What is your usual communication style?

a. I give instructions after considering all the aspects, and expect that these are carried out.
b. I have informal and open communication with my people.
c. I encourage people to directly seek information from knowledgeable colleagues in and outside the department.
d. I made available relevant information to all who need and use it for achieving high performance.
e. I have concern for my people, and communicate with them (including their criticism) out of such concern.
f. I give information only to the deserving people.

8. How do you take decisions?

a. While taking decision I take special care to maintain cordial relations with all concerned.
b. I do not take decision, but only communicate the decision, made at the higher levels, to my people.
c. I encourage higher performance to participate in the decisions being made.
d. I take the decisions myself, and inform my people.
e. I consult the specialists and knowledgeable people and give great weight to their opinions.
f. The good of the organisation and the people mainly guide me in taking decisions.

31A11 SUPERVISORY BELIEFS QUESTIONNAIRE

Author : T.V. Rao.

Availability : Indian Institute of Management, Ahmedabad.
Language : English.
Uses : To study beliefs underlying supervisory styles.
Level : Supervisors and executives.
Main features : Nine items distribution of weighted scores.
Time : Ten minutes.
Reference : Jain Uma; Life style of Indian managers : A study of district collectors. Unpublished Doctoral Dissertation in Management, Indian Institute of Management, Ahmedabad, 1981.

31A11 SUPERVISORY BELIEFS QUESTIONNAIRE

1. a. My workers are capable of working on their own, there is no need to supervise them. They only need to be helped once in a while.
   b. Workers are generally lazy and avoid work unless they are closely supervised.
   c. Workers need to be constantly guided and helped, what they need is an affectionate supervisor who can understand them and keep telling them what to do and what not to do.

2. a. A good supervisor is one who gives enough freedom to workers and has faith in them.
   b. A good supervisor is one who treats the workers like constantly admising them and telling them what to do and what not to do.
   c. A good supervisor is one who keeps a close eye on the workers and makes them feel that he is constantly watching them.

3. a. How well the workers work depends a great deal on how well his supervisor guides them constantly.
   b. How well a worker works depends a great deal on how strict his supervisor is with him.
   c. How well a worker works depends a great deal on how much his superior keeps confidence on him and gives him freedom.

31A12 MOTIVATIONAL ORIENTATIONS QUESTIONNAIRE

Author : T.V. Rao.
Availability : Indian Institute of Management, Ahmedabad.
Language : English.
Uses : To understand the motivational profile on achievement, power, affiliation, dependence, aggressiveness and extension.

225 Organisational Behaviour

Level : Adult employees.
Main features : It is a Likert's type scale.
Time : Twenty minutes.

31A12 MOTIVATIONAL ORIENTATIONS QUESTIONNAIRE

1. Setting difficult goals for myself.
2. Competing with others in my environment for better performance.
3. Doing something difficult to prove that I can do it.
4. Doing things that would help me stand out uniquely.
5. Taking up things with determination and working for accomplishing them.
6. Meeting a lot of people.
7. Joining a social club or group.
8. Inviting people home for tea-parties, and get-togethers.
9. Having a lot of friends.
10. Attending parties and social activities.
11. Getting what I deserve even if I have to fight for it.
12. Doing something that might provoke criticism.
13. Arguing with a superior or subordinate.
14. Teasing someone who is conceited.
15. Annoying people I don't like.
16. Helping someone in trouble even if I have to go out of my way.
17. Taking personal care of workers and their problems.
18. Fighting for national goals.
19. Sacrificing things for the sake of others.
20. Counselling someone who is disturbed.
21. Doing tasks my superiors ask me to do.
22. Pleasing my superiors.
23. Observing the rules and regulations outlined for me very strictly.
24. Checking things with superiors before I make decisions.
25. Consulting people for most of the decisions.
26. Having workers who do whatever I ask them to do.
27. Getting people to accept my point to view.
28. Framing rules and regulations.
29. Demonstrating my knowledge and sharing it with others.
30. Controlling the workers through various techniques.

31A13 WHAT WOULD YOU SAY

Author : T.V. Rao.

Availability : Indian Institute of Management, Ahmedabad.
Language : English.
Uses : To study the sales styles of salesmen using TA models.
Level : Salesmen.
Main features : It is open ended questionnaire.

31A13 WHAT WOULD YOU SAY

1. "Pfizer is better than your company, and I prefer its products".
2. "I just bought this item the other day, I do not need any more".
3. "You sales people promise all kinds of things at the time of selling but never do anything afterwards".
4. "I have a very bad opinion of your company".
5. "New products are not reliable as no one knows how well it has done".
6. "I do not believe in this therapy".
7. "I do not understand how Kanamycine works, I am interested in knowing how it works."
8. "I have bad experiences with your company; they do not provide timely supplies".
9. "Would you like to have tea?"
10. "This is too costly, my patients cannot afford this".
11. "I do not have time talk to you".
12. "I would not like to buy your item at the price you are quoting. I wish it was a little less".
13. "I will decide later".
14. "I like to be convinced more about your product".
15. "I like to know the experiences of other doctors".
16. "Give me a ring some time later".
17. "This is an outdated therapy".
18. "This is a risky, toxic item, how can I use it?"
19. "Whatever amount of samples you keep, that much business you will get".
20. "It seems this time there is no specific programme by your company? These are all common products you kept here".
21. "Why are you leaving only two pieces? Leave more, it will move in the market".
22. "Surprisingly, you are promoting Erythrocin and .... no samples?"
23. "For so many months I have not seen any literature or samples. I thought your company is not interested in this product".
24. "Have you stopped marketing this?"

25. "Where is your supervisor? I am getting this product for lesser price. If you want me to accommodate, see that I do not get into a loss.
26. "How much can you reduce the price?"
27. "I have enough stock! Come next time"

31A14 ORGANISATIONAL EFFECTIVENESS SCALE

Author : C.N. Daftuar.
Availability : Author, Department of Psychology, M.S. University, Baroda.
Language : English.
Uses : To measure nine dimensions/soft criteria of organisational effectiveness.
Level : Supervisors and above in organisation.
Main features : A 46 items Likert's type scale, measures 9 dimensions—Organisational attachment, Job involvement, Self control, Legitimatization, Organisational commitment, Innovation, Consensus and Satisfaction of organisational effectiveness.
Reliability : Alpha coefficient of reliability for 9 dimensions ranges between .51 to .99.
Validity : Validated on the basis of data from effective and non-effective organisation.
Time : Twenty minutes.
Norms : Not available.

31A14 ORGANISATIONAL EFFECTIVENESS SCALE

(The following statements have to be checked on a 5 point scale).

1. Is the standard of the time schedule in your organisation fair?
2. Are your superiors ahead of time in planning organisation and scheduling work?
3. Are the objectives of your factory realistic and worthwhile?
4. If ever a discussion is sought by your superiors regarding an issue, do you think that they are genuine?
5. Do you believe that the communication you receive from above are well intentioned and well thought off?
6. Are the actions of your superiors guided by legal provisions?
7. Are you likely to be put in hot water for the discharge of your responsibilities and duties?

8. How much do you usually want your immediate superior to tell you what to do.
9. When you have a problem related to your work, how much do you like to solve it yourself, without any body's help?
10. Regarding your job, how often do you like to act according to your own judgement?
11. Will the people here do their duties irrespective of the fact that the management do not bother to reward for their sincerity on job?
12. Will the people here do their duties irrespective of the fact that the management will not care to punish them for their lapses in job?

How you agree with the following statements?

13. I will stay overtime to finish a job, even if I am not paid for it.
14. I usually show up for work a little early, to get things ready.
15. Sometimes, I lie awake at night thinking ahead of the next day's work.
16. I used to be more ambitious about my work than I am now.
17. If a problem comes up in your mind and it is not all settled by the time you go home, is it likely that you will find yourself thinking about it after work?
18. How often do you try on your own to find a better or faster way of doing something on your job?
19. How often do you try to express your ideas on the job, either or after checking with your boss?
20. I am willing to put a great deal of effort beyond that normally expected in order to help this organisation be successful.
21. I would accept almost any type of job assignment in order to keep working here.
22. I find that my values & the organisation's 'values' are very similar.
23. I really care about the fate of this organisation.
24. I feel that this organisation is a large family.
25. I feel a sense of pride in working in this organisation.
26. I feel that the organisation's problems are my own.
27. I feel that the achievement of organisation's goal is the fulfilment of my own personal goals.

Ask yourself : How satisfied I am with this aspect of my job? On my present job, this is - how I feel about :

28. The chance to do different things from time to time.
29. The chance to the "somebody" in the community.
30. The competence of my supervisor in taking decision.
31. The way my job provides for steady employment.
32. The chance to do something that makes use of my abilities.
33. My pay.
34. The chances for advancement on this job.
35. The working conditions.
36. The way my co-workers get along with each other.
37. The feeling of accomplishment I get from the job.
38. General management of the company.
39. My past-advancement in this organisation.
40. Chances for future growth (in efficiency).
41. Social conditions within the organisation.
42. Recognition for my work.
43. Responsibilities given to me.
44. Company's policies.
45. All things considered, my work as a whole.
46. All things considered, my company/organisation as a whole.

31A15 MANAGERIAL BEHAVIOUR QUESTIONNAIRE (MBQ)

Author : C.N. Daftuar.
Availability : Author, Department of Psychology, M.S. University, Baroda.
Language : English.
Uses : To measure six managerial or leadership style in organisations.
Level : Supervisors & executives.
Main features : Likerts scaling, 24 items. 4 items for each dimensions.
Reliability : Cronback's Alpha for each subscales has been worked out and it ranges from .89 to .97.
Validity : Validated on data from different organisations.
Times : Fifteen minutes.
Norms : Not available.

31A15 MANAGERIAL BEHAVIOUR QUESTIONNAIRE (MBQ)

(The following statements have to be checked as true or false on a five point scale).

1. I take special care that work gets top priority.
2. I believe that most of the interpersonal troubles start because people try to be over friendly and in-

formal on the job.

3. It is human warmth and feeling for each other that makes an organisation prosper.
4. I believe that subordinates keep a sense of responsibility under the guidance and care of a good superior.
5. I feel that power and prestige are necessary so that subordinates will listen to me.
6. If my subordinates need help, I help as much as I can.
7. I appreciate the subordinates who are efficient and hardworking.
8. I believe that even indisciplined workers can be improved by friendly support and persuasion.
9. I believe that human nature is such that the more you share ideas, the more worth-living life becomes.
10. Whenever, I face a problem on the job, I try to look calm and cheerful.
11. I always keep track of the work progress.
12. I help my subordinates in their career planning.
13. I believe that persons at the top are in the best position to make major decisions.
14. I maintain fair but impersonal relationship in the group.
15. I like to be friend-type, caring and receptive.
16. I see that subordinates work to their capacity.
17. I appreciate the subordinates who are loyal and grateful.
18. I always seek my subordinates opinion and abide by them.
19. I appreciate the subordinates who are quite free in dealing with me.
20. I help my subordinates to grow up and assume greater responsibility.
21. I always follow standard rules and regulations in organisational matters.
22. I provide all information to my subordinates and let them jointly find out the solution of a problem.
23. I believe that human nature is such that there will always be conflict and friction in any organisation.
24. Whenever I face a problem on the job, I gather the relevant persons and try to work out through them an agreed solution.

31A16 JOB SATISFACTION SCALE

Author : C.N. Daftuar.
Availability : Department of Psychology, M.S. University,

Baroda.
Language : English.
Uses : To measure job satisfaction or employees.
Level : Any level of employees.
Main features : The scale has 19 items including 2 which measure separately overall satisfaction with the company and overall satisfaction with the work.
Reliability : Cronbach's alpha reliability = .95.
Validity : Each items correlation with the total score are high ranging between .67 to .89.

31A16 JOB SATISFACTION SCALE (JSS)

(The following items have to be checked on a 5-point scale of satisfaction).

1. The chance to do different things from time to time.
2. The chance to be "some body" in the community.
3. The competence of my supervisor in making decision.
4. The way my job provides for steady employment.
5. The chance to do something that makes use of my abilities.
6. My pay.
7. The chances for advancement on this job.
8. The working conditions.
9. The way my co-workers get along with each other.
10. The feeling of accomplishment I get from the job.
11. General management of the company.
12. My past-advancement in this organisation.
13. Chances for future growth (in efficiency).
14. Social conditions within the organisation.
15. Recognition for my work.
16. Responsibilities given to me.
17. Company's policies.
18. All things considered, my work as a whole.
19. All things considered, my company/organisation as a whole.

31A17 DYSFUNCTIONAL CONSEQUENCES OF CONTROL SYSTEM SCALE

Author : C.N. Daftuar.
Availability : Department of Psychology, M.S. University, Baroda.
Language : English.
Uses : To measure dysfunctional consequences of control system in organisation.
Level : Any level of employees in an organisation.
Main features : The scale has five items and measures three

dimensions of dysfunctional consequences of control system - rigid bureaucracy, reward-punishment interaction, and sources of generation of invalid data within the organisation.

Reliability : Cronbach's alpha reliability = .97.

Validity : Not known.

31A17 DYSFUNCTIONAL CONSEQUENCES OF CONTROL SYSTEM

(The respondents have to give their opinion about the following questions).

1. In a situation when the rules and regulations of the company is strictly followed, the objective of your organisation cannot be attained. What do you think, you or your colleagues will do in such a situation?

(i) _______ will meet the target even at the cost of rules, (ii) _______ will try to achieve the target, (iii) _______ will try to meet the target and follow the rules as well, (iv) _______ will follow the rules, in the first place, and then care for the target, (v) _______ will strictly follow the rules, irrespective of target.

2. In the same type of situation, will the management punish any employee who tries to flout the rules even if such an act is done to achieve the target?

(i) _______ they will never punish, (ii) _______ will not punish, (iii) _______ may not like it, (iv) _______ likely to punish, (v) _______ will definitely punish.

3. How the management will react if an employee strictly follows rules to the extent that it ultimately hampers in achieving the target?

(i) _______ immediately fire him, (ii) _______ they will not approve and will warn him, (iii) _______ they will not appreciate, (iv) _______ they will like it, (v) _______ they will very much appreciate.

4. Are the rewards in this organisation (physical like pay rise, etc. or psychological like appreciation, recognition, etc), are as per your expectations?

(i) _______ No, never, (ii) _______ rarely, (iii) _______

not sure, (iv) _______ yes, often, (v) _______ always.

5. Management scientists have shown that often department supply wrong information (for example, production data) to higher management. They have also listed some more common reasons (given below) for that. Is this true in case of your department also?

Yes/No

a. Wrong information in case of budgetary estimate.
b. Because of low trust in higher ups.
c. Regarding application of rules for regard of punishment.
d. Unknowingly wrong information are given.
e. To fail management's technique of collecting information.
f. When data which are asked for are not available
g. Any other (kindly name it).

31A18 DELEGATION OF AUTHORITY SCALE

Author : C.N. Daftuar.
Availability : Department of Psychology, M.S. University, aroda.
anguage : English.
Uses : To measure employees attitude towards delegation of authority in organisations
Level : Workers and supervisors.
Main features : The scale has four items rated on a 5-point scale.
Reliability : Cronbach's alpha coefficient of reliability = .95.
Validity : Not available.

31A18 DELEGATION OF AUTHORITY

(The following items have to be checked on a 5-point scale).

1. Does your supervisor allow you to decide about your work related problems?
2. Do you think that centralisation of authority at top always helps in uniformity of policy and minimises discrepancies?
3. Do you think that you have got sufficient authority also to discharge your job related responsibilities?
4. Do you allow your subordinates to make their own

decision regarding their job matters?

31A19 POWER STRATEGY SCALE

Authors : C.N. Daftuar & Shubhada Pange.
Availability : Department of Psychology, M.S. University, Baroda.
Language : English.
Uses : To measure power strategy of employees in organisations.
Main features : The scale consists of 41 items and measures 13 strategies which people employ to reach a power position in most organisations. The scale is scored on a 5-point scale.
Reliability & Validity : The alpha coefficient for the scale = .65.

31A19 POWER STRATEGY SCALE

(The following items have to be checked on a 5-point scale relevancy).

1. Make a subordinate feel great by asking them for a personal favour.
2. By being too helpful towards a person attracts attention.
3. When one disagrees with a decision, it is better to get it hanged.
4. Some people refuse to compromise with their colleagues in order to show their worth.
5. Trying to command others is a way of showing personal importance.
6. It is better to depend on your superior for decision making.
7. Acting friendly has a great effect on another person.
8. Talking politely is one way of making the other person favourable.
9. Inflating the importance of a request shows a sort of interest on other person.
10. Expressing values, opinion and attitudes similar to those of his boss.
11. The assignment of uninterested tasks are often used to punish.
12. By threatening an employee's job security.
13. Pointing to the lapses in other's work.
14. Giving extra time for relaxation in place of get-

ting some urgent work.

15. By being obliging to get a particular work done.
16. Having direct contact with the top bosses rather than going through the usual channels.
17. Influencing bosses through their friends and relations.
18. Implementing new ideas and carrying out the superior's job.
19. In the boss's absence, an effort to finish his work.
20. Pushed by someone in one's cares is very helpful.
21. Getting help by some important person to reach greater heights.
22. Being pulled up is much more effective than exerting your own upward force.
23. It is proper to have a sponsor to recommend you as far as jobs are concerned.
24. Influencing superiors by being obliging to them for certain work helps to gain importance.
25. Aggressive actions towards an individual is hint for outcasting that particular individual.
26. Spreading false informations is one way of gaining importance and popularity.
27. Using this strategy for compensating his own misdeeds.
28. Social get together and informal meetings with seniors helps to brake the ice for further considerations.
29. An attractive feature is to have close contacts with powerful people.
30. It is the general feeling that if prown to the higher authorities there are chances of rising fast.
31. Influence makes a person grow fast.
32. Stirring up rivalry between two departments is a means of achieving power.
33. Uniting forces and forming coalition to work against someone is a path to power.
34. A subordinate tries to reach his boss's level by creating confusion in the department.
35. Creating misunderstanding and confusion in an organisation helps being important.
36. Informing the senior about the latest information helps one to feel important.
37. Keeping all the details to oneself and informing at the correct time makes one feel great.
38. Manipulating information can exert influence on others.

39. In Indian culture the tendency is to misinform one's own colleague in order to gain popularity.
40. Being in the notice of one's superiors is useful in the long run.
41. Threatening or blackmailing is booking for popularity.

31A20 ORGANISATIONAL BEHAVIOUR QUESTIONNAIRE

Author : R.P. Singh and Janak Pandey.
Availability : Department of Postgraduate studies in Psychology, Feroze Gandhi College, Rae-Bareli, UP.
Languages : English and Hindi.
Uses : Assessment of as to how much influence the organisation has over its members.
Level : Macro and Meso levels of large size organisations.
Main features : Likert type five point scale, 166 items under four subscales, i.e., organisational power, climate, control and personal consequences.
Reliability : Cronbach alpha reported.
Validity : Construct validity : Twenty two predictors significantly explain the variance of each of the ten criterion variables.
Time : About one hour.
Norms : No norms.
Reference : D. Phil. thesis in Psychology. Allahabad University, Allahabad.

31A20 ORGANISATIONAL BEHAVIOUR QUESTIONNAIRE

SCALE 1 : ORGANISATIONAL POWER

(The following statements have to be checked as always true, frequently true, true, seldom true, or never true).

1. Persons identified as members of one's own group are perceived as powerful.
2. Popularity of a worker/executive makes one power-
3. te, religion, region identities enhance the power.
4. Those who make people feel good are in demand.
5. Keeping information, though not part of duty; is a source of power.
6. Those who manage rare information carry weight.
7. Those who say the truth against all odds influence

people.

8. Those who convince others only on the basis of logic and arguments are powerful.
9. Those who mediate the rewards are looked upon as powerful
10. Those who manage good posting for others are treated with respect.
11. Those who give positive feedback weild power over others.
12. Those who are perceived helpful in career-development are powerful.
13. Fear of stoppage of material benefits influences the people.
14. The authorities who can deny promotion are influential.
15. Perception of social boycott keeps people under influence.
16. Perception of termination of job is a deterrent.
17. Those who know all the intricacies and technicalities of their jobs are influential.
18. Those who know their job and also the job of higher and lower positions are influential.
19. Those who help others without any ulterior motive command respect.
20. Those who make sacrifices influence other.
21. People follow those who have similar political ideology.
22. Hard working people become an example for others to follow.
23. Those perceived to pass on information with no ulterior motive command respect.
24. Those who give timely information weild influence.
25. Those who informally circulate the information weild power.
26. Those who grant the material rewards like pay-hike, promotion etc. are looked as powerful.
2 Those who manage only good words are not considered powerful.
28. Those who allow others to have their way are loved and liked.
29. Those who provide opportunities of developing new skills attract people.
30. Perception of disciplinary proceedings creates awe in people.
31. Erring, non-compliant lazy ones are afraid of public denouncement.
32. Fear of the curtailment of power keeps people under organisational influence.

33. Being put on an undesired assignment influences people.
34. People with the knowledge of law, rules and procedures of company are perceived powerful.
35. People with keen insight into human affairs weild power over others.
36. Even those who are difficult to be replaced do not get recognition.
37. No one bothers about the authorities if one has no axe to grind (R).
38. Persons with legitimate power can reject the consensus.
39. Many have too much responsibility but no legal authority (R).
40. Clear-cut distribution of rights and duties has made the legitimate power effective.
41. Importance is given to refresher courses to keep pace with recent developments.
42. Those who come out with innovations are given special treatment.
43. Those whose legal right extend over many levels and department weild wide influence.
44. The final say is always with the top position.
45. Those who depend on informal power prove very effective (R).
46. Those with positions of authority carry weight.
47. In case of disagreement the company prefers the expert over authority, staff number, age, caste, membership of union/association, total experience of the present job, grade/category and scale of pay, department, post, number of dependents, education, mother tongue, and total monthly pay.

SCALE 2 : ORGANISATIONAL CLIMATE

(The following statements have to be checked as always true, frequently true, true, seldom true, or never true).

1. Both labour and management fully accept the importance of the institution of collective bargaining.
2. Any decision we make has to have our boss's approval.
3. The parties recognize that they have certain goals in common.
4. There can be little action taken here until a superior approves the decision.

5. The contract is understood and effectively administered in good faith by both parties.
6. We participate in the decision on the promotions of any of the professional.
7. A person who wants to make his decision will be quickly discouraged.
8. Employees feel a sense of participation in their general welfare as a result of collective bargaining.
9. Negotiations are carried out with intelligence, preparations and a sincere desire to achieve results.
10. We participate in the decision to hire new staff.
11. We participate in interpersonal conflicts resolution.
12. We feel we are our own boss in most matters.
13. Although each party identifies most strongly with its own interests, the parties know and respect each other's goals.
14. The union is strong enough to create a balance of power between labour and management.
15. We have to ask our boss before we do almost anything.
16. Even small matters have to be referred to someone higher up for a final answer.
17. Communication between the parties, other than the negotiations, is highly developed.
18. We participate in evaluating the performance.
19. Both parties continually evaluate the effectiveness of their relationship with the other party.
20. We participate in decisions on the adoption of new policies.
21. The grievance procedure is comprehensively structured with a binding final step.
22. We participate in the decisions of the adoption of new programme.
23. Management (Organisation) has a strong, well organised labour relations programme.
24. We participate in the decisions on budget preparation.
25. Most jobs have something new happening every day.
26. We are to follow strict operating procedures at all times.
27. Whatever situations arise we have procedures to follow in dealing with them.
28. People here are allowed to do almost as they please.
29. There is something different everyday to do.

30. Whenever we have a problem we are supposed to go to some person for opinion.
31. Everyone has a specific job to do.
32. Most people here make their own rules on the job.
33. One thing people like around here is the variety of work.
34. This organisation keeps written records of everyone's job performance.
35. People here feel they are constantly being checked to see that they obey all rules.
36. How things are done here is left to persons doing the work.
37. A person can make one's own decisions without checking with anybody else.
38. The employees here are constantly being checked for rule violation.
39. Going through proper channel is constantly stressed.
40. People here do the same job in the same way everyday.
41. People here would not do anything else except the task assigned by the organisation.
42. Supervisors emphasize meeting targets.
43. Superiors take offence if subordinates do not pay them respects.
44. Job specification is not liked as it fixes individual responsibility.
45. Workers/officers would remain in their seat/chamber/office but engage themselves in gossips.
46. Superiors and subordinates have clear understanding of each other.
47. Superiors and subordinates have differing interests.
48. People work vigorously when put together on some organisational task. (R)
49. Superiors drive subordinates to work hard.
50. Superiors/supervisors give specific directions to their subordinates.
51. Superiors demand personal loyalty and blind obedience.
52. People would remain in their seat/office but would do the job only for name sake.
53. Superiors enforce rules and regulations uniformly over subordinates.
54. Vanity and whims of a superior get priority over everything.
55. Superiors show their superiority by letting their

subordinates down.

SCALE 3 : ORGANISATIONAL CONTROL

(The following statements have to be checked as most of the time, frequently, sometime, seldom, or rarely).

1. Efficient workers/executives are given special increments.
2. Annual Increments are stopped of those who do not work well.
3. The hot headed snub, sniff and sneer and control others effectively.
4. Superficial concern is shown to assuage the feelings of the complainant.
5. People describe themselves to their targets as most weak and powerless.
6. Any means are adopted to get the work done.
7. Rowdyism brings people to their knees.
8. Undue financial or other favours are given to buy loyalty from individuals or groups.
9. Card punching arrangement ensures attendance.
10. Positions with possibility of bribe are given to loyal ones.
11. Fear of insecurity of job keeps people under control.
12. Efficient and compliant workers/executives are put on committees.
13 Fringe benefits are withdrawn if someone is found misusing it.
14. Quality and quantity checks are carried on regularly.
15. Efficient workers/executives are sent on higher course/skill training.
16. None gets promotion if his/her tackling of subordinates is ineffective.
17. A constant watch; through men and machine is kept to ensure that everybody is working.
18. Good behaviour is rewarded by giving them desired posting.
19. Communication channels are kept alive to anticipate exigencies.
20. Accountancy rule violation results in snatching of financial power.
21. Annual confidential report keeps the subordinates under control.
22. At times friends mediate and sort out the dif-

ferences.

23. To get things done from a person his ideas and opinions are praised.
24. Erring ones are sent to higher authority for being taken to task.
25. Consensus is sought and the course of action follows thereafter.
26. People change themselves quickly with the changes in the person whom they intend to influence.
27. Good ones are sent to higher authority to receive bouquet.
28. Where there is no law, the writ of the authority runs large.
29. Deviants are controlled through group pressure.
30. At the most, things go to the tribunal level and everybody takes it as final.
31. Those indulging in theft, physical violence are handed over to police.
32. To keep everybody at par, people support one another.
33. To win over someone people pose themselves fully dependent upon him/her.
34. Anyone found guilty is never promoted.
35. Use of unparliamentary language shows positive results.
36. Those who manage gangs are obeyed well.
37. Disliked ones are tucked up to obscure positions in the name of reorganisation.
38. People communicate explicitly their achievement with their targets.
39. °Tit for tat' tactic works well.
40. Individuals/groups are played against each other.

SCALE 4 : PERSONAL CONSEQUENCES

(The following items have to be checked as most of the time, frequently, sometime, seldom, or rarely).

1. I am willing to put in a great deal of effort beyond that normally expected in order to help this organisation to be successful.
2. I would accept almost any type of job assignment in order to keep working for this organisation.
3. This organisation really inspires the very best in me in the way of job performance.
4. I talk of this organisation to my friends as great organisation to work for.

5. I am proud to tell others that I am part of this organisation.
6. I feel very little loyalty to this organisation.
7. I could just as well be working for a different organisation as long as the type of work is similar.
8. I find that my values and the organisation's values are very similar.
9. It would take very little change in my present circumstances to cause me to leave this organisation.
10. There is always a feeling of worthwhile accomplishment here.
11. I am very secure in my position as this job assures a regular steady income sufficient for my family.
12. Often, I find it difficult to agree with the policies of this organisation on important matters related to its employees.
13. I feel free to do my job and also participate in the setting of goals in this company.
14. Deciding to work for this organisation was a definite mistake on my part.
15. There is not too much to be gained by sticking with the organisation indefinitely.
16. I receive affection, esteem from the colleagues, subordinates and superiors regularly.
17. For me this is the best of all possible organisations for which to work.
18. I am extremely glad that I chose this organisation to work for over others I was considering at the time I joined.
19. I find sufficient opportunity for intermingling with employees and officers of my section or department of company and work together.
20. I really care about the fate of this organisation.
21. There is sufficient scope to take over the next position as the gap is minimum and easily accessible.
22. In the course of work I have all the rights to direct and regulate the activities of the people.
23. In my work I always have a feeling that I have done this.

31A21 WORK SATISFACTION QUESTIONNAIRE (FOR WORKERS).

Authors : Prayag Mehta and Mahaveer Jain.
Availability : National Labour Institute, AB-6, Safdarjang Enclave, New Delhi.

Language : English and Hindi.
Uses : To measure the level of satisfaction with work.
Level : Industrial workers.
Main features : It contains 26 questions covering following dimensions : influence and autonomy, trust, and support; supervisory behaviour, intrinsic job satisfaction and relation with peers.
Reliability : Item analysis was carried, KR-20 reliability coefficient is 0.85 and split-half reliability is 0.67 (N = 90).
Validity : Factorial validity and face validity established.
Time : No time limit (about 15 minutes).
Norms : Scores of skilled and unskilled workers are available.
References :

(1) Prayag Mehta; From Economism to democratic commitment : The role of worker participation. Vikalpa : The Journal of Decision Makers, 1976, 1(4), 39-46.
(2) Prayag Mehta; Employee motivation and work satisfaction in a public enterprise. Vikalpa : A Journal of Decision Makers, 1977, 2(3), 231-236.
(3) Prayag Mehta; Work satisfaction and democratic outlook : The role of worker participation. National Labour Institute Bulletin, 1976, 2, 231-236.
(4) Prayag Mehta; Worker participation for increased satisfaction and production. Productivity, 1977, 17(4), 571-578.
(5) Prayag Mehta; Education for promoting worker participation : The case of a public sector organisation. ASCT Journal of Management, 1977, 7(1), 12-22.
(6) Prayag Mehta; Workers' rising aspirations and work organisation. Yojana, 1978, 2181.
(7) Prayag Mehta; Objective and subjective factors is employees' satisfaction in life and work. Indian Journal of Industrial Relations, 1978, 2, 3(4), 433-444.
(8) Prayag Mehta; A note on some suggested research in management of work organisations. Indian Journal of Industrial Relations, 1980, 16(2), 277-285.
(9) Prayag Mehta; Rising aspirations, quality, of life and work satisfaction. Productivity, 1982 (forthcoming).
(10) Prayag Mehta; Making participation work Workers Education, 1981, January.
(11) Prayag Mehta; Motivational approach to organisational development National Labour Institute Bulletin, 1980, 134-139.
(12) Prayag Mehta; Participative Decision Making and

Democratisation of Management : Impediments and problems. New Delhi : National Labour Institute, Occasional, Paper No. 1, 1979.

(13) Prayag Mehta; Worker participation and democraticve consciousness, New Delhi : National Labour Institute, 1978 (Mimeo)

(14) Prayag Mehta; Work Motivation in Indian Public Sector : Some conceptualisations. National Labour Institute Bulletin, 1978, 4(3), 90-99.

(15) Prayag Mehta & Jain, Mahaveer; Measuring employees satisfaction and personality. New Delhi : National Labour Institute, 1982 (forthcoming).

31A21 WORK SATISFACTION QUESTIONNAIRE

1. At the place of work we may have opportunity to learn something new, for example, skills of our co-workers. In some Companies, the organisation helps workers to learn new jobs and skills. What is the position in your Company?

(a) We have good opportunities for learning new jobs and skills.
(b) Sometimes there is some opportunity.
(c) We do not have any such opportunity here.

2. People working together develop friendship with each other. In some places, however, such a thing may not be possible. What is the situation in your organisation? Are people generally friendly?

(a) People here are very friendly.
(b) People here are sometimes friendly.
(c) People are generally not friendly here.

3. Employees like to have good welfare facilities from the company, for example, education of their children, medical facilities for their families, etc. On the whole how are the welfare facilities provided in vour organisation?

(a) Our welfare facilities are quite good.
(b) There are only few such facilities available here.
(c) Such facilities are quite poor here.

4. Looking to the nature of work and the organisation, what do you think about your wages?

(a) We are receiving good wages.
(b) The wages are not so good.
(c) The wages are poor and inadequate.

5. In all organisations there are people who supervise the work. How are the people who supervise your work? Are you happy with them?

(a) People here are generally happy with their supervisors.
(b) People here are not very happy with their supervisors.
(c) People here are not at all happy with their supervisors.

6. In industry fresh drinking water is provided at the work place by the Company. How are the facilities for drinking water provided by your Company?

(a) Facilities for drinking water are satisfactory.
(b) Facilities for drinking water are not so good.
(c) The facilities for drinking water are poor.

7. It is natural to have curiosity about whatever is happening in the organisation. You may also be sometimes curious to know about the events in your Company. How far you are able to get such information?

(a) We get all the information about the events in the Company.
(b) We get enough information.
(c) We do not have adequate information about the affairs of the Company.

8. If any of your colleagues express opinions and give suggestions to senior officers, do they really care for it?

(a) Yes, they do care for our suggestions.
(b) Only sometimes they look into them.
(c) They never care for them.

9. How far do you have a feeling that the job you are doing is useful for the society?

(a) I think my job is very useful to the society.
(b) My job is useful to the society only to some extent.
(c) It is not useful to the society at all.

10. We do want appreciation for good work. Do you receive appreciation for good work in your Company?

(a) Good work is always appreciated here.
(b) Good work is appreciated only sometimes.
(c) No one cares to appreciate good work.

11. Very few people like to do the same thing again and again. How is the situation in your Company? Do people like to get variety in their work?

(a) Here people have to do the same kind of routine over and over again.
(b) Sometimes we get some novelty in our work here.
(c) Here, we frequently get new and interesting things to do.

12. In work organisations canteen facilities are provided to the employees. How is your canteen?

(a) Our canteen is quite good.
(b) Our canteen is not good.
(c) There is no or hardly any canteen.

13. People wish to have a job in which there is maximum scope for using one's skills and abilities. How do you feel about your job?

(a) My job is not matched with my skills and abilities.
(b) My job is matched with my skills and abilities.
(c) My job is very much upto my skills and abilities.

14. In work organisations differences of opinion and conflicts are inevitable. There are ways to deal with such disputes. How far you are satisfied the way such disputes and grievances are dealt with in your Company?

(a) There is no proper way to settle disputes and grievances.
(b) Sometimes some attempts are made to settle.
(c) There is good arrangement for settlement of disputes and redressal of our grievances.

15. Companies provide medical facilities to employees. How are these facilities provided by your Company?

(a) Medical facilities are good here.

(b) There is hardly any medical facility available.
(c) There are some such facilities available here.

16. Normally, people who work together develop trust in each other; but it does not happen all the time. In your experience how much trust people in your organisation have of each other?

(a) People here trust each other very much.
(b) People here have very little trust in each other.
(c) They do not have much trust in each other.

17. Work organisations provide facilities for recreation. How are the facilities for recreation provided by your Company?

(a) There are good facilities for recreation available here to the employees, after work.
(b) There are hardly any facilities available for recreation.
(c) There are some facilities for recreation available here.

18. When decisions concerning the workers are taken by the management, in what measure are you able to influence these decisions?

(a) We have considerable influence over the decisions.
(b) We can influence the decisions only sometimes.
(c) We have almost no influence on the decisions.

19. There is a general tendency to be on one's own while doing his job. How much freedom do you have in doing your job without interference from your supervisors?

(a) We have full freedom to do our own work.
(b) Sometimes we have freedom to do our own work.
(c) We have always to carry out the wishes of our supervisor and do work according to his instructions.

20. It is expected of each employee to put in his best. But in your Company, do your supervisors expect you to do your best?

(a) They always expect good work from us.
(b) Good or bad whatever we do is alright here.
(c) Good work is not particularly expected from us here.

21. Sometimes you might feel that injustice is being done to you by the management. Is there any forum where such grievances can be redressed?

(a) There is proper arrangement for redressal of such grievances.
(b) Only sometimes attention is paid to such grievances.
(c) No attention whatsoever is paid to such grievances.

22. When decisions about work and workers are taken, the employees are involved in such decision making. Is it done in your Company?

(a) Before taking any decision everyone is asked for his opinion.
(b) Only sometimes opinions are asked for.
(c) Nobody is ever asked to give his opinion.

23. In your job there must be certain things which you could do by using your own judgment. In some Companies, the management encourages the workers to use their own judgment about their job. How is the situation in your Company?

(a) Here we are encouraged to take up our own decisions in day-today work.
(b) Such encouragement is sometimes available here.
(c) For each and every thing one has to look to the orders of the management.

24. When your union takes any decision, does it ask for your opinion? How much influence do the members have in the decisions of the union?

(a) Our opinions are asked for and we can influence the decisions of the union.
(b) Union only sometimes asks for your opinions.
(c) The union never asks for our opinion and we have no influence on the decisions of the union.

25. How are the interpersonal relations among the workers here? Do people quarrel with each other?

(a) People cooperate with each other and there are no quarrels.
(b) People do not have very good relations with each other.
(c) People have very bad relations with each other.

26. It is sometimes felt that the supervisors do not plan things properly and alterations have to be made frequently. How is your experience in your Company?

(a) Jobs are properly planned here.
(b) Jobs are only sometimes planned properly.
(c) Jobs are not at all planned and frequent alterations are necessary.

31A22 WORK SATISFACTION QUESTIONNAIRE (FOR MANAGERS)

Authors : Prayag Mehta and Mahaveer Jain.
Availability : National Labour Institute, AB-6, Safdarjang Enclave, New Delhi.
Language : English.
Uses : To measure the level of satisfaction with work.
Level : Industrial managers.
Main features : It contains 23 questions covering the following dimensions : influence and autonomous; working conditions; trust and support; intrinsic job satisfaction; supervisory satisfaction and relations with peers.
Reliability : Item analysis, KR-20 reliability coefficient is 0.71 and split-half reliability coefficient is 0.29 (N = 77).
Validity : Factorial validity established.
Time : No time limit.
Norms : Scores of coal managers are available.
References :

(1) Prayag Mehta; From economism to democratic commitment : The role of workers participations. Vikalpa : A Journal of Decision Makers, 1976, 1(4) 39-46.
(2) Prayag Mehta; Employee motivation and work satisfaction in a public enterprise. Vikalpa : A Journal of Decision Makers, 1977, 2(3), 231-236.
(3) Prayag Mehta and Mahaveer Jain; Measuring work satisfaction and personality, New Delhi : National Labour Institute (forthcoming).
(4) Prayag Mehta; Work satisfaction and democratic outlook : The role of worker participation. National Labour Institute Bulletin, 1976, 2, 231-236.

31A22 WORK SATISFACTION QUESTIONNAIRE

1. At the place of work we may have opportunity to

learn something new, for example, skills of management. In some companies, the organisation helps people to learn new jobs and skills. What is the position in your Company?

(a) We have good opportunities for learning new jobs and skills.
(b) Sometimes there is some opportunity.
(c) We do not have any such opportunity here.

2. People working together develop friendship with each other. In some places, however, such a thing may not be possible. What is the situation in your organisation? Are people generally friendly?

(a) People here are very friendly.
(b) People here are sometimes friendly.
(c) People are generally indifferent here.

3. Employees like to have good fringe benefits from the company, for example, education of their children, medical facilities for their families, etc. On the whole how are such benefits in your organisation?

(a) Our fringe benefits are quite good.
(b) There are only few such benefits available here.
(c) Such facilities are quite poor here.

4. Looking to the nature of work and the organisation. What do you think about your salary?

(a) Salary scales are good.
(b) They are not so good.
(c) Scales are poor and inadequate

5. In all organisations there are people who supervise subordinates' work. How are the people who supervise your work? Are people happy with them?

(a) People here are generally happy with their supervisors.
(b) People here are not very happy with their supervisors.
(c) People here are not at all happy with their supervisors.

6. In industry fresh drinking water is provided at the work place by the company. How are the facilities

for drinking water in your company?

(a) Facilities for drinking water are satisfactory.
(b) Facilities for drinking water are not so good.
(c) The facilities for drinking water are poor.

7. It is natural to have curiosity about whatever is happening in the organisation. You may sometimes be curious to know about the events in your company. How far you are able to get such information?

(a) We get all the information about the events in the company.
(b) We get enough information.
(c) We do not get adequate information about the affairs of the company.

8. If any of your colleagues express opinions and give suggestions to senior officers, do they care for your suggestions?

(a) Yes, they do care and listen to our suggestions.
(b) There is no pattern, sometimes they take note of our suggestions, sometimes, they don't care.
(c) They never care for our suggestions.

9. We do want appreciation for good work. Do you receive appreciation for good work in your company?

(a) Good work is always appreciated here.
(b) Good work is appreciated only sometimes.
(c) No one here cares to appreciate good work.

10. Very few people like to do the same thing again and again. How is the situation in your company? Do you get variety in your work?

(a) Here people have to do the same kind of routine over again.
(b) Sometimes we get some novelty in our work here.
(c) Here, we frequently get new and interesting things to do.

11. In work organisations canteen facilities are provided to the employees. How is your canteen?

(a) Our canteen is quite good.
(b) Our canteen s not good.

(c) There is hardly any canteen here.

12. People wish to have a job in which there is maximum scope for using one's skills and abilities. How do you feel about your job?

(a) My job is below my skills and abilities.
(b) My job is matched with my skills and abilities.
(c) My job is very much upto my skills and abilities.

13. Companies provide medical facilities to employees. How are these facilities provided by your company?

(a) Medical facilities are good here.
(b) There is hardly any medical facilities available.
(c) Medical facilities are not adequate.

14. Normally, people who work together develop trust in each other; but it does not happen all the time. In your experience how much trust people in your organisation have of each other?

(a) People here trust each other very much.
(b) People here have very little trust in each other.
(c) They do not have much trust in each other.

15. Work Organisations provide facilities for recreation. How are the facilities for recreation provided by your company?

(a) There are good facilities for recreation available here to the employees, after work.
(b) There are hardly any facilities available for recreation.
(c) There are some facilities for recreation available here.

16. When decisions concerning you and your colleagues are taken by the management, in what measure are you able to influence these decisions?

(a) We have considerable influence over the decisions.
(b) We can influence the decisions only sometimes.
(c) We have almost no influence on the decisions.

17. There is a general tendency to be on one's own while doing his job. How much freedom do you have in doing your job without interference from your supervisors?

(a) We have full freedom to do our own work.
(b) Sometimes we have freedom to do our own work.
(c) We have always to carry out the wishes of our supervisor and do work according to his instructions.

18. It is expected of each employee to put in his best. In your company, do your supervisors expect you to do your best?

(a) They always expect good work from us.
(b) Good or bad whatever we do is alright with them.
(c) Good work is not particularly expected from us here.

19. Sometimes you might feel that injustice is being done to you by the management. Is there any forum where such grievances can be redressed?

(a) There is proper arrangement for redressal of such grievances.
(b) Only sometimes attention is paid to such grievances.
(c) No attention whatsoever is paid to such grievances.

20. When decisions about work and workers are taken, the employees are involved in such decision making. Is it done in your company?

(a) Before taking any decision everyone is asked for his opinion.
(b) Only sometimes opinions are asked for.
(c) Nobody is ever asked to give his opinion.

21. In your job there must be certain things which you could do by using your own judgment. In some companies, the management encourages people to use their own judgment about their job. How is the situation in your company?

(a) Here we are encouraged to take up our own decisions in day-today work.
(b) Such encouragement is sometimes available here for taking initiative in day-today work.
(c) For each and every thing one has to look to the orders of the higher ups.

22. How are the interpersonal relations among the officers here? Do people quarrel with each other?

(a) People cooperate with each other and there are no quarrels.
(b) People do not have very good relations with each other.
(c) People here tend to down grade each other.

23. It is sometimes felt that the higher ups do not plan things properly and changes in plans etc. have to be made frequently. How is your experience in your company?

(a) Things are properly planned here.
(b) Planning is weak and sometimes we get contradictory messages.
(c) Things are not at all planned and frequent changes in instructions and plans are done.

31A23 GENERAL OPINION QUESTIONNAIRE

Authors : Prayag Mehta and Mahaveer Jain.
Availability : National Labour Institute, AB-6, Safdarjang Enclave, New Delhi.
Language : English and Hindi.
Uses : To find out authoritarian tendency among industrial employees.
Level : Adults working in industry.
Main features : It contains 20 questions covering following dimensions : misanthropism, powerlessness, normlessness and dogmatism.
Reliability : Item analysis was carried, spilt half reliability = 0.31 (N = 73).
Validity : Factorial validity and content validity established.
Time : No time limit.
Norms : Scores of skilled workers, unskilled workers, supervisors and middle managers are available.
References :

1. Prayag Mehta and Mahaveer Jain; Measuring work satisfaction and personality. New Delhi, National Labour Institute, 1982 (Memeo forthcoming).
2. Prayag Mehta; Form economism to democratic commitment : The role of worker participation. Vikalpa : A Journal of Decision Makers, 1976, 1(4), 39-46.
3. Prayag Mehta; Work satisfaction and democratic outlook; The role of worker participant. National Labour Institute Bulletin, 1976, 2, 231-236.
4. Prayag Mehta; The alienated middle manager. National Labour Institute Bulletin, 1976, (2), 94-96.

31A23 GENERAL OPINION QUESTIONNAIRE

(The following items have to be checked on a 5-point scale of agreement).

1. The God has divided society into two classes the rich and the poor.
2. Family planning can never succeed in this country.
3. It is futile to hope that bad persons will be able to work with good persons.
4. There is some supreme power above us and we should accept his decision without any reservation.
5. Natural calamities can alone bring an end to social evils and personal quarrels.
6. We should not mix too much with others because too much mixing produces mutual hatred.
7. Nationalisation of large scale industries is bound to lead to inefficiency and loss.
8. Military training must be compulsory for every citizen of India.
9. Most problems of our country are due to our low moral character.
10. For happy life it is necessary to have faith in religion and God.
11. Persons belonging to different religious groups will always find it difficult to work together.
12. It is the duty of the Government to respect and continue the former princes.
13. Political parties are so big that an average member has not got much say in what goes on there.
14. Politics and Government are so complicated that an average man like me cannot really understand what is going on.
15. It seems to me whoever you vote for, things remain pretty much the same.
16. Nothing I can do seems to have any effect on what happens in politics.
17. Some people or groups have so much influence over the Government that interests of the majority are ignored.
18. We talk of participation but common people like me have really no say in what the Government does.
19. It is no use worrying my head about the public affairs; I cannot do anything about them anyhow.
20. Elections have generally no meaning to me.

31A24 ROLE-CONFLICT INVENTORY

Author : B.A. Parikh.
Availability : Rupa Psychological Centre, Bhelupura, Varanasi.
Language : English.
Uses : To measure the level of adjustment and degree of conflict among married working women.
Levels : Married working women.
Main features : Likert type scale, 40 items.
Reliability : Test-retest reliability = .84, and split-half (odd-even) correlated with S.B. formula = .79.
Validity : Validated against (i) self evaluation and (ii) opinion by other near relative friends.
Time : Twenty minutes.

31A24 À ROLE CONFLICT INVENTORY

(The following statements have to be checked on a 5-point scale).

1. Can you perform your duties as a mother satisfactorily?
2. Can you perform your duties as a wife satisfactorily?
3. Can you perform your duties as a caretaker of the house satisfactorily?
4. Can you perform your duties as a social individual satisfactorily?
5. Do you feel tired and boring that you have to carry out house hold duties after coming from the job?
6. Do you nurse the guilt feeling that you are not able to pay as much attention to the house and family as you should?
7. Do you feel that your husband should share the responsibility in the household work?
8. Do you feel that other members of the family should share the burden of the household?
9. Does your husband feel that running the house is entirely the responsibility of a wife?
10. Do you have a feeling that you should compensate your absence in the house in some special ways?
11. Do you try to make other members of the family feel that you are a financial support?
12. Do you feel that because you are earning you should be given a special treatment in the family?
13. Do you feel that because you are earning your status in the house and social circles is higher than otherwise?

14. Does your husband adjust his needs to suit your job programmes?
15. Do the children adjust their needs to suit your programme?
16. Does your husband appreciate that you are holding two responsibilities, the house and the job?
17. Do the children and other members of the family appreciate that you are holding two responsibilities, the house and the job?
18. Do you feel that your family life is happy?
19. Sometimes when you have overtime on late hours on job do the members of the family accept it without grudge?
20. Do you feel that you have most agreeably synchronised your role as a housewife with the role of the working woman?
21. What is the opinion of your boss about a woman doing a job?
22. What is the opinion of your coworkers about woman doing a job?
23. What is the attitude of your superiors towards you?
24. What is the attitude of your coworkers towards you?
25. If you are late or asking leave because of family work what is the attitude of your boss?
26. Do your supervisors appreciate that you are doing job along with your household responsibilities?
27. Do your coworkers appreciate your doing a job with the responsibility of the family?
28. Do you feel the pleasure in doing the job?
29. Do you feel that you have satisfaction of doing a job?
30. Do you feel that you are doing the job most efficiently?
31. When you have to make adjustments in the type of work and hours of the job, do you do it without grumbling?
32. Do you have worries about the home when on job?
33. Are their occasions of friction in the office because of your household responsibilities?
34. Do you feel that as a married woman you have some limitations in performing the job efficiently?
35. Do you feel that married women on job should be granted some special concessions?
36. Do you feel like giving up the job?
37. Do you feel that you have most agreeably adjusted with your role as a working woman?
38. What do you feel whether a married woman should do a job or not?

39. If you are given the freedom of decision what would you decide about your doing the job?
40. What is your preference job or home?

31A25 JOB MOTIVATION SCALE (JMS)

Authors : S. Sultan Akhtar and Yog Bhargava.
Availability : Pili Kothi, Jaiganj, Aligarh, UP.
Language : English & Hindi.
Uses : To compare the job motivation of various professions.
Level : Various professional personnel.
Main features : Five point rating scale, number of items used 25.
Reliability : Reliability coefficient is 0.87.
Validity : Not given.
Time : Eight minutes.
Norms : Not given.
References :

1. Akhtar, S.S. & Bhargava Yog; Job motivational factors under different organisational climates : Proceedings of 18th International Congress of Applied Psychology, Montreal, Canada (Qubec), 1974.
2. Bhargava Yog; A pilot study of job motivation of salaried class and wage earners. Unpublished M. Phil. Dissertation, Department of Psychology, Aligarh Muslim University, Aligarh, 1975.
3. Bhargava Yog; A comparative study of job motivation of various professional groups. Unpublished Ph.D. thesis, Department of Psychology, Aligarh Muslim University, Aligarh, 1978.

31A25 JOB MOTIVATION SCALE

1. Think of a time in the past when you feel specially good or bad about your present job, that is, when you were very happy and satisfied or unhappy and dis-satisfied with your job. Can you think of such a high or low point in your feelings about your job?
2. People like to have many things in their job. When they get the desired things in the job they become satisfied. Their absence leads to dissatisfaction.

Can you tell us as to what things have made you satisfied with your job? You have to write them below in order of preference. The aspect that has been most satisfying is to be written first. In this manner you have to write three satisfying aspects.

(A) (B) (C)

Similarly the aspects of job that led to your dis-satisfaction have to be written below in order of preference.

The aspect that has been most dis-satisfying is to be written first. In this manner you have to write three dis-satisfying aspects.

(A) (B) (C)

3. Out of the factors given below, you have to indicate those which have been satisfying to you for most of the time, that is, for most of your working life and also those which have been dis-satisfying to you for most of the time.

1. To complete a job successfully.
2. To be singled out for praise.
3. To like the actual tasks involved in getting the job done.
4. To gain responsibility for own or other's work in a job.
5. To change status through promotion.
6. To be happy with ones' earnings.
7. Change in a job which could lead to further growth.
8. To experience satisfying social interactions with one's subordinates.
9. To obtain social status through job.
10. To experience satisfying social interactions with one's boss.
11. To experience satisfying social interactions with one's co-workers.
12. To have competent supervisor.
13. To be in a company with good policies and administrative procedures.
14. To have good physical surroundings on the job.
15. To have one's personal life affected for good by occurrences on the job.
16. Objective indications of security (such as job tenure and company stability).
17. To have housing facilities.
18. To get transportation facilities.

19. To get medical facilities.
20. Health suitable for the job.
21. To like leave policies.
22. To have opportunities for recreations.
23. Experiencing no feelings of casteism on the job.
24. Possibility of mobility with regard to work.
25. Participation in decision making processes.

4. Now you are required to rank the first three satisfying as well as the first three dis-satisfying factors, which have been satisfying or dis-satisfying to you most of the time in your working life.

Factors satisfying
1,2,3.

Factors dis-satisfying
1,2,3.

31A26 EMPLOYEES' MOTIVATION SCHEDULE

Author : A.K. Srivastava.
Availability : Department of Psychology, Banaras Hindu university, Varanasi.
Language : English and Hindi.
Uses : To assess the level of various needs of the employees which motivate them at job.
Level : It is most suitable for the employees of rank and file and supervisory cadres of production and non-production organisation, but may also be administered to the employees of higher level.
Main features : The motivation schedule consists of 70 °true-keyed' items with four categories of responses (never, sometimes, mostly, and always). The scale assess employees' level of following seven needs which motivate them to work efficiently :
(1) Achievement (A) : Competence and self improvement.
(2) Achievement (B) : High production, goal achievement and competition.
(3) Self control at work.
(4) Monetary gains.
(5) Non-financial rewards (recognition, appreciation, status and prospects).
(6) Autonomy and self actualisation needs.
(7) Social relation and social control at work.

Reliability : The following table records the reliability co-efficients of the seven subscales of the Employees' Motivation Schedule :

Sub-Scales	Index of reliability	
	Split-half (N = 200)	Retest (N = 95)
1	.79	.84
2	.55	.64
3	.74	.73
4	.68	.70
5	.71	.78
6	.56	.71
7	.63	.61

Validity : Employees' scores on the Employees' Motivation Schedule and on a measure of occupational stress were found to be inversely related. The coefficient of correlation was .44 (N = 200).

31A26 EMPLOYEES' MOTIVATION SCHEDULE

(The following items have to be checked on a 4-point scale - Always, Mostly, Sometimes and Never).

1. I am willing to improve my capability and competence.
2. I like to bear more and more responsibilities on my shoulders.
3. I would prefer such works which provide opportunities of increasing competence.
4. It gives me pleasure to find out easy ways for doing the work.
5. I like promotion based on °ability' rather than promotion based on °seniority'.
6. I like such new (original) and extra ordinary tasks which provide opportunity to learn something.
7. I feel like having better ways for performing the job.
8. Increment in the efficiency develops positive job attitudes.
9. "What can I do" is more important for me than "what I know"?
10. I want to be totally self-dependent by increasing my ability and competence.
11. I concentrate on a higher goal.

12. I do not consider any work very hard, for I like to work.
13. I think that inspite of obstacles and hindrances I can do my work very well.
14. I want to maintain a high level of my performance/production.
15. I keep prepared to face the unforeseen and emergent situations on the job.
16. I like such goals which require more effort in achieving them.
17. I take pleasure in performing new and challenging works.
18. I believe in goal setting and its attainment.
19. I take genuine risks for increasing the output/production.
20. I like competing with other efficient co-workers/colleagues.
21 I consider myself personally responsible for the jobs assigned to be.
22. Finishing the work within given time is a challenge for me.
23. I stay overtime to finish the work started.
24. I am alert at job and keep wholly prepared to do my work.
25. Time is valuable. I feel uneasy when it is wasted.
26. I do not postpone for tomorrow what I can do today.
27. I can be wholly trusted for the delegation of my responsibilities.
28. Instead of my higher authorities I myself fix up a deadline to finish my work.
29. I think that in comparison to other colleagues I notice such small tasks which must be done.
30. When needed I myself come early and stay late at work.
31. I would like to have more pay instead of higher position and prestige.
32. Money is important for getting rid of every kind of worries.
33. I like buying new things immediately not in the coming times.
34. One immediate promotion is equal to two promotions due in the future.
35. I would like to work overtime if paid extra for it.
36. Money is the main determinant of social status.
37. I want to be capable of buying every thing of my need and liking.
38. In return of my efficient performance I prefer monetary rewards to praise and recognition.

39. I like the principle of "more pay for more work".
40. I like earning more money and spending it.
41. I try to pave my own way to reach a higher position ultimately.
42. I wish to be acknowleded as a popular officer/worker.
43. I wish to be a good example for others.
44. I want to associate myself witn successful and respectable persons.
45. I like such officers who appreciate the work.
46. I feel dejected when my good performance is neglected.
47. I like the appreciation of my distinct skills and performance.
48. I want to create good impression on others through my performance.
49. I labour hard from the view point of promotion.
50. Where will I be in the next five years is important for me.
51. I like to be responsible for more and more persons.
52. I am willing to have my say in the decisions about policies and goals of my Department/Organisation.
53. I like independent thinking and want to decide the work-method myself.
54. I wish to have dominance over other people.
55. I want to have more and more authority.
56. I take pride in using my abilities and skills.
57. I get self-satisfaction through my position and job.
58. I try to make proper adjustment between my original ideas and performance of job activities.
59. I wish to make proper use of my special abilities and skills.
60. I want to make personal-development by making full use of my abilities and aptitudes.
61. I want to earn confidence and faith of my colleagues.
62. I make all efforts to maintain confirmity with my work-group.
63. I like having informal and intimate relations with my colleagues.
64. Proper relations with my colleagues gives me strength and enhances my morale.
65. My feeling of attachment with the organisation motivates me to work more effectively.
66. Good relations with higher authorities increases my involvement with the job.
67. More presence of the colleagues impel me to be en-

gaged in the work.

68. I work more to achieve popularity and prestige among the colleagues.
69. I like to give advice in problems related to my work..
70. I co-operate in the activities and functioning of my Section/Organisation.

31A27 JOB ANXIETY SCALE

Authors : A.K. Srivastava and M.M. Sinha.
Availability : Rupa Psychological Centre, B-19/60-B Deoriabir, Bhelupur, Varanasi.
Language : English and Hindi.
Uses : To assess the level of anxiety pertaining to various constituents of the job life of the employees.
Level : The employees of every level operating in the context of industries and other non-production organisations.
Main features : The scale consists of 80 items, with yes/no response pattern, pertaining to following seven constituents of the job life : (1) Job-security, (2) Recognition and fair evaluation, (3) Human relations at work, (4) Rewards and punishment, (5) Self-esteem and status of the job, (6) Future prospects and (7) Capacity and confidence to shoulder job responsibilities.
Reliability : The following table records the indices of split-half and retest reliability of the seven subscales of the JAS :

Method	Sub-Scales 1	2	3	4	5	6	7	The scale as a whole
Split-half (N = 414)	.93	.82	.93	.94	.87	.83	.85	.92
Retest (N = 110)	.91	.78	.90	.92	.84	.81	.83	.90

Validity : The coefficients of correlation between the scores of on the Job Anxiety Scale and the Sinha W.A. Self-Analysis from (Anxiety Scale), Sarason's General Anxiety Text, and Taylor Manifest Anxiety Scale were found to be .54 (N = 100), .56 (N = 60) and .48 (N = 51) respectively.

Employees' tendency for neuroticism, measured by Eysenck's Mandsley Personality inventory was found to be positively correlated with their job anxiety (r = .32).

Time : Twenty-five to thirty minutes.

Norms : Norms are provided in the manual.

31A27 JOB ANXIETY SCALE

(The following items have to be checked as °yes' or °no').

1. I usually fear I may be terminated from my job.
2. Our officers consider us to be hardworking and competent workers.
3. Our officers behave sympathetically and nicely with us.
4. I usually think and worry about my promotions.
5. I get here enough of opportunity to improve and display my abilities and efficiency.
6. I often feel that my officers and colleagues neglect and disregard me.
7. I often feel that I am not capable of performing my work as efficiently as I can.
8. Sometimes I think of what will happen to my family if I am turned out of my job.
9. It is my experience that hardworking, competent, and honest workers are given respect and promotions here.
10. There exist good relations between officers and workers of this company (organisation).
11. I apprehend that my officers and co-workers criticise me and my work.
12. I am confident that I can achieve the goal of my life through this job.
13. Very often I feel that there are good chances of my promotion in this job.
14. I often feel that here the workers are paid less in comparison to there abilities and efforts.
15. I often get worried that I would come under some catastrophe.
16. I hope that here I can get better opportunities to learn work and increase my efficiency.
17. In want of cordial relations and co-operation between officials and workers I often feel frustrated and mentally tense.
18. Here the employees are dealt with the principle of

equality and honesty.
19. Due to this job I am deprived of respect from the society and sympathy from relations.
20. Our officers punish us severely for trivial mistakes.
21. I often get worried that I would not be able to progress.
22. Often I am afraid thinking I may be suspended.
23. My officers and co-workers misunderstand me.
24. Often I am to restrain my anger and emotions for fear of the cruelty of my officers and employer.
25. I am very often worried that I may be given some punishment.
26. My job is not given due honour in society.
27. The idea that I would not get a job in some reputed company or organisation after working over here for a long period worries me.
28. I often feel that this job is not befitting to my capabilities and aptitudes.
29. I often apprehend and worry that my promotion would be barred.
30. Our officers give rewards to honest, hardworking, and efficient workers.
31. Here officers and rank-and-file workers sympathize with each other.
32. Often I am blamed for others' mistakes.
33. Sometimes I feel that I am good for nothing.
34. The chances of promotion on merit are few in this company.
35. I do my work under heavy mental strain.
36. I often apprehend that I would be involved in some accident.
37. I often experience that here the workers are neither appreciated for their abilities and efficiency nor encouraged.
38. Here I have to work with certain persons whom I do not like.
39. My officers chafe at my work (performance) without reasons.
40. I often realize that the rights and responsibilities given to me fall too short to the real requirements.
41. I often feel that by staying over here I cannot improve my competency and efficiency.
42. I sometimes feel that I can do some other job with more ease and efficiency.
43. I think of changing over to some other job.
44. I often feel that I have not selected a suitable

job.

45. Most of the time I find that there is no person among my colleagues in whom I can confide.
46. Sometimes I am afraid of false allegations being levelled against me.
47. I am often worried with the probabilities of humiliations from the dealings of the officials.
48. Though expenditure go on increasing, the probability of an increase in salary is very thin here.
49. I often feel that my work is interesting and simple.
50. I cannot advise any of my friends or relatives to come to this job.
51. It is my experience that employees of this factory are in a better position than those in other factories.
52. Often I am afraid my co-workers will get annoyed with me or leave my company.
53. Workers are treated here in the way they should be treated.
54. It often pricks me that my performance lacks special significance to the society.
55. Screening is made very often here and so chances of our promotion and increment are lesser.
56. I usually feel that this life and job is a kind of burden for me.
57. In this company ordinary workers are not treated as human beings.
58. Even among my friends I often feel lonely.
59. In this company an ordinary worker can rise very high through his abilities and efforts.
60. In this factory ordinary workers cannot speak in favour of their welfare.
61. Here even after several years of service there is not any special increment in the salary.
62. I often apprehend that my colleagues may be promoted earlier than me.
63. I am often afraid of my officers and employer without any apparent cause for it.
64. Whenever any of my friends is promoted I feel disappointed.
65. I often apprehend and fear that my officers and employer might misunderstand me.
66. In five or seven years, here money cannot be earned as much as elsewhere.
67. Here officers think of their own welfare only and not of the ordinary workers.
68. I often feel that I shall not be able to achieve

inner satisfaction through this job.

69. My friends often complain against or criticise me before my officers and employer.
70. I often feel whether I shall be able to discharge my duties and responsibilities successfully.
71. I often feel that I am working in a horrible and exciting environment.
72. Here the workers get more opportunities to make use of their abilities and experience than those in other companies.
73. I observe that my colleagues do not express real happiness on my promotion or success.
74. Whenever my officers or supervisors observe my activities I undergo a sort of tension and fear.
75. My co-workers try to take undue advantage of my trivial mistakes.
76. I often apprehend that my officers may get annoyed with me.
77. Here I get enough opportunity to make independent use of my ability and competency.
78. I hesitate in meeting my friends and relatives because of the low status of my job.
79. My co-workers neither have faith in me nor like to tell me their personal matters.
80. I think that the services of workers of other companies are more secure than those of the workers of this company.

31A28 OCCUPATIONAL STRESS INDEX (OSI)

Authors : A.K. Srivastava and A.P. Singh.

Availability : Authors, Department of Psychology, Banaras Hindu University, Varanasi.

Language : English and Hindi.

Uses : To Assess the degree of perceived stress arising from various aspect of the job of the employees.

Level : The employees of any level engaged with organisations. But would prove more suitable for the employees of supervisory cadre and above.

Main features : The scale consists of 46 items, with 5 alternative response, selected on the basis of their significantly high indices of homogeneity (rbis) with the cut-off-point of 0.20. Out of 46 items 28 are °true-keyed' and 18 are °false-keyed'. The items relate to almost all relevant components of the job like which cause stress in some way or the other such as role overload; role ambiguity; role conflict; group and political pressures; responsibility for persons;

underparticipation; powerlessness; poor peer relations; intrinsic impoverishment; low status; strenuous working conditions; and unprofitability.

Reliability : The split-half reliability coefficient by odd-even method and Cronbach's alpha coefficient for the scale were found to be 0.935 and 0.90 respectively.

Validity : The employees' scores on the occupational stress index negatively correlate with their scores on the measures of certain attitudinal, motivational and personality variables which have been proved to lowering or moderating the level of stress. The coefficients of correlation between the scores on the occupational stress index and the measures of job involvement, age strength and employees' motivation were found to be -.80 (N = 120), -.40(N = 120), -.44 (N = 200) respectively. The employees' scores on the OSI have been found to be positively correlated with their scores on the measures (indicators) of ill mental health.

Time : It takes normally 20 to 25 minutes.

Norms : Available with authors.

Reference : Srivastava, A.K. & Singh, A.P. Construction and standardization of an Occupational Stress Index : A pilot study. Indian Jr. Clinical Psychology, 1981, 8, 133-136.

31A28 OCCUPATIONAL STRESS INDEX

(The following items have to be checked on a 5-point scale of agreement).

1. I have to do a lot of work in this job.
2. The available informations relating to my job-role and its outcomes are vague and insufficient.
3. My different officers often give contradictory instructions regarding my works.
4. Sometimes it becomes complex problem for me to make adjustment between political/group pressures and formal rules and instructions.
5. The responsibility for the efficiency and productivity of many employees is thrust upon me.
6. Most of suggestions are heeded and implemented here.
7. My decisions and instructions concerning distribution of assignments among employees are properly followed.
8. I have to work with persons whom I like.
9. My assignments are of monotonous nature.

10. Higher authorities do care for my self-respect.
11. I get less salary in comparison to the quantum of my labour/work.
12. I do my work under tense circumstances.
13. Owing to excessive work load I have to manage with insufficient number of employees and resources.
14. The objectives of my work-role are quite clear and adequately planned.
15. Officials do not interfere with my jurisdiction and working methods.
16. I have to do some work unwillingly owing to certain group/political pressures.
17. I am responsible for the future of a number of employees.
18. My co-operation is frequently sought in solving the administrative or industrial problems at higher level.
19. My suggestions regarding the training-programmes of the employees are given due significance.
20. Some of my colleagues and subordinates try to defame and malign me as unsuccessful.
21. I get ample opportunity to utilize my abilities and experience independently.
22. This job has enhanced my social status.
23. I am seldom rewarded for my hard labour and efficient performance.
24. Some of my assignments are quite risky and complicated.
25. I have to dispose off my work hurriedly owing to excessive work load.
26. I am unable to perform my duties smoothly owing to uncertainty and ambiguity of the scope of my jurisdiction and authorities.
27. I am not provided with clear instructions and sufficient facilities regarding the new assignments trusted to me.
28. In order to maintain group-confirmity sometimes I have to do/produce more than the usual.
29. I bear the great responsibility for the progress and prosperity of this organisation/department, company.
30. My opinions are sought in forming important policies of the organisation/department.
31. Our interests and opinion are duly considered in making appointments for important posts.
32. My colleagues do co-operate with me voluntarily in solving administrative and industrial problem.
33. I got ample opportunity to develop my aptitude and

proficiency properly.

34. My higher authorities do not give due significance to my post and work.
35. I often feel that this job has made my life cumbersome.
36. Being too busy with official work I am not able to devote sufficient time to my domestic and personal problems.
37. It is not clear that what type of work and behaviour my higher authorities and colleagues expect from me.
38. Employees attach due importance to the official instructions and formal working procedures.
39. I am compelled to violate the formal and administrative procedures and policies owing to group/political pressures.
40. My opinion is sought in changing or modifying the working system, implements and conditions.
41. There exists sufficient mutual co-operation and team-spirit among the employees of this organisation/ department.
42. My suggestions and co-operation are not sought in solving even those problems for which I am quite competent.
43. Working conditions are satisfactory here from the point of view of our welfare and convenience.
44. I have to do such work as ought to be done by others.
45. It becomes difficult to implement all of a sudden the new dealing procedures and policies in place of those already in practice.
46. I am unable to carry out my assigments to my satisfaction on account of excessive load of work and lack of time.

31A29 RESISTANCE TO CHANGE SCALE

Author : D.M. Pestonjee.
Availability : Indian Institute of Management, Ahmedabad.
Language : English.
Uses : To measure organisational change.
Level : Industrial workers and supervisors.
Main features : The scale contains 50 items on social, economic and personal aspects which are likely to be affected by introduction of change.
Reliability : Split-half reliability = +.96.
Validity : Validated by item-test correlation method and

also by known group technique.

Time : Untimed.

Norms : Available with author.

References :

(1) Pestonjee, D.M. An investigation into job satisfaction and resistance to change. Psychological Studies, 1972, 17(2), 8-12.

(2) Pestonjee, D.M. Employees' Morale and Resistance to Change. Paper presented at the XVIII International Congress of Applied Psychology, Montreal, Canada, July-August, 1974.

(3) Pestonjee, D.M. Attitudes of blue-collar textile mill workers towards automation and rationalisation in textile industry as a function of job satisfaction and morale. Unpublished Research Report, Banaras Hindu University.

(4) Pestonjee, D.M., Akhtar, S.S. and Siddiqui, M.M. Attitudes of different levels of employees towards electronic data processing system. Psychological Studies, 1971, 16(1), 9-14.

31A29 R-C SCALE

1. There would be better coordination between departments.
2. Workers will become more efficient.
3. Management will suffer financial losses.
4. There would be retrenchment.
5. Condition of work will improve.
6. Will lead to strikes and °gheeraos'.
7. Productivity will increase.
8. Work simplification will lead to a decrease in interest.
9. Employe-employee relations will improve.
10. Workers will get higher wages.
11. There will be decrease in accidents and low quality behaviour.
12. There will be new problems on the job.
13. Promotions will depend on the wishes of superiors, not on the ability of the worker.
14. Hazard to health will decrease.
15. There will be no recognition for good work.
16. Transfer from one job to another will lead to dissatisfaction.
17. Public will get better service.
18. Experienced workers will suffer a loss.
19. Efficiency of the organisation will increase.

20. This will lead to an increase in unemployment in the country.
21. There will be greater freedom to work.
22. Earlier training will go waste.
23. There will be an increase in competition between workers.
24. The standard of living of the workers will go up.
25. Workers will get greater opportunity to participate in social activities.
26. Pride in doing the job will decrease.
27. Economic conditions of the country will improve.
28. There would be greater availability of leisure.
29. Worker's initiative will vanish.
30. There will be a joy in doing new and difficult jobs.
31. Abilities of workers will not be properly utilised.
32. There would be frequent °lock-outs'.
33. Management will be able to extend more facilities to workers.
34. Many people will have to change their vocations.
35. There will be no sense of success on the job.
36. Workers will get an opportunity to participate in management functions.
37. One's vocation (job) will go down in the esteem of the public.
38. There will be an increase in improved relations between workers.
39. Work environment will become more congenial.
40. Many more persons will boss over you.
41. Management will give more sympathetic hearing to workers' complaints and problems.
42. Conversation and social interaction during working time will decrease.
43. Workers will be happy due to an increase in responsibilities.
44. There will be greater mental fatigue.
45. Jobs will be in jeopardy.
46. Prestige of the organisation will go up.
47. The worker will get a greater opportunity to display his ability.
48. The pace of work will not depend on the wishes of the worker.
49. Re-training will lead to big expenses.
50. Promotions will be quicker.

31A30 PERFORMANCE RATING SCALE

275 Organisational Behaviour

Authors : A.P. Singh & D.M. Pestonjee.
Availability : M/s Banaras Psychological Corporation, Rajputana Uttar, Maunath Bhanjan, Azamgarh.
Languages : English and Hindi.
Uses : To ascertain the level of efficiency.
Level : Blue collar as well as white collar workers and supervisory cadre employees.
Main features : It is a likert type scale consisting of 14 items with 5 response alternatives. The immediate officers are required to rate how well the particular subordinate was doing on such of the 14 items.
Reliability : Cronbach's alpha coefficient was found to be +.99.
Validity : The index of homogeniety and internal validity of the items were tested by point biserial correlation. The coefficient of correlation between actual performance and the scores on this scale was found to be .84 (N = 200).
Time : No time limit.
Norms : Not available.
Reference :

(1) Srivastava, G.P. An empirical study of the ego strength as a moderator of the relationship of supervisory orientation with industrial morale and job performance of blue collar workers. Unpublished Ph.D. Dissertation, Banaras Hindu University, 1980.
(2) Singh, A.P. & Srivastava, G.P. Performance in relation to different styles of supervision. Decision, 1979, 6(3), 271-275.
(3) Singh, A.P. & Srivastava, G.P. Effect of ego-strength on the relationship of different styles of supervision with morale and performance. Psychological Studies, 1980, 25(2), 98-104.
(4) Singh, A.P. & others : Effect of morale and ego-strength on performance of blue-collar industrial workers. Indian Psychological Review, 1981, 20(3).

31A30 PERFORMANCE SCALE

(The following items have to be rated on a 4-point scale).

1. Quality of work performance.
2. Amount of effort expended on job.
3. Speed on the job.
4. Quantity of work.
5. Capacity of work performance.
6. Care in handling company property.
7. Ability to work without supervision.

8. Ability to handle different jobs.
9. Dependability.
10. Ability to get along with others.
11. Attendance and punctuality.
12. Planning ability.
13. Initiative on the job.
14. Overall work performance.

31A31 PSYCHOLOGICAL PARTICIPATION INDEX

Authors : A.P. Singh & D.M. Pestonjee.

Availability : M/s Banaras Psychological Corporation, Rajputana Uttar, Mannath Bhanjan, Azamgarh, UP.

Languages : English and Hindi.

Uses : To find out the levels of participation in decision-making allowed by the employees or immediate higher cadre.

Level : For employees of all categories in any type of organisation.

Main features : Psychological Participation Index comprises of fifteen items which cover four areas, namely, decision-making, autonomy, opinion-seeking, and involvement. The items are in the form of positively and negatively worded statements with five response alternatives for each item, namely, definitely true, mostly true, sometimes true/sometimes false, mostly false, and definitely false.

Reliability : Reliability has been determined areawise by computing Cronbach's alpha coefficient. It was found to be .86 for decision-seeking, .79 for autonomy, .82 for opinion seeking and .73 for involvement.

Validity : The index of homogeniety and internal validity of the items has been determined by computing point-biserial coefficient of correlation (rpb). The scores on °sense of participation' (Pestonjee, 1973) was used as one of the validation criteria for the psychological participation index. The coefficient of correlation between the scores on the two tests was found to be +.48 on a representative sample of 200 blue-collar industrial workers.

Time : No time limit.

Norms : Not available.

References :

(1) Singh, B.V. Ego-strength, participation and job-anxiety as factors influencing the performance of blue-collars industrial workers. Unpublished Ph.D Thesis, Banaras Hindu University, Varanasi, 1982.

(2) Singh, S.P. Job satisfaction, participation, and alienation as factors influencing production in case of blue-collar industrial workers. Unpublished Ph.D. Thesis, Banaras Hindu University, 1980.

31A31 PSYCHOLOGICAL PARTICIPATION INDEX

(The following statements have to be checked on a 5-point scale; definitely true, mostly true, sometimes true, mostly false, definitely false).

1. In general, your say or influence carries weight for what goes on in your company.
2. You feel that you can influence the decisions of your immediate supervisor regarding things about which you are concerned.
3. Your immediate supervisor asks your opinion when a problem comes up that involves your work.
4. When you have a suggestion for improving the job, it is easy for you to get your ideas acrossed to your immediate supervisor.
5. Everybody is consulted for the welfare of the company.
6. Workers are encouraged for suggesting new ideas about the work.
7. No changes are introduced in the work method without consulting the workers.
8. Suggestions given by the workers are not respected (recognised)
9. Supervisors (officers) do everything according to their own wishes : workers are not consulted for anything.
10. Your believe that workers get full opportunity to use their abilities and experiences here.
11. It is not considered desirable for the workers to adopt now methods of work.
12. Work of the group is left to those who are considered most capable for the job.
13. Members are interested in the group but not all of them want to work for it.
14. Each member of the group is on one or more active committees.
15. The work of the group is weldivided among members.

31A32 WORKMEN PERSONALITY INVENTORY

Author : Prabhakar Singh.
Availability : Author, Department of IEM, Indian School of Mines, Dhanbad.
Language : Hindi.
Uses : To assess the workmen personality.
Level : Workmen (5th to 8th standard education).
Main features : Forced choice, 78 items covering ten areas of personality.
Reliability : All the consistency reliability values are significant beyond .01 level.
Validity : Factorial validity established.
Time : Thirty minutes.

31A32 WORKMEN PERSONALITY INVENTORY

(The respondents have to choose one of the alternatives).

Scale I : Traditional vs Progressive

1. (a) If you get ten thousand rupees from the lottery, will you keep the entire sum with you?
   (b) Will you give a part of it to temple/church/mosque?
2. (a) Do you think that new values of life are good?
   (b) Do you think that old values of life are good and should be retained?
3. (a) Will it be good if every one goes to the temple/church/mosque daily?
   (b) Is it not very important to go to temple/church/mosque daily?
4. (a) Do you think observing religious rites on auspicious days should be made necessary for every one?
   (b) Should every one be left free to do/not to do it as he likes?
5. (a) If you have Rs. 10 to give as donation, will you give to some educational institution?
   (b) Will you give it to the temple/church/mosque?
6. (a) Should we follow old customs and traditions?
   (c) Should we follow new social costums and traditions?
7. (a) Are you in favour of family planning and do you think it will bring prosperity?
   (b) Are you against it because it is against the will of God?

Scale II : Socially Bold vs Inhibited

1. (a) If you are invited to attend some function, will you make efforts to get it started as soon as you find every one has come?
   (b) Will you leave it to some one else to do?
2. (a) if you take a job in a new factory will you take a long time to mix with the workers there?
   (b) Will you take less time in mixing with people there?
3. (a) Do you hesitate and feel shy while talking to others?
   (b) Do you talk without any hesitation or feeling of shyness?
4. (a) if given a chance to address a gathering of labourers, will you feel any difficulty?
   (b) Would you do it without any difficulty?
5. (a) Would you like to take a job in which you are not required to meet many people?
   (b) Would you like to take a job which requires you to meet many people?
6. (a) If required, can you meet renowned and important persons easily?
   (b) Do you find it difficult?
7. (a) Do you show off well in functions?
   (b) Do you sit quietly?
8. (a) In a gathering of laborers can you verbalize your feelings easily?
   (b) Would you rather suppress it?

Scale III : Dependent vs Independent

1. (a) When you travel alone, do you look out of the window (sit quietly)?
   (b) Do you often talk with people sitting by your side?
2. (a) Do you take active part in all social functions, even if you do not like it?
   (b) Would you rather like to do things which you like and think you can do by yourself?
3. (a) Do you ask others' opinion before doing any thing?
   (b) Do you do things according to your own will and in you own way?
4. (a) Would you like to pass your day-offs at a quiet place?

(b) Would you prefer to go to one who is your well-wisher?

5. (a) If you are requested not to talk for about two hours, could you do it without any difficulty?

(b) Would you not find it difficult even to think of it?

6. (a) Would you like your son to read some story (paint picture in his leisure hours)?

(b) Would you like him to run some social club in cooperation?

7. (a) Would you like your son to take a job in which he has to work with a group of people?

(b) Would you like your son to take a job in which he has to work alone and on his own?

8. (a) In a social function would you like to work with a group of people?

(b) Would you like to do some thing all by yourself?

Scale IV : Participating vs Reserved

1. (a) Do you talk over factory problems with your fellow workers?

(b) Not?

2. (a) Would you like your son to take a job which requires him to meet and work with people one after another (active participation)?

(b) Would you like him to take a job he has to do by himself?

3. (a) Would you be a bit perplexed if in a gathering every one gets interested in you and you become the centre of attention?

(b) Would you enjoy it?

4. (a) Do you share your feelings with others?

(b) Not?

5. (a) Given similar facilities, would you like to have a house which is at a quiet place and away from town?

6. (a) Would you like to discuss with others about their own problems/feelings?

(b) Would you not like to discuss with others about their own problems/feelings?

7. (a) Do others say that you are talkative?

(b) Do others consider you to be a quiet person?

8. (a) In your leisure time would you like to go for a walk alone?

(b) Would you like to go to a social club which

helps others?

Scale V : Suspicious vs Confident

1. (a) Do you some times feel sorry for yourself, for things which you do?
   (b) Do you never feel sorry for yourself, for things which you do?
2. (a) Do you some times suspect the presence of some danger without any cause?
   (b) Do you never suspect the presence of some danger without any cause?
3. (a) In a group of people do you sometimes feel lonely and thing you are of no worth?
   (b) Do you think you are of some worth?
4. (a) Do you often have baseless fear-feeling?
   (b) Do you like to be a worker only?
5. (a) Would you like to be promoted as supervisor (responsible for activities of a group of workers)?
   (b) Would you like to be a worker only?
6. (a) If at a public place two or more people look at you and whisper, would you not think that they are conspiring against you?
   (b) Would you become upset and think they are conspiring against you?
7. (a) Did you never blame yourself for any mishappening?
   (b) Do you often blame yourself and think you could make an effort to avoid it?
8. (a) When you are called by a company officer, do you feel happy to get a chance to show your competence?
   (b) Do you feel that you are called for giving an explanation for mistakes you have committed?

Scale VI : Emotionally Stable vs Emotionally Unstable

1. (a) Do you work on your plans?
   (b) Do you neglect the plans you have made?
2. (a) Do you get impatient and worried when people do not pay any attention to what you say?
   (b) Do you never get annoyed?
3. (a) Do you become angry very easily?
   (b) Are you slow to get angry?
4. (a) Are you sometimes badly disturbed by small

things/happenings?
(b) Do small things/happenings never disturb you?

5. (a) Do you thing your strong feelings are related to what goes on around you?
(b) Do you think your strong feelings never have any association with what goes on around you?

6. (a) In case you become upset do you get over it very soon?
(b) Do you never cool down soon?

7. (a) Do you feel energetic when you have to start a day's work?
(b) Do you feel tired?

Scale VII : Sober vs Vivacious

1. (a) Would you appreciate a person telling jokes quite often?
(b) Would you dislike him?

2. (a) Would you like to pass your evenings quietly at home?
(b) Would you like to go and see a dance?

3. (a) Would you prefer a calm and quiet environment?
(b) Would you prefer an exciting environment?

4. (a) Do you thing one should be serious most of the time?
(b) Do you thing one should be cheerful most of the time?

5. (a) Do you entertain others by telling funny stories?
(b) Do you not like to do it?

6. (a) If you go for a dance do you enjoy it with others and make funny remarks?
(b) Do you sit alone and quietly?

7. (a) Do people say you are a happy-go-lucky person?
(b) Do People say you are serious person?

8. (a) Do people say you are vivacious?
(b) Do people say you are quiet?

Scale VIII : Disturbed vs Relaxed

1. (a) If your supervisor/coworkers/others get angry with you, do you forget it soon?
(b) Do you get upset very much and think over it for long?

2. (a) Do you not suffer from the feeling of jealousy?

(b) Do you suffer from the feeling of jealousy?

3. (a) Do you get very much disturbed by minor happenings/irrelevant events?
   (b) Do you never get disturbed by them?
4. (a) Do you often have fearful dreams which disturb your sleep?
   (b) Do you never have fearful dreams and sleep well?
5. (a) Do you often feel relaxed?
   (b) Do you often feel disturbed?
6. (a) Do you feel you are surrounded by problems?
   (b) Do you never feel you have major problems?
7. (a) Whenever you have to go anywhere do you feel tense and always fearful of being late?
   (b) Do you feel you have enough time and you will reach in time?
8. (a) Do you get along with your problems well?
   (b) Do you feel sad and become low when you have problems?

Scale IX : Assertive vs Humble

1. (a) If you have to tell a lie to your supervisor/manager, could you tell it without hesitation?
   (b) Is it that you can never do it?
2. (a) Could you take a chance and invest your small savings in business?
   (b) Is it that you will not take a chance, and would rather keep the money with you?
3. (a) Do you very often get angry with your parents/supervisors?
   (b) Do you think it is bad?
4. (a) If some day you do not get the right tool to work with, would you stop working?
   (b) Would you just go on working with the tools available?
5. (a) Do you sometimes make pinching remarks?
   (b) Do you always try not to make this type of remarks?
6. (a) Suppose you have to tell an obvious lie to your manager, would you look at his face and tell it?
   (b) Would you look down and tell a lie?
7. (a) At a new place would you stay away from the place you are told to be disturbed?
   (b) Would you rather go there without paying at-

tention to what you are told?
8. (a) Can you criticise others openly?
   (b) Is it that you cannot?

Scale X : Conscientious vs Unscrupulous

1. (a) Are you a man who tries his best to complete every work?
   (b) Do you try to get through with it somehow?
2. (a) Do you always try to avoid saying which you think may worry others?
   (b) Do you sometimes say what you think may worry (hurt) others?
3. (a) Do you think all the laws are good and should be observed?
   (b) Do you think some laws are bad and need not be observed?
4. (a) Do narrow and dirty lanes of the city worry you very much?
   (b) Do they never worry you at all?
5. (a) Do you think laws should be observed fully?
   (b) Do you think every one should be free?
6. (a) Would you like to do only that which is beneficial to you?
   (b) Would you like to do only that which is beneficial also to others?
7. (a) Do you think some jobs, in comparison with others, are not important hence should not be done perfectly?
   (b) Do you think every job is important and should be done perfectly?
8. (a) Do you feel happy even after violating factory rules?
   (b) Do you feel sorry if any factory rule is violated by you?

31A33 FATIGUE INVENTORY

Author : S. Narayanan.
Availability : Department of Psychology, University of Madras, Autonomous P.G. Centre, Coimbatore.
Language : English.
Main features : It is a 32 items °yes' °no' type inventory and measures the subjective feelings related to fatigue.
Reliability : Reliability coefficient =.50.
Validity : Validity coefficient = .85.

31A33 THE FATIGUE INVENTORY

(The following items have to be checked as °yes' or °no').

1. Do you usually feel carefree sometimes or worried at other times on work days?
2. Have you ever tried at times to be evasive on your job?
3. Have you ever lost your consciousness completely for certain seconds when doing work?
4. Are you more alert in your work in the morning than in the afternoon?
5. Is your sleep affected if you do heavy work in the day?
6. Does the quantity of your production go down if you are fatigued?
7. Does fatigue set in often in your on working days?
8. Have you ever tried to have rest by completing the work quickly?
9. Have mistakes crept in your work, because of fatigue?
10. Are your dreams confusing when they occur during nights of your working days?
11. Do you feel that you need rest often?
12. Do you find difficult to concentrate on your work?
13. Do you feel that you can work better if you do not get fatigued quickly?
14. Does your interest in work decline as working hours increase?
15. Is it easier to work in the morning than in the evening?
16. Have you ever reduced the speed of your work due to fatigue?
17. Do you get a feeling of dullness as work progresses?
18. Do other thoughts come often while doing work?
19. Have you ever feared that the work would suffer due to fatigue?
20. Do you more often take leave to stay at home to take rest?
21. Do you often yawn during working days?
22. Are you often disturbed when doing work?
23. Does your briskness in doing work declines as the working hours increase?
24. Are you in the habit of trying to talk to other workers when doing work?

25. Do you feel that your efficiency in work decrease as the working hours increase?
26. Do you day-dream often when doing work?
27. Do you long for the conclusion of the work day even during noon time?
28. Do you get irritated easily during working hours?
29. Are you fatigued most of the times during working days?
30. Do you find your speed at work decreases as you go on doing work?
31. Do you feel that you need more rest during your work days?
32. Do you feel that the quality of the products you produced has gone down because of fatigue?

31A34 BUSINESS ETHICS INVENTORY

Author : R. Venkatapathy.
Availability : Department of Psychology, University of Madras, Autonomous P.G. Centre, Coimbatore.
Language : English.
Uses : To measure the business ethics present among the entrepreneurs.
Main features : It is a 26 items °yes' °no' type inventory measuring general belief one has in his business.
Reliability : Split-half reliability = .632.
Validity : To be established.

31A34 BUSINESS ETHICS INVENTORY

(The following items have to be checked as °yes' or °no').

1. In business exploitation is inevitable.
2. Earning money is not a sin, if it is spent on good causes.
3. Man does not nave faith in his own fellow men.
4. People engaged in business cannot always be honest.
5. Wealth and status can be achieved only through hard work.
6. Even the close friends seem to be ungrateful.
7. Hard work alone can convert a desert into a beautiful garden.
8. Ability and willingness to work hard conceed success in life.
9. I am proud to say that I'm a hard worker.

10. One should trust his business and effort instead of other human beings.
11. It is correct that how much we earn than how we earn.
12. The attainment of social status is the hall mark of success.
13. A hard worker will do any job with utmost care.
14. Mutual trust among one another will lead to progress.
15. Hard work is most essential to succeed.
16. Lack of confidence in one's own ability will lead to labour in vain.
17. One should have the tendency to admit his/her shortcomings.
18. Faith in all the fellowmen will lead one to go out of his business.
19. Work is equivalent to worship.
20. Highly religious man cannot succeed in his business.
21. There is no substitute for hard work.
22. One who shirks labour will find even an easy job as tremendous.
23. The hard earned money should be reinvested.
24. Effort and confidence will even shatter mountains to smithereens.
25. Man is basically a Sycophant.
26. Lazy people cannot function effectively.

31A35 AN INVENTORY ON OFF-THE-JOB ACTIVITIES

Author : Anima Sen.
Availability : The Author, Department of Psychology, University of Delhi, Delhi.
Language : English.
Uses :

(1) To assess the off-the-job activities of an individual belonging in any profession.
(2) Individuals from different professions indulge in different types of activities. The present inventory can provide a comparison among various professions in terms of preference for off-the-job activities.
(3) Further, it can also be used to determine relationship between leisure activities and different aspects of personality and other psychological variables.

Level : The inventory is to be used for individuals who are above 20 years of age and who are in some kind of profession.

Main features : The inventory consists of 60 different possible off-the-job pursuits. Each activity has five choices i.e., like very much, like, undecided, dislike and dislike very much.

At the end of this inventory the subject is then required to write the names of the activity or activities which one actually performs during this leisure time in order of priority.

Reliability : The reliability was determined by applying the formula,

$$r_{tt} = 1 - \frac{ve}{vt}$$

Where,

v_e = Error variance, v_t = Total variance.

The reliability coefficient thus calculated was found to be 0.88.

Validity : The inventory was analysed for determining content validity.

Time : There is no time limit, but it takes about ten minutes.

Norms : No norms are available.

References :

(1) Sen, Anima; A study on the personality make-up and off-the-job activities in a group of executives. Journal of Applied Psychology, 1976, 13,16-20.

(2) Sen, Anima & Opal, P. Relationship between personality make-up and preference for off-the-job activities among executives. Psychological Research Journal, 1980, 1(2), 56-61.

31A35 AN INVENTORY ON OFF-THE-JOB ACTIVITIES

(The following items have to be checked on a 5-point scale of like and dislike).

1. Arts & craft/painting.
2. Bird watching.
3. Beating.
4. Camping.
5. Clubs.
6. Collecting antiques/vintage cars.
7. Collecting stamps & coins.

8. Conversation.
9. Cooking.
10. Crossword puzzle/quiz.
11. Cycling/horseriding.
12. Dancing.
13. Daydreaming.
14. Debating.
15. Diving.
16. Driving.
17. Entertaining people.
18. Fishing.
19. Flying.
20. Gambling.
21. Gardening.
22. Gymnastic/physical training.
23. Hitchhiking.
24. Homemaking/household chores.
25. Hunting.
26. Indoor sports/games.
27. Keeping diaries.
28. Keeping pets.
29. Letter writing.
30. Listening to music.
31. Listening to radio/television programmes.
32. Mountaineering.
33. Movies/plays.
34. Outdoor sports.
35. Palmistry/Astrology
36. Photography.
37. Picnics.
38. Play with children.
39. Racing cars/horses/motor bykes.
40. Reading.
41. Recording daily/monthly expenditure.
42. Reviewing past memories.
43. Sewing/knitting.
44. Shopping.
45. Sightseeing.
46. Singing/playing on musical instrument.
47. Skating.
48. Sleeping/taking rest.
49. Social work.
50. Stargazing.
51. Studying for further education.
52. Swimming.
53. Teaching children.
54. Travelling.
55. Visiting religious places.

56. Visiting relatives/friends/parties.

So far you have expressed your feelings about different activities. One can imagine, however, that it may not be possible for you to pursue all the activities of your choice. Please mention below in order of importance the activity/activities you do practice whenever you find leisure. In case you indulge in any other activity/ activities which are not mentioned in the schedule, you may include them as well in your preference list now. 1,2,3,4,5 etc.

31A36 ATTITUDE SCALE FOR LOCATING PRO AND ANTI-MANAGEMENT INDUSTRIAL EMPLOYEES.

Author : K.D. Kapoor.
Availability : Agra Psychological Research Cell, Tiwari Kothi, Belanganj, Agra.
Languages : English and Hindi.
Uses : To locate pro and anti-management industrial employees.
Level : Industrial workers.
Main features : Opinions expressed in each statement has a Thurstonian scale value and each response to it has a fibertian weight. Number of items 20.
Reliability : Reliability was found to be .82 by the odd-even method.
Validity : The present scale was validated against supervising ratings about anti-management.
Time : Approximately twenty minutes - no exact time limit.

31A36 ATTITUDE SCALE FOR LOCATING PRO AND ANTI-MANAGEMENT INDUSTRIAL EMPLOYEES

1. From time to time the managers distribute bonus among the workers.
2. Our supervisors do not at all boss over the workers.
3. If workers go out for smoking management people take disciplinary action against them.
4. Managers are not paying any heed to the increasing resentment among the workers against the management.
5. Supervisors very easily understand all matters related to the work.
6. The management people raise the morale of the

workers by rewarding good workers with appreciation.

7. In political elections management people unduly pressurise workers to cast vote in favour of their own candidate.
8. To management pays the workers their salary regularly in time.
9. Due to the fear of the management workers arrive before time for their duty (work).
10. If workers talk with their colleagues during the working hours the managers take strict action against them.
11. The management acts on prejudice at the time of promotions.
12. The managers assign work to the workers according to their interests.
13. The present managers are lazy and shirk work.
14. In the sections most of the workers are satisfied with their supervisors.
15. Workers have feelings of belongingness for the factory due to the sympathetic behaviour of the managers.
16. The management people indulge in nepotism in appointing workers.
17. The management people do not pay any heed to even just complaints of the workers.
18. During the long working hours of the factory there is no source of recreation for the workers.
19. The management people do not fulfill promises given to the workers.
20. Managers take good care of the problems of the workers.

31A37 MEASUREMENT OF HAPPINESS

Authors : P. Sinha and A.K. Sharma.
Availability : The Author, HSS Department, IIT, Kanpur.
Language : English.
Uses : Studying the level and determinants of happiness.
Level : Industrial workers.
Main features : The scale ranges from least i.e., 1 to complete/most satisfied i.e., 7; number of items is 21.
Reliability : Test-retest reliability = 0.51.
Validity : Peer rating validation between 0.55 to 0.75.
Time : Thirty minutes.
Reference : Sinha, P and Sharma, A.K. Happy Life : Dimensions of satisfaction, Indian Journal of Social Work,

Vol. XL, No. 4 January 1980, pp. 369-79.

31A37 MEASUREMENT OF HAPPINESS

(The following items have to be checked on a 7-point scale).

1. How much are you satisfied with your food (with respect to your family).
2. To what extent the present national scene (political, economic and so on) satisfies you?
3. To what extent does your prestige and status satisfy you?
4. How much are you satisfied with cloths and dresses?
5. To what extent are entertainments present for your satisfaction?
6. How for are you satisfied with your children's welfare?
7. How much facility do you have regarding travel and transport?
8. How much are you satisfied with respect to your values and ideals?
9. How satisfactory your family relations are?
10. How much are you satisfied with your place of residence/housing facilities?
11. To what extent are you satisfied in fulfilling your aspirations to achieve better and higher (need for achievement)?
12. How much are you satisfied in terms of assistance from state or any agency of the state?
13. To what extent do your social relations satisfy you?
14. How satisfactory is your financial condition (money)?
15. Sometime back (i.e. before getting married) you must have had a desire for family with certain characteristics. To what extent are you satisfied with them now?
16. How satisfied are you with your service and job?
17. To what extent are you free from worries and thoughts which are mentally disturbing?
18. How far are you content with your land and property?
19. How far are you satisfied with the general health conditions of yourself and your family members?
20. It is a man's natural desire to be of some help utility to the society in which he lives. How far are you satisfied with this aspect in your connection?

21. To what extent are you satisfied with the education of and educational facilities available to you and your family?

31A38 JOB SATISFACTION INSTRUMENT

Authors : R.S. Mishra, M. Tiwari and D.N. Pandey.
Availability : Agra Psychological Research Cell, Tiwari Kothi, Agra.
Languages : English & Hindi.
Uses : To assess the efficiency of a worker in relation to job satisfaction.
Main features : The present test includes 11 areas as security, monetary remuneration service conditions, future advancement, recognition, of good work, social circle, working condition, nature of job, supervision, accommodation and leave facilities. The 11 areas have been split up into 41 statements. Each statement is scored on a 5-point scale.
Reliability : Split-half (N = 75) = .78 and Test-retest (N = 50) = .69.
Validity : Validity is established by correlating the test scores with scores of rating by the Head/Supervisors of the workers. Coefficient of correlation was found to be .68 (N = 50).
Time : Fifteen minutes.
Norms : On the basis of the total scores, three categories are made.

31A38 JOB SATISFACTION INSTRUMENT

(The following statements have to be checked on a 5-point scale of agreement).

1. The working hours are not fit for me.
2. I feel that I have got opportunities of promotion in my job.
3. My job is quite interesting and according to my liking.
4. The present working hours though hinder in my entertainment, yet like them.
5. The present employment though good yet I do not get leisure.
6. Being on present employment I can not display good results.
7. I feel that I should get more pay in my present

employment.

8. Usually I am dissatisfied as I am not getting residence.
9. My service is more secure than other service.
10. My employment gives me all facilities but no status.
11. My colleagues are not very helpful in my work.
12. The basis of my employment is less work and more pay.
13. People less educated than me get more pay.
14. I feel that this employment is not more secure than other services.
15. I get more pay than others whose work is as important than mine.
16. My colleagues are of helping nature.
17. I do not see many opportunities of progress in this job.
18. My working hours are such that I remain too busy.
19. I feel satisfied with my work by working more.
20. My work is not very attractive.
21. I always suffer with a feeling that I may not lose my job.
22. My service gives me opportunities of good residence.
23. Quick transfers give me great trouble.
24. I feel that I work with full responsibility.
25. Leave applications are not accepted though there are facilities for it.
26. I get recognition for my good works.
27. I get very little co-operation from the public in my work.
28. I feel that my services is not according to my taste.
29. I am not more able than other worker in this field.
30. I usually feel to change my work according to my wish.
31. I like to do some other work in this salary.
32. There are many problems in working in rural areas.
33. I remain very worried for not having facility of transport.
34. I am suppressed by my officer for not attaining the request target.
35. My colleagues are happy in my joys.
36. I feel that I am considered an indespensable person in this field.
37. I have given more importance in this institution that others.
38. I do not get co-operation when I need it.

39. I feel that my work is not interesting.
40. Sometimes transfer is not an obstacle in my work.
41. I feel that my work is comfortable.

31A39 TRADE UNION AFFILIATION QUESTIONNAIRE

Author : Babu Thomas.
Availability : The Author, Department of Psychology, M.S. University, Baroda.
Language : English.
Uses : To assess the affiliation of trade unions.
Main features : There are 30 questions covering five areas like Security, Economic, Ideology, Political and Leadership. It is a 5-point scale ranging from strongly agree to strongly disagree.
Reliability : Test-retest reliability of all the dimensions combined = .87.
Validity : The data obtained on the two groups i.e., active and non-active yields a biserial r = .614.

31A39 TRADE UNION AFFILIATION QUESTIONNAIRE

(The subjects have to rate each statement on a 5-point scale of agreement).

1. The true prosperity of the nation is based on true prosperity of the workers.
2. Union guarantees security to its members and other workers.
3. A strong and united trade union is a foundation for the security of workers.
4. The ideas of the workers have been nullified by the management to a great extent.
5. Becoming the member of the union, it should serve the social security to its members and other workers.
6. Workers education is the best method to stop the exploitation of the workers.
7. Socialistic pattern of economy is good for the workers.
8. Workers right to hold a job is more important than investor's right to have a profit.
9. Opportunity should be given to workers to participate in the field of administration and wage policy.
10. There is too much economic exploitation in our industry.

11. It is always good to have a representative of judges from the union in the panel of judges in the Labour Court.
12. Employers always think about their profits only and care little about the employee's welfare.
13. Free, stable and independent trade union movement can contribute to the progress of working class.
14. Trade union should take part in the upliftment of socio economic condition of our society.
15. All the union members have a common philosophy to safeguard the interest of the workers.
16. Worker's unity is important to keep their identity.
17. Trade union should always be above all social antagonism like caste, creed, religion and language.
18. Trade union activities will help to develop moral, intellectual, social and cultural development of the members and their family.
19. The growth of the trade union in our country has made the democracy stronger and stronger.
20. All the trade unions should merge together and form a labour party as it is in England.
21. The workers are not better off because the workers do not have much influence in the political circles as the employers and the business man have.
22. Most of the strikes are broken because the police and the military are controlled by the politicians who sympathise more with the management than the trade union.
23. it is always good to have a democratic set up within the union.
24. Workers have been exploited by the political parties very much.
25. Democratic method of selection is good while electing the union leaders.
26. Leaders should take much interest to keep away the trade union from political influence.
27. Good leaders can maintain good industrial relation and peace in the factory.
28. Democratic leaders are better than autocratic leaders.
29. The grievance of the workers should be solved by the leaders alone.
30. A full time trade union leader is essential in all the industries.

31A40 WORKER'S MOTIVATION SCALE

Author : Babu Thomas.

297 Organisational Behaviour

Availability : The Author, Department of Psychology, M.S. University, Baroda.
Language : English.
Uses : To assess the areas of motivation.
Level : Industrial workers.
Main features : The scale consists of 32 pairs of questions each of which has two self descriptive statement arranged in a force-choice format. The scale assesses eight areas of motivation as adequate earning, achievement, opportunity for promotion, suitable type of job, comfortable working condition, opportunity to learn a job, job security and competition. Each of the statement is paired with different areas.

31A40 WORKER'S MOTIVATION SCALE

(The subjects have to choose one of the two statements which is more acceptable).

1. (a) I like to do something which make me wealthy.
   (b) I like to have a comfortable working condition in my factory.
2. (a) I like to earn money by hard work.
   (b) I find real enjoyment in my work since it is very interesting.
3. (a) I like to have honest means of getting money.
   (b) I experiment new things in my job.
4. (a) I frequently aspire to be very rich.
   (b) I believe that joining a Union gives me a job security.
5. (a) My secret ambition in life is to get highly paid job.
   (b) I am of the opinion that promotion opportunities are very much necessary to discharge the duties effectively and efficiently.
6. (a) I believe that I am able to earn enough according to my basic needs.
   (b) I have a tendency to work a task till it is completed.
7. (a) Our present economic system should be reformed so that the profits made by the company can be used for the betterment of workers.
   (b) I believe that competition among the workers improve the general living standard of the workers.
8. (a) Adequate earning is positively related to social security.

(b) Very often, I feel that there is too much mental tension due to adverse environmental conditions which are adversely affecting work output.

9. (a) The work gives me opportunity to express myself completely.

(b) I would like to get a work according to my taste.

10. (a) I like to have good hygienic conditions in my factory.

(b) I am keeping keen observation around my surroundings especially when novel and unfamiliar things are going on.

11. (a) I like to work in a place where less accident-prone machines are installed.

(b) I am of the opinion that job security should be guaranteed by the Govt. in the present condition.

12. (a) I believe that better and comfortable working conditions will increase the efficiency of labour.

(b) I would like to change my present job, because promotion chances are very meagure here.

13. (a) I feel that workers should fight with tooth and nail to improve the working conditions in the factory.

(b) It is my nature to undertake difficult task.

14. (a) I will be very happy if the Govt. intervenes to improve the overall working conditions.

(b) I like to do things better than other people.

15. (a) I do my work irrespective of any reward or recognition.

(b) I always look out for a new method of techniques which enhance production.

16. (a) Very often, I feel that the present work facinates me very much.

(b) I ask question to my supervisors when I do not understand technical problems related to my work.

17. (a) I believe that job satisfaction is based on suitable type of work.

(b) I believe that production will increase if we get job security in an industry.

18. (a) Very often, I feel that I am part and parcel of this factory.

(b) I believe that better training and higher qualification will help us to get promotion immediately.

19. (a) I am enjoying good prestige in my job.
    (b) I feel my success depend upon my hard work.
20. (a) I get due recognition for my work here.
    (b) I believe that industries are not progressing very much because of lack of competition among the workers.
21. (a) I am not discharging my duties without fear or favour because I may lose my job.
    (b) When high posts are created in the industry, they should be filled by people from the same industry.
22. (a) I like to know and implement new things in my life.
    (b) I believe that job security is a must in industrial set up.
23. (a) I try to keep up-to-date information pertaining to my work.
    (b) I like to get frequent promotion because my contribution is extremely good here.
24. (a) In these days of rapid progress, all round us, we cannot afford to be slow to learn new ways of doing things.
    (b) I frequently aspire to be a man with wonderful achievement.
25. (a) I seek help from superiors in learning new things.
    (b) Qualitative and quantitative improvement is possible only through tough competition among the workers.
26. (a) I have general tendency to continue to my work till it is finished.
    (b) Competition has more advantages than disadvantages.
27. (a) Sometime I feel that I will lose my job without any reason.
    (b) I do believe that if all the workers promote more profits, more industries would spring up which will help us to get more promotion opportunities.
28. (a) I will continue my job as long as I do it sincerely.
    (b) My secret ambition in my life is to establish a glorious record to achievement.
29. (a) Friends and co-workers are the best security that a person can have.
    (b) Competition with ones own performance increases efficiency.
30. (a) For me prestige is of vital importance and so

I plead for promotion.
(b) It gives me a great satisfaction to undertak very difficult task.

31. (a) Promotion should be done on the basis o seniority.
(b) Society is changing from the traditional t the modern type. So competition is the onl way to keep us up-to-date.

32. (a) I like others to think of me as very in dustrious.
(b) I like the competitive workers because com petition is a good quality.

31A41 S-D EMPLOYEE INVENTORY (WHILE-COLLAR PROFESSIONALS)

Author : D.M. Pestonjee.
Availability : With the Author.
Languages : English and Hindi.
Uses : To evaluate job satisfaction of white-collar profes sionals.
Levels : Rank and file workers, supervisory professional and middle management.
Main features : Evaluates job satisfaction in four areas namely, job, management, social relations, and persona adjustment.
Time : Untimed.
Technical data reference : MBA Thesis of Shri Preoborot Ganguly, entitled "Effect of Professional Training o Job Satisfaction and Job Performance." Banaras Hind University, Varanasi, 1981.

31A41 S-D EMPLOYEE INVENTORY (WHITE-COLLAR PROFESSIONALS)

(The following items have to be checked as 'yes' or 'no').

1. Are you satisfied with your work environment?
2. Do your supervisors reward good employees?
3. Do you think that good people are respected Society?
4. Does the thought of future mishaps make yo worried?
5. Are most of your acquaintances reliable?
6. Do your supervisors sympathetically hear yo difficulties?
7. Does this job provide good opportunities f promotion?
8. Do you feel that due to poor health you could n get ahead in your job?

9. Do your neighbours help you when you are in some difficulties?
10. Do you sometimes think that you do not have those qualities which others have?
11. Do you have to work with some such people whom you don't like much?
12. Do you often feel that you are alone in this wide world?
13. Do you feel satisfied with the over-time rules of your organisation?
14. Do your supervisors think that most of the people are hardworking?
15. Do you sometimes feel that there is none in whom you can confide?
16. Do you often get such ideas at the time of going to bed which make sleep difficult?
17. Do your superiors behave well with the employees?
18. Do you think that the work you are doing is interesting?
19. Do you thing that promotions to employees are given impartially?
20. Do you get upset for a long time when criticised by somebody?
21. Do you feel satisfied with the condition of the place where you work?
22. Do you believe that in case of emergency (such as illness or marriage) the management would help you?
23. Do you hesitate in accepting the responsibilities of social functions?
24. Are you frequently worried due to illness of your family members?
25. Are most of your neighbours gentle and worth mixing with?
26. Do your superiors invite suggestions from you for the welfare of your organisation?
27. Do you thing that you have selected the right job for yourself?
28. Do you sometimes think that your family members do not care for you sufficiently?
29. Do you sometimes think of changing your house due to the neighbours?
30. Are there any such members in your family whose presence causes you annoyance?
31. Do you sometimes think that you can earn more in some other job?
32. Do you thing that bad people outnumber good people in the society?
33. Does your job allow you sufficient time for rest

and recreation?

34. Do your superiors respect your skills and abilities?
35. Do you think that most people exploit the weaknesses and shortcomings of others?
36. Do small things also hurt you?
37. Do your superiors harshly punish employees for simple mistakes?
38. Do your fellow workers help you?
39. Do you think that people get promotions due to personal pulls?
40. Do your relatives frequently bother or trouble you?
41. If you are offered elsewhere the same facilities which you are enjoying in your present job, would you like to change your job?
42. Are the employees dismissed from the job on simple and trivial matters?
43. Do you feel hesitation in talking to strangers?
44. Do you often have to leave tasks unfinished?
45. Do you think that your friends are sincere to you?
46. If you were an officer would you treat your subordinates the same way as your officers do ?
47. Do you think that you have to work too much here?
48. Had there been some unpleasant experience in your childhood, which you cannot forget?
49. Do you believe that most of the social customs and traditions are troublesome?
50. Do you pass your time pleasantly in your home?
51. Do you think that your work is hard and difficult?
52. Are most of the people in society selfish?
53. Is your profession respected by others?
54. Do your superiors believe that the employees welfare is their own welfare?
55. Do you think that people do not make lasting friendship with you?
56. Do the members of your family often do things against your wishes?
57. Do most of your colleagues work under duress and fear?
58. Would you advise any of your close relatives to do the job which you are doing?
59. Do you think that the employees are treated here the way they should be treated?
60. Do you sometimes get worried without any apparent cause?
61. Do you sometimes feel like giving up this job and taking up some other job?
62. Do your superiors praise efficient employees?

63. Do most of the people misunderstand you?
64. Do you earn enough money so that you don't have to seek help from others?
65. Are you troubled by feelings of caste and creed in society?
66. Are you often given such orders by your superiors which are difficult to carry out?
67. Do you thing that this work provides you opportunities to display your talent and skills?
68. Do you generally feel tired after doing ordinary jobs?
69. Do you think that your fellow workers generally avoid your company?
70. Do you think that things go wrong without any fault of yours?
71. Do you think that you need some more training on this job?
72. Do you feel hesitant in seeking advice from others?
73. Do you think that inspite of your lack of interest in this job, you work because you get good money?
74. Are you often asked to work at odd hours?
75. Do you easily make friends with new people?
76. Do the members of your family live cordially?
77. Do your superiors think that their employees are efficient?
78. Do you think that your present job is a respectable job for a person like you?
79. Do you think that you can place your problems before your superiors without any hesitation?
80. Do you get worried often thinking about the goal or purpose of life?

instruments with technical information **B**

31B1 ROLE PICS (0)

Author : Udai Pareek.

Availability : Navin Publication, P.B. No. 4105, Gulbai Takra, Ahmedabad.

Language : English.

Uses : To measure styles of coping with stress.

Level : University students Organisations and Training Institutions.

Main features : It is a semi-projective instrument and measures the 8 styles of coping with stress. It contained 24 pictures, in each picture two person are shown and one of them is making statement.

Reliability : Reliability is established, available in the manual.

Validity : Principal components analysis was used. Details are available in the manual.
Time : Fifteen to twenty minutes.
Norms : Available in the manual.
References :

(1) Sen, P.C. Personal and organisational correlates of role stress and coping strategies in some public sector banks. Unpublished Ph.D. Dissertation, University of Gujarat, 1982.

(2) Surti, K. Some psychological correlates of role stress and copying styles in working women. Unpublished Ph.D. Thesis, University of Gujarat, 1982.

31B2 ORS SCALE

Author : Udai Pareek.
Availability : Navin Publications, Post Box No. 4105, Gulbai Tekra, Ahmedabad.
Language : English.
Uses : To measure role stress in organisations.
Level : University students, organisations and Training Institutions.
Main features : There are 50 items for 10 organisational role stresses.
Reliability : Test-retest reliability calculated. Details are given in the manual.
Validity : Validity against correlation with the total score. All the coefficients are highly significant.
Time : Fifteen to twenty minutes.
Norms : Norms are available in the manual.
References :

(1) Sen, P.C. Personal and organisational correlates of role stress and coping strategies in some public sector banks. Unpublished Ph.D. Dissertation, University of Gujarat, 1982.

(2) Surti, K. Some psychological correlates of role stress and coping styles in working women. Unpublished Ph.D. Dissertation, University of Gujarat, 1982.

31B3 SUPERVISOR'S RATING SCALE

Author : M.C. Agarwal.
Availability : Author, National Institute for Training in Industrial Engineering, P.O. NITIE, Vihar Lake Road, Bombay.
Language : English.
Uses : To determine effectiveness of supervisors.

Level : Middle level supervisors.
Main features : Likert method used with 5 points scale (number of items 22).
Reliability : Correlational method of item analysis used. All items found significant at 1% level.
Validity : As mentioned above.
Time : Twenty to twenty-five minutes.
Norms : No.
Reference : Agrawal, M.C. "Effective and less-effective first-line supervisors" - Indian Journal of Social Work, Vol. XXI, No. 3, October, 1980.

31B4 SUPERVISORS' ORIENTATION SCHEDULE

Author : A.P. Singh.
Availability : Banaras Psychological Corporation, Rajputana Uttar, Maunath Bhanjan, Azamgarh.
Languages : English & Hindi.
Uses : To determine the types of supervisory behaviour of first level supervisors in industries.
Level : First-level supervisors.
Main features : The schedule comprises of 60 items which cover two dimension - employee-oriented and production-oriented. The items are positively and negatively worded with two response alternatives, i.e., °yes' or °no'.
Reliability : The split-half reliability was found to be .84 for production-oriented and .86 for employee-oriented dimensions.
Validity : The index of homogeneity and internal validity of the items were tested by computing point biserial correlation.
Time : No time limit.
Norms : Available with the author.
References :

(1) Pestonjee, D.M. & Singh, A.P. Supervisory behaviour and job satisfaction. Indian Journal of Industrial Relations, 1974, 9(3), 407-416.
(2) Pestonjee, D.M. & Singh, A.P. Supervisory Orientation and Employee's Morale. Jr. Occupational Psychology, 1977, 50(2), 85-91.
(3) Singh, A.P. & Srivastava, G.P. Performance in relation to different styles of supervision. Decision, 1979, 6(3), 271-275.
(4) Singh, A.P. & Srivastava, G.P. Effect of ego-strength on the relationship of different styles of supervision with morale and performance. Psychological studies, 1980, 25(2), 98-104.

31B5 ASPIRATION INVENTORY FOR INDUSTRIAL WORKERS

Authors : S.K. Sarkar & A.K. Basu.
Uses : To assess the aspiration level of industrial workers.
Reliability : Reliability coefficient = .877.
Validity : Content validity was established.
Reference : Sarkar, S.K. & Basu, A.K. Construction and standardisation of an aspiration scale for industrial workers : Proceeds 69th session of Indian Science Congress, Part III, Mysore, 1982.

31B6 U-SCALE OR UNION SCALE

Authors : D.M. Pestonjee, A.P. Singh & S.P. Singh.
Availability : M/s Banaras Psychological Corporation, Rajputan Uttar, Maunath Bhanjan, Azamgarh, UP.
Languages : English & Hindi.
Uses : To ascertain the employees' attitude towards Union. They can be classified into two categories, i.e., pro-union and anti-union.
Level : Workers and supervisors.
Main features : U-Scale has fourty-six items with four response alternatives, namely, never, rarely, often, and always. The scale assesses attitude towards union in six areas, namely grievance settlement, safeguarding the rights of workers, quality of working life, organisational effectiveness, care and concern for health, and compensation.
Reliability : The reliability of scale was computed by the Cronbach's alpha coefficient technique and its found to be +.80
Validity : The index of homogeneity and internal validity of the scale were tested by computing the point biserial correlation (rpb).
Time : No time limit.
Norms : Not available.
References :

(1) Pestonjee, D.M., Singh, A.P. and Singh, S.P. Attitude towards union as related to morale and job involvement. International Review of Applied Psychology, 1981, 30, 209-216.

(2) Pestonjee, D.M., Singh, A.P. and Singh, S.P. Productivity and attitude towards union, National Labour Institute Bulletin, 1980, 3-4.

(3) Srivastava, N.L. Effect of supervisor's attitude towards union on workers' morale and job involvement. Master's dissertation, Department of Psychology, Banaras Hindu University, Varanasi.

31B7 MEASUREMENT OF JOB AND WORK INVOLVEMENT

Authors : R.N. Kanungo and Sasi Misra.
Availability : The Second Author, Indian Institute of Management, Ahmedabad.
Reliability : Internal consistency coefficient (Cronbach alpha) worked out.
Validity : Validity Established by factor analysis.
References :

(1) Kanungo, R.N. Measurement of job and work involvement. Journal of Applied Psychology, 1982, 67, 341-349.

(2) Misra, S.; Kanungo, R.N.; Rosenstiel Lutz Von; & Stuhler, E.A. The Motivational Formulation of job and work involvement : A cross national study. Unpublished manuscript, Indian Institute of Management, Ahmedabad, 1983.

citations C

31C1 AN INVENTORY TO MEASURE QUALITY OF WORKING LIFE

Authors : Prakash Sinha & O.B. Sayeed.
Reference : Measuring quality of working life : Development of an inventory, Indian Journal of Social Work, 1980, XLI(3), 219-226.

31C2 WORK ALIENATION SCALE

Author : U.N. Agarwala.
Availability : Department of Psychology, University of Allahabad, Allahabad.

31C3 WORK COMMITMENT SCALE

Authors : P.K. Shrivastava & A.M. Dholke.
Availability : Ahmedabad Textile Industries Research Association, Ahmedabad.

31C4 ORGANISATIONAL IDENTIFICATION SCALE

Authors : P.K. Shrivastava & A.M. Dholke.
Availability : Ahmedabad Textile Industries Research Association, Ahmedabad.

31C5 HUMAN RELATIONS IN INDUSTRY

Author : Baldev R. Sharma.
Availability : Xavier Labour Relations Institute, Jamshedpur.
Language : English.

adaptations D

31D1 STRESS QUESTIONNAIRE

Author : O.N. Ganguly.
Availability : Industrial Psychology Division, Central Labour Institute, Sion, Bombay.
Language : English.
Uses : To measure job stress.
Level : Educated-English knowing industrial population.
Main features : Forty-seven items from 3 scale.
Reliability : Not known.
Validity : Not known.
Time : Fifteen to twenty minutes.
Norms : Available with author.

31D2 JOB INVOLVEMENT SCALE

Authors : Reeta Kapoor & Ashok Pratap Singh.
Availability : M/s Banaras Psychological Corporation, Rajputan Uttar, Maunath Bhanjan, Azamgarh, UP.
Language : Hindi.
Uses : It can be used to assess the level of job involvement of workers and immediate first-level supervisors.
Level : Workers and supervisors.
Main features : It is an Indian adaptation of Lodahl and Kejner's job involvement scale. The scale comprises of twenty items which cover six areas namely, work motivation, organisational identification, fulfillment of organisational demands, commitment for work, internalisation of organisational goals and need for achievement. The items are positively and negatively worded with four response alternatives, namely strongly agree, agree, disagree, and strongly disagree.
Reliability : The reliability of the scale was computed by the alpha coefficient technique which was found to be +.82. The split-half reliability coefficient by odd-even method, on a sample of 200 employees, was found to be .73.
Validity : The index of homogeneity and internal validity of

the items were tested by computing the point-biserial coefficient of correlation (rpb). The scores of Lodahl and Kejner's job involvement scale was used as one of the validation criteria for this job involvement scale. The coefficient of correlation between the scores on the two scales was found to be .58 (N = 100).

Time : No time limit.

Norms : Not available.

References :

(1) Pestonjee, D.M., Singh, A.P. & Singh, Y.K. Alienation as a moderator variable of job performance - job involvement relationship. Communicated for publication to Group and Organisational Study, 1981.

(2) Pestonjee, D.M. & Singh, Y.K. Productivity in relation to anxiety and job involvement. Presented at the 20th International Association of Applied Psychology, 1982.

(3) Singh, Y.K. Alienation, anxiety and job involvement as factors related to the productivity of blue-collar industrial workers. Doctoral dissertation, Banaras Hindu University, Varanasi, 1981.

(4) Singh, S.B. Perceived occupational stress as a function of ego-strength and job involvement of management personnel. Unpublished Master's dissertation, Banaras Hindu University, Varanasi.

2. Health Organisations

complete instruments A

32A1 HOSPITAL CLIMATE QUESTIONNAIRE

Author : C.N. Daftuar.

Availability : Department of Psychology, M.S. University, Baroda.

Language : English.

Level : Literate English knowing employees.

Main features : The scale is based on managerial behaviour questionnaire. It consists of 33 items and covers 8 dimensions of organisational climate. It is rated on a 5-point scale.

Reliability & Validity : Cronbach's alpha = .63.

32A1 HOSPITAL CLIMATE QUESTIONNAIRE

(The following items have to be checked on a 5-point scale).

1. In this hospital a special care is taken that work gets top priority.
2. In this hospital it is believed that most of the interpersonal troubles start because people try to be over friendly and informal on the job.
3. People here, generally believe that it is the human warmth and feelings for each other that makes an organisation prosper.
4. In this hospital it is believed that subordinates keep a sense of responsibility under the guidance and care of a good superior.
5. Officers in the hospital generally believe that the subordinates will listen to them only when they have enough power and prestige.
6. Here subordinates are helped and cared by their superiors, as much as they need.
7. In this hospital, subordinates who are efficient and hard working are appreciated.
8. The general impression is that even the indisciplined worked can improve by friendly support and persuasion.
9. Human nature is such that the more you share ideas, the more worth living life becomes.
10. In this hospital, whenever there is a problem related to the job people try to look calm and cheerful.
11. Officers here always keep track of the progress of the work.
12. Superiors in this hospital help their subordinates in their career planning.
13. In this hospital it is believed that persons at the top are in the best position to make major decisions.
14. Here, people maintain fair but impersonal relationship in the group.
15. In this hospital people are friend type, caring and receptive.
16. People in authority have to see to it that their subordinates work to their capacity.
17. In this hospital, people appreciate those subordinates who are loyal and grateful.
18. Superiors in this hospital always seek their subordinates opinion and abide by them.
19. In this hospital, the subordinates who are quite free in dealing with their superiors are appreciated.
20. In this hospital, subordinates are helped to grow

up and assume greater responsibility.

21. In this hospital, we always follow standard rules and regulations in organisational matters.
22. In this hospital, all necessary information are provided to subordinates and they are allowed to find out their solution jointly.
23. We believe that human nature is such that there will always be conflict and friction in any organisation.
24. In this hospital, whenever one faces a problem on the job, he can gather the relevant person and try to work out through them an agreed solution.
25. People here are allowed to do almost as they please.
26. The employees are constantly being checked for rule violations.
27. There is no rules manual.
28. There is a complete written discription for your jobs.
29. We are to follow strict operating procedures at all times.

32A2 JOB SATISFACTION MEASURING SCALE

Authors : M.B. Paliwal and Nirmal Sawhney.
Availability : Population Centre, Indira Nagar, Lucknow.
Language : English.
Level : Family welfare personnel.
Main features : The scale consists of 14 items rated on a 5-point scale. The items include the factors causing satisfaction-dissatisfaction among the family welfare personnel.
Reliability : Split-half reliability (S.B. Formula) = .82.
Validity : Content and face validity established.
Reference : Sawhney, Nirmal; Paliwal, M.B. & Saxena, P.K. A study on programme perception, motivation and morale of family welfare programme workers, PC/RT/31.

32A2 SCALE TO MEASURE THE JOB SATISFACTION AMONGST FAMILY WELFARE WORKER

1. Do you feel secure in the present job?

(a) Yes, fully secure.
(b) Yes, secure till complete target achieved.
(c) Yes, secure till fixed percentage of target achieved.
(d) Always worried because of temporary nature of the

job.
(e) Not secured at all.

2. Is there any departmental promotion avenue for you?

(a) Yes, after a specified period of service.
(b) Yes, after under-gone specified training.
(c) Yes, there are chances of promotion.
(d) No possibility of promotion at all.
(e) Not at all.

3. Are you confident to get promotion if opportunity arises?

(a) Yes, fully confident.
(b) Yes, if authorities are satisfied.
(c) Yes, after getting training and requisite experience.
(d) No hope for promotion.
(e) No chance.

4. Have you been assigned the job as per requirements of the post?

(a) Yes, assigned duties are fully connected with my job.
(b) Yes, most of the job functions are connected with job.
(c) Assigned job functions are not clearly defined.
(d) Job functions are not for which I am appointed.
(e) Not at all.

5. You feel that your job does carry value in this department?

(a) Yes, my work is very valuable.
(b) Yes, authorities give weightage to my work.
(c) Yes, I have been given facilities to perform the assigned jobs.
(d) Officers are not prepared to listen to my suggestions.
(e) Don't think so.

6. Is the present job interesting?

(a) Job in hand is highly interesting.
(b) This job is alright.
(c) It is not interesting because of the nature of the

job.
(d) I have accepted this job by force of circumstances.
(e) Not interesting.

7. Do you get support in the form of supervision and guidance from your officers in your work?

(a) Yes, get excellent support.
(b) Yes, adequate support.
(c) Yes, get the work checked by the higher authorities.
(d) Do not get any support.
(e) Not at all .

8. Do you get opportunity of advanced training connected with your specialisation?

(a) Yes, get ample opportunity.
(b) Yes, get some opportunity.
(c) Yes, get opportunity once.
(d) Did not get any opportunity.
(e) Not hope at all.

9. Do you get support from your colleagues in performing your duties?

(a) Receive sufficient support.
(b) Receive some support.
(c) Support not needed.
(d) Support not given.
(e) Not at all.

10. If you are offered the same wage and benefits in some other organisation would you like to shift to that job?

(a) Highly satisfied and not interested in shifting from this job.
(b) Not interested to shift the job on same status.
(c) Family circumstances do not permit to shift.
(d) May shift to other job irrespective of post & pay.
(e) Ready to shift to other job.

11. Do you think that the salary matches with the assigned job?

(a) Salary is higher than the assigned work.
(b) Salary matches with assigned work.
(c) Salary is lower than the job requirements.

(d) Salary is low compared to job functions.
(e) Salary is very inadequate considering the job functions.

12. Are you satisfied with the procedures of promotion adopted in this department?

(a) Yes, fully satisfied.
(b) Yes, satisfied.
(c) No, sometimes favouritism prevails because of out-agency involvement.
(d) No, most of time extreme favouritism.
(e) No, comments.

13. Do you feel depressed or fatigued after whole day's activities?

(a) No, enjoy my job very much.
(b) No, enjoy this job.
(c) No, consider my job as duty.
(d) Yes, sometimes feel fatigued.
(e) Yes, always feel fatigued.

14. Do you get support from the masses of the area in which you serve?

(a) Receive support from every community in the area I work.
(b) Receive support from majority of population.
(c) Receive support from some sections only.
(d) Majority do not give support.
(e) Nobody gives support.

32A3 S-D EMPLOYEE INVENTORY (HEALTH PROFESSIONALS)

Author : D.M. Pestonjee.
Availability : With the Author.
Languages : English and Hindi.
Uses : To evalusate job satisfaction of Doctors and other health professionals.
Levels : Doctors and para-medical staff.
Main features : Evaluates job satisfaction in four areas, namely, job, management, social relations, and personal adjustment.
Time : Unitimed.
Technical data reference : Research Report entitled "Factors Affecting Motivations of Health Professionals". IIMA Report.

32A3 S-D EMPLOYEE INVENTORY (HEALTH PROFESSIONALS)

(The following items have to be checked as °yes' or °no').

1. Do you work with good materials, equipments and drugs?
2. Are you rewarded for good work?
3. Do you think that good people are respected in society?
4. Does the thought of future mishaps make you worried?
5. Are most of your acquaintances reliable?
6. Do your superiors sympathetically listen to your difficulties?
7. Does this job provide good opportunities for promotion?
8. Do you feel that due to poor health you could not get ahead in your job?
9. Do your neighbours help you when you are in some difficulties?
10. Do you sometimes think that you do not have those qualities which others have?
11. Do you have to work with some such people whom you don't like much?
12. Do you often feel that you are alone in this wide world?
13. Do you feel satisfied with the various service rules of your organisation?
14. Do your superiors think that most of you are hardworking?
15. Do you sometimes feel that there is none in whom you can confide?
16. Do you often get such ideas at the time of going to bed which keep you awake?
17. Do your superiors behave well with their subordinates?
18. Do you think that the work you are doing is interesting?
19. Do you think that promotions are given impartially?
20. Do you get upset for a long time when criticised by somebody?
21. Do you feel satisfied with the condition of the place where you work?
22. Do you believe that in case of emergency (such as illness or marriage) your organisation would help you?
23. Do you hesitate in accepting the responsibilities of social functions?

24. Are you frequently worried due to illness of your family members?
25. Are most of your neighbours gentle and worth mixing with?
26. Do your superiors invite suggestions from you for the welfare of your organisation?
27. Do you think that you have selected the right job for yourself?
28. Do you sometimes think that your family members do not care for you sufficiently?
29. Do you sometimes think of changing your house due to the neighbours?
30. Are there any such members in your family whose presence cauces you annoyance?
31. Do you sometimes think that you can earn more in some other job?
32. Do you think that bad people outnumber good people in the society?
33. Does your job allow you sufficient time for rest and recreation?
34. Do your superiors respect your skills and abilities?
35. Do you think that most people exploit the weaknesses and shortcomings of others?
36. Do small things also hurt you?
37. Do your superiors harshly punish people for simple mistakes?
38. Do your colleagues help you?
39. Do you think that people get promotions due to personal pulls?
40. Do your relatives frequently bother or trouble you?
41. If you are offered elsewhere the same facilities which you are enjoying in your present job, would you like to change your job?
42. Are people dismissed from the job on simple and trivial matters?
43. Do you feel hesitation in talking to strangers?
44. Do you often have to leave tasks unfinished?
45. Do you think that your friends are sincere to you?
46. Would you like to treat your subordinates the same way as your superiors?
47. Do you think that you have to work too much here?
48. Has there been some unpleasant experience in your childhood which you can not forget?
49. Do you believe that most of the social customs and traditions are troublesome?
50. Do you pass your time pleasantly in your home?
51. Do you think that your work is hard and difficult?

52. Do you believe that most of the people in society are selfish.
53. Is your profession respected by others?
54. Do your superiors care enough for the welfare of their subordinates?
55. Do you think that people do not make lasting friendships with you?
56. Do the members of your family often do things against your wishes?
57. Do most of your colleagues work under duress and fear?
58. Would you advise any of your close relatives to do the job which you are doing?
59. Do you think that the people are treated here the way they should be treated?
60. Do you sometimes get worried without any apparent cause?
61. Do you sometimes feel like giving up from this job and taking up some other job?
62. Do your superiors praise good workers?
63. Do most of the people misunderstand you?
64. Do you earn enough money so that you do not have to seek help from others?
65. Are you troubled by feelings of caste and creed in society?
66. Are you often given such orders by your superiors which are difficult to carry out?
67. Do you think that this work provides you opportunities to display your talent and skills?
68. Do you generally feel tired after doing ordinary jobs?
69. Do you think that your colleagues generally avoid your company?
70. Do you think that things go wrong without any fault of yours?
71. Do you think that you need some more training on this job?
72. Do you feel hesitant in seeking advice from others?
73. Do you think that in spite of your lack of interest in this job you work because you get good money?
74. Are you often asked to work at odd hours?
75. Do you easily make friends with new people?
76. Do the members of your family live cordially?
77. Do your superiors think that their subordinates are efficient?
78. Do you think that your present job is a respectable job for a person like you?
79. Do you think that you can place your problems

before your superiors without any hesitation?

80. Do you get worried often thinking about the goal or purpose of life?

PART FOUR

SOCIAL PHENOMENA

Social Phenomena

This part of the Handbook reports instruments dealing with several social dimensions. The instruments are reported under six sections :

i. Values
ii. Stratification
iii. Social distance and group attitudes
iv. Modernisation and social change
v. Religion and morality, and
vi. Other social attitudes.

The classification is based on the consideration of a number of instruments forming into a distinct category rather than on any theoretical basis. For example, the instruments reported under Social Distance and group attitudes, modernisation and social change, religion and morality and other social attitudes are by and large, the instruments which deal with social attitudes. The section of modernisation and social change includes a few specific dimensions like Family Planning, Agricultural Innovations, Social and Cultural Modernisation Scales. Although sufficient number of these instruments are available and may be grouped separately, but these have been grouped under modernisation and social change to avoid any specific-issue-based classification. The instruments on other social attitudes include several dimensions of social issues like attitudes towards Governmental family planning, mentally retarded, alienation, political awareness, socio-political attitudes, national integration, parent-child relation and social supports etc. In a way most of the miscellaneous categories of instruments dealing with social phenomena and social issues have been included in this section.

In all, 69 instruments have been reported in this part

of the Handbook. Twenty-one instruments have been originally reproduced here. Information has been provided for other 28 instruments. Sixteen are citations and 4 are adaptations. The detailed break-up of the instruments is given in Table 4.

TABLE 4

Details of the instruments related to social phenomena

Area	Originals Reproduced	Information Provided	Citations	Adaptations	Total
Values	-	4	2	1	7
Stratification	2	1	2	-	5
Social Distance & Group Attitudes	4	2	1	-	7
Modernisation & Social Change	6	5	6	1	18
Religion & Morality	-	4	-	-	4
Other Social Attitudes	9	12	5	2	28
Total	21	28	16	4	69

Values :

The instruments in this section cover value dimensions like achievement values, values dominating life style etc. Only seven instruments have been reported in this section. No original scale is available. Out of seven, one scale measures values dominating the life style of a person. The scale is available in Hindi and is useful for 17 to 22+ adults. The scale has reported significantly high reliabilities like test-retest, split-half and rational equivalence. Validity is also ensured against correlation with other standardised tests. Norms are also provided.

The other one is a brief scale of Values available in Hindi assessing the personal values of individuals. This scale includes paired-comparison type items and reports fairly high reliability and validity. There is an other Value Dimension Indicator which determines the value types. The other one is an Achievement Value Index. Standardization data for these two instruments are not available. Two are citations and one instrument is adaptation of a foreign instrument.

Instruments in this section are very few and do not cover any specific sector. Some specific scales are needed for specific professions like teaching, management, engineering, social work, medicines etc., as these professions require some specific value-dimensions.

Stratification :

The instruments dealing with the socio-economic status are reported in this section. There are only 5 instruments available of which 2 are original and reproduced here in full. Information about other one is reported and two are cited. There instruments are generally to be administered on adult population for information about the parental income, material possessions, education etc. of the family members.

The first one to be reproduced here is a Socio-Economic Status Scale by R.A. Singh and S.K. Saxena. This scale reports fairly high reliability and validity data. The scale is available for urban and rural people separately. Norms are also provided for the two scales. The other one is an Individual and Family Status Measure by R.P. Gupta meant for adolescents and adults. Standardization data are available in the manual. It has also two forms : A-short and B-complete.

Information about one Social Class Evaluation Scale is provided which is available for urban populations. It has also reported fairly high reliability and validity. Two socio-economic scales are cited add details are not available. Besides these socio-economic status scales some more scales for castes, social classes etc. are also needed in this area of stratification.

Social Distance and Group Attitudes :

This section includes information about the instruments dealing with social distance, discrimination and sociometric choices. In all seven instruments have been included in this section of which 4 have been reproduced here. Details have been provided for the other two. One is cited here. Out of seven, three instruments are dealing with social distance, one is a discrimination scale, one is contact scale and the other one is a sociometric test.

Several instruments are reproduced here. One is a Social Distance Scale by Kamal Dwivedi based on Bogardus S-D Scale and reports good reliability and validity data. There are a set of instruments by P.K. Muttagi. One is a Social Distance Scale available for linguistic and religious groups separately. The other one is a Discrimination Scale measuring perceptual or cognitive component of the attitude towards discrimination. The third one is a Contact Scale measuring contact of respondents with five communities - Buddhist, Christian, Hindu, Muslim and Parsee. These instruments deal with important aspects of social phenomena. Standardization data are not provided.

The information about other two instruments is provided which deal with Social Distance and Sociometric Choices. Standardization data is available for these two instruments.

Instruments dealing with other social problems like communal and racial conflict etc., are very much lacking. We used to have more instruments on these themes as social scientists in general believe that psychologists have not contributed their might to larger social and national issues.

Modernisation and Social Change :

There are in all 18 instruments listed under this title of which six have been originally reproduced here. Information is provided for other five instruments. One is an adaptation and six have been cited. These instruments deal with several indicators of modernization and social change, like attitude towards social and cultural modernisation, family planning, awareness of congruence, differential perceptions of adopters and non-adopters, level of farm mechanisation, and womens' social freedom etc.

Among the instruments reproduced here, two are scales measuring attitude towards modernization. These instruments are meant for literate adolescents and adults but can also be used with illiterate populations (the statements have to be read). The first one is by Mamta Agrawal and measures attitudes of Muslims and Hindus towards various aspects of social and cultural modernization in India. This scale is based on Thurstone's method of "Equal Appearing Intervals". Fairly high reliability values have been reported. Validity is established by judge's rating. Another one by Singh and others measures attitude of modernity of college students and adults. Reliability and validity are fairly high.

There is a Likert's type scale by Dhillan and others which measures attitude towards Family Planning. This scale also seems to be well standardized. Two instruments by Ingle and Deshpande have been reproduced here which deal with the study of congruence as a factor influencing adoption of agricultural innovations. The other one by Murthy and others is meant for farmers and measures the differential perception of adopters and non-adopters. Fairly satisfactory reliability and validity data for these instruments are reported.

Information is provided for other five instruments of which one is available in Gujarati and measures attitude towards modernization. The other one is a Family Planning Attitude Inventory. There is one scale meant for farmers and measures level of farm mechanisation. The other one measures the desire for social freedom among women. The other scale measures the modernity attitude. All these instruments have reported fairly high reliability and validity data.

On the whole, the instruments reported in this section deal with important aspects of social issues and sufficient attention has been paid to the standardization of these instruments.

Religion and Morality :

There are only four instruments reported under this section. No original instrument is available which may be reproduced here.

There are two instruments which measure religious attitudes. One is Likert type and the other one is a Thurstone type of scale. Reliability and validity have been reported for the two instruments which are fairly high. There is one Moral Judgement Test meant for children of 6-11 years and measures the ability to make moral judgement. The test is developed on the model of a general intelligence test. Fairly high split-half reliability is reported. Validity is established by correlating with the moral knowledge scores. Norms are also available with the authors. The other one is a Moral Development Test Battery and reports high reliability and validity. This is one area where more instruments on various other aspects are very much needed.

Other Social Attitudes :

In this section, 28 instruments have been included. The instruments relate to social phenomena other than those reported earlier. Out of 28 instruments, 9 have been reproduced here. Information is given for 12 and other two are adaptations. Five instruments have been cited and full information is not available. The areas covered by these instruments include general attitude of people, attitude towards governmental family planning programme, alienation, relationships, political attitudes and awareness, life satisfaction, national integration and social supports etc. As the variety of dimensions indicates, instruments in social research are concerned with a variety of areas relevant to the emerging needs of the society.

There is a scale by Dhillon available in Punjabi and English which measures attitude towards Governmental Family Planning Programme. It is a Likert type scale reporting fairly high reliability and validity. The other instruments reproduced here measure sibling-relationship, alienation, political efficacy, socio-political attitudes, and political awareness. Alienation scale by Kureshi and Dutt is available in English, Hindi, Urdu and Gujarati languages and is well used instrument. Reliability and validity have been reported for all these instruments.

Among the other instruments reported here, one is a TAT type projective test which measures feelings of political efficacy among adult populations. Another scale measures attitude towards the mentally retarded. There is one Likert-type National Integration Scale available in Urdu and Hindi Languages. Further researches are in progress on this scale. Two instruments are related to parent-child relations. The other instruments reported here measure life satisfaction and social supports and report fairly high standardization data.

Two instruments are adaptations. One is a Personal Reaction Inventory which is Hindi adaptation of the Marlowe-Crowne Social Desirability Scale. Satisfactory reliability and validity for the Hindi adaptation is reported. The other one is the Hindi adaptation of Parental Attitude Research Inventory of Schaefer and Bell. Reliability and validity has been established and norms are also prepared for this instrument.

There are several other social phenomena on which scales and instruments need to be developed. These are the areas of special significance like group conflicts, work alienation, social commitment, poverty, power and social deprivation.

SOCIAL PHENOMENA

1. Values

instruments with technical information B

41B1 VALUES SCALE

Authors : Q.G. Alam & Ramji Srivastava.
Availability : M/s Prasad Trading Corporation, J-1/53, Daranagar, Varanasi.
Language : Hindi.
Uses : To measure values dominating the life style of a person.
Level : 17 + to 22 + (adults).
Main features : The scale consists of 60 positively and negatively worded items covering 6 areas viz. theoretical, economic, aesthetic, social, political and religious. A 5-point Likert type scaling technique is used.
Reliability : The test-retest, split-half and rational equivalence values vary between .65 to .78, .64 to .78 and .65 to .78 respectively for the 6 areas.
Validity : The scale is validated against Ojha's test and Kulshrestha's test. The values were found to be above .80 for the 6 areas on both the tests.
Time : About forty minutes, but there is no time limit.
Norms : Based on °T' scores, available with Authors/Publishers.

41B2 BRIEF SCALE OF VALUES (BSV)

Author : Yashvir Singh.
Availability : Agra Psychological Research Cell, Agra.
Language : Hindi.
Uses : To assess the personal values of individuals.
Main features : The scale includes 16 paired comparision type items. The items consist of short statements which evoke responses regarding six values-aesthetic, political, economic, theoretical, social and religious.
Reliability : Test-retest reliability was calculated on urban and rural sample and was found to be .97 and .98 respectively.
Validity : Validity was determined against Ojha's Hindi version of Allport Vernon Lindzey's study of values and the

validity indices range from .12 to .70 for the six values.
Time : Five to ten minutes.
Norms : Sten-score norms available.
Reference : Singh, Y.V. A study of personal value patterns of 'a' and 'r' groups of family planning programme. Unpublished doctoral dissertation, Agra University, Agra, 1976.

41B3 VALUE DIMENSION INDICATOR

Author : R.P. Gupta.
Availability : Psychological Centre, 569 Ch/26K-2, Prem Nagar, Alambagh, Lucknow.
Language : Hindi.
Uses : To measure values, their categories strength and polarization pattern etc.
Level : Hindi knowing adolescents and adults.
Main features : Twenty main items requiring choice of five responses each from the given alternatives.
Reliability : Given in the manual (+.86).
Validity : given in the manual (+.563).
Time : About 45 minutes, though there is no prescribed time limit.
Reference : Suman Srivastava : Unpublished M.A. Dissertation, Department of Education, Lucknow University, Lucknow, 1981.

41B4 P.G.I. ACHIEVEMENT VALUE INDEX

Authors : D.K. Menon, N.N. Wig & S.K. Verma.
Availability : Department of Psychiatry, P.G.I. Medical Education and Research, Chandigarh.
Language : Hindi.
Main features : The scale consists of 8 statements. The statements are phrased in forms of opinion seeking. Three alternatives are given for each statement.

citations C

41C1 VALUE TEST
Author : M.V. Gopalaswamy
Availability : Department of Psychology, University of Mysore, Mysore.

41C2 AN INVENTORY OF VOCATIONAL VALUES

Author : M.S. Prasad.
Availability : Author, Department of Psychology, Patna University, Patna.

adaptations D

41D1 HINDI ADAPTATION OF ALLPORT-VERNON-LINDZEY STUDY OF VALUES

Author : Madhuri Verma.
Availability : Author, Department of Psychology, Patna University, Patna.
Language : Hindi.
Uses : To measure the relative prominence of six dominant interests, motives or evaluative attitudes in personality, theoretical, economic, aesthetic, social, political and religious.
Main features : The test contains 45 questions and is divided into two parts. There are 30 items in part one and 15 items in part two.
Reliability : Split-half reliability (Spearman Brown formula) for different values ranges from .84 to .95. Mean reliability coefficient (Fisher's Z transformation) = .90. Test-retest reliability = .89.
Validity : Validity established.
Time : Thirty to forty minutes (No time limit).
Norms : Mean & S.D. norms prepared.

2. Stratification

complete instruments A

42A1 SOCIO-ECONOMIC STATUS SCALE (SES)

Authors : R.A. Singh & S.K. Saxena.
Availability : Agra Psychological Research Cell, Agra.
Languages : Hindi & English.
Uses : To evaluate the socio-economic status of students.
Level : Students of III standard and onward.
Main features : There are separate scales for urban and rural people. The urban scale consists of 18 items while there are 21 items in rural scale. The scales reflect social, economical, educational, caste and cultural aspect etc. of the students.
Reliability : The split-half and test-retest reliability

has been established for rural and urban scales as given below :

	Test-retest	Split-half	Coefficient
SES (Rural) N = 100	.83	.85	.87
SES (Urban) N = 100	.89	.91	.93

Validity : Validity is established by correlating the scores of these scales with that of Kulshreshtha's SES scale (N = 50). The coefficient of validity (N = 50) was found to be .78 and .73 for urban and rural scales respectively.

Time : No time limit but it takes about 35 minutes.

Norms : T-score norms are available for both the urban and rural scale.

42A1 SOCIO-ECONOMIC STATUS SCALE

1. What is the education of your family members?
   (a) University's high degree e.g., Ph.D., D.Litt. D.Sc., M.S., M.D. or similar professional degree.
   (b) Post graduate education (M.A., M.Sc, M.Com, M.Ed.).
   (c) Graduate level education (B.A., B.Sc., B.Com., B.Ed., L.L.B. etc.) or any other equivalent degree after Intermediate.
   (d) Higher Secondary, Intermediate, any other professional certificate or any diploma after High School.
   (e) Middle School (Class VIII passed) or equivalent training certificate.
   (f) Primary education (class V passed).
   (g) Literate (did not pass classes but know little reading and writing).
   (h) Illiterate.

2. What is the occupation of your family members (father/guardian, mother, eldest sister)?
   (a) High Administrative, Managerial or professional work, such profession in which high education is required, e.g., High Govt. officer, Proprietor of professional institutions, Advocate, University Professor, Engineer etc.
   (b) Middle class professional, Managerial or Technical Work, e.g., Middle class Advocate, Shop-keeper, College lecturer.
   (c) Ordinary professional, such profession which requires education upto B.A. e.g., teacher of high

school classes, technician.
(d) Skilled profession, e.g., Electrician, Carpenter etc.
(e) Service - Clerk, Typist, P.A., Steno, Policeman etc.
(f) Middle class, skilled profession.
(g) Very ordinary work - Servant, Labourer, Peon etc.

3. What is the income of your family?
(a) Above Rs. 1501/-
(b) Between 1001/- and 1500/-
(c) Between 501/- and 1000/-
(d) Between 201/- and 500/-
(e) Between 101/- and 200/-
(f) 100/- or below.

4. What is the Deposit and Debt of your family?
(a) Above Rs. 1501/-
(b) Between 1001/- and 1500/-
(c) Between 501/- and 1000/-
(d) Between 201/- and 500/-
(e) Between 101/- and 200/-
(f) 100/- or below.

5. If your family requires an urgent sum of money how much sum of money could be collected?
(a) Above Rs. 1501/-
(b) Between 1001/- and 1500/-
(c) Between 501/- and 1000/-
(d) Between 201/- and 500/-
(e) Between 101/- and 200/-
(f) 100/- or below.

6. The house in which you reside is :
(a) Your own
(b) A part of the house is on rent
(c) Reside on rent
(d) Reside on rent and have let your own house.

7. How is your house?
(a) Big bungalow, big lawn, electricity and telephone.
(b) Small bungalow, small lawn, electricity.
(c) Pucca house, electricity.
(d) Pucca house but quite small.
(e) Tile-shed, Kachha floor.
(f) Kachha house.

8. Tick (/) the articles which you possess at home.

(a) Car..... Auto-rickshaw ...... Motor Cycle or Scooter..... Rickshaw ...... Bicycle .....
(b) Stereo ...... Television ...... Recordplayer..... Radio or Transistor ..... Gramophone ......
(c) Refrigerator ...... Cooler ...... Safe .... Steel Almirah ..... Dinning table ...... Dinning Set-Steel ....
(d) Sofa-Set ...... Good chair table ...... Wooden chairs .....
(e) Ordinary chair table .... Wall-Clock, Time Piece .... Wrist Watch ......
(f) Gasburner ...... Electric Stove ..... Pressure Cooker ..... Water boiler ......
(g) Mixi.....Electric automatic-press......Grinder .... Sewing-machine .....
(h) Camera ...... Taperecorder .... Tea-set .... Lemon-set ...... Picnic-set .....

9. What type of News paper/Magazine do you purchase. If they are more than one tick them also.
(a) Daily
(b) Weekly
(c) Monthly
(d) Quarterly
(e) Sometime
(f) Never.

10. What is the average expenditure on Newspapers/Magazine.
(a) Rs. 10/-
(b) 20/-
(c) 30/-
(d) 50/-
(e) Above 50/-

11. In the opinion of your family caste system is right. ( )

12. The place where you reside, mostly :
(a) Such people live who possess motor car, telephone good or are quite resourceful.
(b) Neither too prosperous or too poor people live.
(c) Service class ordinary people live.
(d) Such people live who if they do not earn daily cannot manage their meals.

13. Often the basis of social work is religion and people carry out such activities on the basis of religion and caste system. Do the members of your family keep this in mind?

Yes ( ) Sometime ( ) Never ( )

14. Are your family members, the members of social, cultural and caste organisations?

Yes ( ) No ( )

15. Do your family members participate in social functions held either in your locality (Mohalla) or in the city?
(a) Always
(b) Sometime
(c) Never.

16. The elder members of your family keep contact with the class of people : (More than one answer is possible)
(a) Caste or Community.
(b) Same profession.
(c) Political field.
(d) Neighbour and locality (Mohalla).

17. What is the opinion of your friend/other people about you and your family?
(a) Most prosperous family.
(b) Prosperous family.
(c) Middle class.
(d) Average class.
(e) Low class.

18. What should be the basis of social status according to the members of your family?
(a) According to profession and work.
(b) On the basis of property and economic condition.
(c) According to caste.

42A2 INDIVIDUAL & FAMILY STATUS MEASURE

Author : R.P. Gupta.
Availability : Psychological Centre, 569 Ch/26K-2, Prem Nagar, Alambagh, Lucknow.
Languages : English & Hindi.
Uses : To measure the prestige level or status of individuals and family groups.
Level : Literate Adolescents and adults.
Main features : It is like a battery of ten associated factors for being filled in by the respondent about himself and his family. It is in two forms : A-short and B-complete.

Reliability : +.9 see the manual for details.
Validity : +.55, see the manual for details.
Time : 1.5 hours for detailed version. Only half an hour for the short version.
Norms : In the form of status index points available in the manual from the publisher.
References :

(1) Sinha Mukul : Unpublished Dissertation, Department of Education, University of Lucknow, Lucknow, 1981.
(2) Srivastava, Suman : Unpublished Dissertation, Department of Education, Lucknow University, Lucknow, 1981.

42A2 INDIVIDUAL AND FAMILY STATUS MEASURE (SHORT FORM)

I. About the Respondent :

Institution, name, age, sex, qualification, status, occupation, monthly income, address, married or unmarried, earning or non-earning, with children or without children, settled or unsettled, Are you the head? (Yes-No), family liabilities (supporting his parents, brothers, sisters, other relations etc.), His Authority in the family (complete, sufficient, some, nil).

II. About the Family :

(1) Kind of Family - (a) Single or joint, (b) Rural or urban or mixed (c) Compact or distributed.
(2) Size of Family :
 (a) Total number of members ......
 (b) No. of males .... and females ....
 (c) No. of adults ..... and minors ....
 (d) No. of earners ..... and dependents .....
(3) Residence Type :
 (a) Structure (Bungalow, Kothi, Simple house, Cottage)
 (b) Quality (Pucca, Kachha, Mixed)
 (c) Size (Big, Medium, Small)
 (d) No. of rooms
 (e) Open land (Yes-No)
 (f) Other facts - (i) self owned or rented (ii) using the complete building and compound or just a part of it with co-tenants or owners.
(4) Amenities enjoyed :
 (a) Water tap (Yes-No)
 (b) Electricity (Yes-No)
 (c) Fan (Yes-No)

(d) Cooler (Yes-No)
(e) Fridge (Yes-No)
(f) Cooking gas (Yes-No).

(5) Usual Family Conveyance and Vehicle Owned :
Cycle, Scooter or Motor Cycle, Jeep. Car, Rickshaw, Tonga, Cart.

(6) Other Property and Machinery Owned :
(a) Property items (Farm land, Plot, House, Garden, Shop, Factory premises, Movie centre etc.).
(b) Machinery items (Sewing machine, Thrasher, Grass cutting machine, Tractor, Pumping set, Oil or cane crusher, Flour or Rice Mills etc.).

(7) Servants if any (Yes-No) Number
No. of part time servants niose and whole time servants

(8) Educational Qualifications of Adult Members :
(Write their last qualification for the adult members).
A, B, C, D, E, F, G, H.

(9) Academic Distinction Obtained by any Members of the Family Such as ....
(a) Position in class or school or Board etc.
(b) Gold medals for obtaining top marks etc.
(c) Scholarship or Fellowship for merit rank etc.

(10) Family Occupation or Occupations (if there are more than one earning member).
A B C

(11) Total Family Income per month -

(12) Any positions of social responsibility held by members apart from their occupation or work e.g., Office bearers of some associations or elected bodies etc. (Yes-No).
A B C D

(13) Caste and Community :

(14) Use of Reading Materials :
(a) In Hindi (Books - Yes-No; Magazines -Yes-No; Newspaper-Yes-No).
(b) In English - (Books - Yes-No; Magazines - Yes-No; Newspaper - Yes-No).
(c) Regularly self-contributed or got from other sources.

(15) Usual Family Entertainment :
Radio, Cinema, Television, Playing Cards, Ludo, Carrom, Chess, Music, Reading stories and Novels etc.)

(16) Frequency of Postal Exchange :
Daily, Weekly or Monthly.

(17) Any Special Feature about yourself or your family you may like to mention not given in this form so far.

instruments with technical information **B**

42B1 SOCIAL CLASS EVALUATION SCALE (URBAN)

Author : R.N. Pandey.
Availability : Agra Psychological Research Cell, Agra.
Languages : English & Hindi.
Uses : The scale is meant for the evaluation of social class position of students.
Level : 8th class and onward.
Main features : The scale consists of 18 items on all the variables which go to constitute social class. The responses are scored according to weightage assigned to each item. All the items are objective in nature.
Reliability : The internal consistency of the scale is quite high. Test-retest reliability coefficient was found to be .98.
Validity : Content validity is established. Construct validity is established against, Kuppuswamy's SES scale and the validity coefficient was found to be .50.
Norms : Standard scores norms available.
References :

(1) Pandey, R.N. Development of a questionnaire for social class evaluation. Indian Psychological Review, 1966, 3(1), 53-56.

(2) Pandey, R.N. Differences in mental ability among social classes. Unpublished Ph.D. Dissertation, 1970.

citations **C**

42C1 SOCIO-ECONOMIC STATUS SCALE

Author : B.G. Sudha.
Availability : Department of Education, University of Bangalore, Bangalore.

42C2 THE SOCIO-ECONOMIC STATUS RATING SCALE (SESRS)

Author : S.N. Rao.
Availability : Rupa Psychological Centre, B-19/60,

Deoriabir, Bhelupura, Varanasi.

Social Distance and Group Attitudes

complete instruments | A |

43A1 SOCIAL DISTANCE SCALE

Author : Kamal Dwivedi.
Availability : Agra Psychological Research Cell, Agra.
Languages : English & Hindi.
Level : Educated people.
Main features : The scale is based on Bogardus Social Distance Scale. There are 12 items and the subjects are asked to assign ranks to 12 statements from the point of view of intimacy. Each item has median value as its score value.
Reliability : The split-half reliability ranges from .83 to 1.00 and .52 to .90 for boys and girls separately.
Validity : To determine validity the second group (ranking from distance point of view) was taken as criterion group. The coefficient of correlation by rank order method is 1.00 between the two sample.
Reference : Saxena, S.P. A comparative study of social distance and intimacy among boys and girls. Unpublished M.A. Dissertation, Agra University, Agra, 1966.

43A1 SOCIAL DISTANCE SCALE

(The following items have to be ranked from 1 to 12).

1. Can give them employment in my occupation.
2. Can invite them for lunch or dinner.
3. Can give them citizenship in my country.
4. Would like to shoot them.
5. Can marry them.
6. Can make them friends.
7. Do not want to have relation with them.
8. Would like to excluae them from the country.
9. Can make them my neighbours.
10. Can make them imprisoned.
11. Can accept them as visitors only in my country.
12. Would like to have speaking terms with them.

43A2 SOCIAL DISTANCE SCALE

Author : P.K. Muttagi.

Availability : Unit of Urban Studies, Tata Institute of Social Sciences, Deonar, Bombay.

Language : English.

Uses : To study the distance or behavioural tendencies or affective components of attitudes maintained by religious and linguistic groups.

Main features : The scale measures social distance through social preference of religious and linguistic communities. The scale consists of 40 items. The items intend to determine the degree of acceptance of ethnic groups in personal and family matters. Items revealing degree of intimacy and preferences in public life cover six areas as economic, educational, political, religious, social and cultural.

References :

(1) Muttagi, P.K. An investigation into the cross community attitudes of students of under graduate and post graduate classes in the University of Bombay. Unpublished Ph.D. Dissertation, University of Bombay, 1970.

(2) Muttagi, P.K. Social distances among religious and linguistic communities. Indian Journal of Social Work, 1975, 36(2), 159-171.

43A2 SOCIAL DISTANCE SCALE

(The following statements have to be ranked from 1 to 5 according to preference for Christian, Hindu, Muslim and Parsee for religious groups, for Gujarati, Hindi speaking, Maharashtrian, Sindhi and Tamilian for linguistic groups).

Indicate Your Preferences in Your Personal and Social Matters Like :

1. Growing casual acquaintance
2. Making intimate friendship.
3. Accepting a room mate.
4. Accepting a neighbour.
5. Your marriage.
6. Organising cultural shows or recreational activities.

State the order of preferences for the communities in your Family Matters like :

7. Inviting casual visitors to your home.
8. Accepting boarders in your family.
9. Engaging domestic servants like cooks.

10. Arranging your sister's marriage.
11. Arranging your brother's marriage.

Put marks to suggest your priority in choosing the persons from other communities in matters of Jobs, Vocation or Business as in :

12. Accepting an employer.
13. Accepting a co-worker.
14. Accepting an assistant in service.
15. Engaging an employee in office.
16. Accepting a business partner.
17. Giving credit or loan.
18. Giving other facilities for business like renting out premises etc.

Indicate your order of preferences for these communities in the field of Education as in :

19. Awarding scholarships.
20. Giving loan facilities to pursue higher studies.
21. Admitting students to technical institutions like IIT.
22. Admitting students to schools and colleges.
23. Accepting your teacher.
24. Accepting your class mate.

State your order of preference for the communities in Political Matters like :

25. Accepting a member in political parties.
26. Accepting a labour leader.
27. Electing a member of assemblies.
28. Electing a member to Parliament.
29. Casting votes in elections.

Indicate your order of acceptance of these communities Cultural and Social Matters as in :

30. Allowing people to become members of institutions run by your community.
31. Allowing people to participate in festivals, fairs etc. of your community.
32. Meetings or social gatherings of your community.
33. Engaging a person as an employee in institutions run by your community.
34. Selecting an office-bearer of trusts and institutions of your community.

Put marks to state your priority in selection of the candidates from amongst members of these communities in the Central and State Government Services as in :

35. Military Departments.
36. Department of Atomic Energy.
37. Judicial Departments.
38. Accounts Departments.
39. Census and Election Departments.
40. Hospitals and health Departments.

43A3 DISCRIMINATION SCALE

Author : P.K. Muttagi.
Availability : Unit of Urban Studies, Tata Institute of Social Sciences, Deonar, Bombay.
Language : English.
Uses : To measure the perceptual or cognitive component of the attitude of the respondents towards discrimination.
Main features : The scale consists of 40 items, the first 20 refer to discrimination at the group level. Remaining 20 statements refer to discrimination at the government level. All the 40 statements are based on the fundamental rights of the Indian Constitution.
Reference : Muttagi, P.K. An investigation into the cross-community attitudes of students of under graduate and post graduate classes in the University of Bombay. Unpublished Ph.D. Dissertation, University of Bombay, Bombay, 1970.

43A3 DISCRIMINATION SCALE

(The subjects have to answer the following questions from none to unsure for Buddhist, Christian, Hindu, Muslim and Parsee for religious groups and for Gujarati, Hindi speaking, Maharashtrian, Sindhi and Tamilian for linguistic groups).

In your opinion are there instances of members of these communities preventing the people of other communities.

1. (a) From using public places of utility like wells, bathing ghats etc.?
2. (b) From living in localities mainly inhabited by people of their own community?
3. (c) From entering into eating houses like restaurants or cafes?

4. (d) From organising cultural activities like dramas etc?

In your opinion are there instances of members of these communities denying the people of other communities the opportunities : -

5. (a) Of getting jobs?
6. (b) Of getting credit their due promotions?
7. (c) Of getting credit or loan from banks?
8. (d) Are there instances of members of these communities, forcibly taking away the properties of the people of other communities?

In your opinion are there instances of members of these communities :

9. (a) Denying the educational facilities such as scholarships, hostel etc. which are given to the students of their own community?
10. (a) Denying admissions in educational institutions for deserving students of other communities.
11. (c) Preventing the students of other communities from sitting with students of their community.
12. (d) Showing partiality in promoting, giving ranks or prizes to the students of other communities?

Are there instances of these communities preventing the people of other communities?

13. (a) From voting in an election?
14. (b) From contesting an election?
15. (c) From giving speeches and expressing their views?
16. (d) From canvassing in an election for the candidates of their community?

In your opinion are there instances of members of these communities :

17. (a) Preventing people of other communities from becoming members of the institution run by them?

Are there instances of members of these communities :

18. (a) Destroying or causing damage to cultural institutions of other communities?
19. (b) Forcing their language or script on members of other communities?
20. (c) Forcing their customs and food habits on the people

of other communities.

Are there instances of the Central or State Government preventing the members of these communities :

21. (a) From staying or residing in any part of the country.
22. (b) From forming associations, unions or political parties?
23. (c) From publishing newspapers or periodicals for the benefit of their community?
24. (d) From voting for the candidate or the party of their community?
25. (e) From holding congregations or conferences?

In your opinion are there instances of the Government :

26. (a) Collecting special taxes from members of these communities?
27. (b) Preventing members of these communities from establishing business as in running shops?
28. (c) Preventing members of these communities from buying or selling off their property?
29. (d) Showing partiality in giving grants to the institutions run by these communities?
30. (e) Denying scholarships or freeships to members of these communities?

In your opinion are there instances of the :

31. (a) Police arresting the persons of these communities for their religious affinities?
32. (b) Government failing in its duty to protect the lives of the members of these communities?

Are there instances of the Government :

33. (a) Preventing members of these communities from going to the Court of Law when injustice is done?
34. (b) Failing in its duty of protecting the properties of the members of these communities?
35. (c) Failing in its duty of protecting cultural institutions of these communities from irreverence and destruction?

In your opinion are there instances of members of these communities denied of opportunities of :

36. (a) Joining Defence Services?

37. (b) Getting jobs in Atomic Energy Establishments or Air Craft Factories?
38. (c) Taking up jobs in Essential Services like Posts, Telegraphs or Railways?
39. (d) Getting employments in State Government departments like Police or Revenue?
40. (e) Getting promotions in Government Departments according to their turn?

43A4 CONTACT SCALE

Author : P.K. Muttagi.
Availability : Unit of Urban Studies, Tata Institute of Social Science, Deonar, Bombay.
Language : English.
Uses : To study the contact of respondents with five communities - Buddhist, Christian, Hindu, Muslim and Parsi.
Main features : The scale consists of 20 items on a 5-point scale.
Reference : Muttagi, P.K. An investigation into the cross community attitudes of students of under graduate and post graduate class in the University of Bombay. Unpublished Ph.D. Dissertation, University of Bombay, Bombay, 1970.

43A4 CONTACT SCALE

(The following statements have to be checked on a 5-point scale i.e. none to large number for Buddhist, Christian, Hindu, Muslim and Parsee for religious groups and for Gujarati, Hindi speaking, Maharashtrian, Sindhi and Tamilian for linguistic groups).

1. How many persons of these communities are known to you?
2. With how many persons of these communities do you have-
3. (a) Casual acquaintance?
4. (b) Very intimate personal friendship?
5. Have you ever lived with members of these communities in the same-
6. (a) Locality
7. (b) Building?
8. (c) Room?

Have you ever attended with members of these communities-

9. (a) Trips of picnics?

10. (b) Restaurants or movies?

Have you ever come in contact with members of these communities as _

11. (a) Your classmates?
12. (b) Your teachers?
13. (c) Servants in your house?
14. Have you ever been associated with any organisation or association of these communities?

Have you ever participated in the following functions or activities conducted by members of these communities -

15. (a) Social functions like marriage?
16. (b) Cultural activities like dramas or dances?
17. (c) Political activities like participating in election meeting etc.?
18. (d) Religious activities like prayers etc.?
19. Have you ever contributed anything by way of charities to members or institutions of these communities?
20. Have you ever been an employee in an institution mostly run by members of these communities?
21. When have you come in contact with members of these communities?

instruments with technical information **B**

43B1 SOCIAL DISTANCE SCALE (SDS)

Authors : M.P. Uniyal & Beena Shah.
Availability : Department of Education, Garhwal University, Srinagar, Garhwal.
Language : Hindi.
Uses : For objectively identifying the caste distances among students.
Level : College and University students.
Main features : It contains two areas - (i) Intimate relations (IR) (ii) Friendly co-operation (FC). Total number of items are 10. First area has 3 and the second area has 7 items respectively. Instructions are given to assign ranks for caste groups on each item of SDS from the view point of intimacy.
Reliability : Test-retest reliability coefficients were calculated for male and female students separately on both the dimensions and the test as a whole. Its values

were found to be for IR = .91, FC = .83, SDS = .89 (in case of male students) and IR = .75, FC = .70, SDS = .78 (in case of females).

Validity : With ratings based from the view point of intimacy and distance, value of validity coefficient was found to be .856. Its validity coefficients with Dwivedi's SDS and Bogardus SDS were found to be .76 and .63 respectively.

Time : No time limit, but it takes 15 to 20 minutes.

Norms : Available with the authors.

Reference : Shah, Beena : "A sociological study of educational development of graduate students of Kumaun University with special reference to caste." Unpublished Ph.D. dissertation, Kumaun University, 1981.

43B2 SOCIOMETRIC TEST

Authors : B.B. Chatterjee & S.S. Singh.

Availability : Indian Psychological Corporation, Shanti Sadan, R.D. Road, Lucknow.

Language : Hindi.

Level : 11- 14 years children.

Main features : The subject has to write the name of his 3 friends in such an order as he likes them.

Reliability : Coefficient of stability = .67, and internal consistency = .94.

Validity : Validity is established.

Norms : Norms on the basis of scores, available in the manual.

References :

(1) Chatterjee, B.B. & Nair, H.K. Bias in interpersonal perception among sociometric choice scores. Psychologia, 1963, 6, 101-109.

(2) Chatterjee, B.B. & Lal, C. Reliability of sociometric choice scores. Journal of Indian Academy of Applied Psychology, 1964, 1, 69-76.

citations C

43C1 SOCIOMETRIC QUESTIONNAIRE

Author : C. Biswas.

Reference : Interpersonal relationship in class room situation as reflected on social desirability scale : Ph.D. Thesis, Calcutta University, 1977.

4. Modernisation and Social Change

complete instruments A

44A1 ATTITUDE SCALE TO MEASURE ATTITUDES TOWARDS SOCIAL AND CULTURAL MODERNISATION

Author : Mamta Agrawal.
Availability : Author, Department of Measurement & Evaluation, NCERT, Sri Aurobindo Marg, New Delhi.
Languages : English & Hindi.
Uses : To measure the attitudes of Hindus and Muslims towards various aspects of social and cultural modernization in India.
Level : Educated and uneducated people (with uneducated people the statements have to be read).
Main features : The technique used for making the scale was Thurstone's °Equal Appearing Intervals'. There are 60 items in the scale. The scale is based on six indices of modernization grouped in 3 sections - (i) marriage & family, (ii) women's status and education, and (iii) religion and caste.
Reliability : Split-half method is used. The correlation between the two forms was .82 (N = 300). The reliability coefficient = .90.
Validity : In addition to the validity implied by the judging procedure, it was shown that educated women scored higher than the uneducated women (i.e., were modern), that the Hindu women scored higher than the Muslim women.
Time : No time limit.

44A1 ATTITUDE SCALE TO MEASURE ATTITUDES TOWARDS SOCIAL AND CULTURAL MODERNISATION

(The following statements have to be checked as agreed or not agreed. The item values are given in parentheses).

1. (3.75) Arranged marriage prove more successful.
2. (3.50) Love marriage are based only on physical attraction.
3. (8.50) Dowry is a social evil.
4. (2.37) Dowry has to be given for getting a good husband for the daughter.
5. (4.50) Dowry is a way of allowing the daughter to share parental wealth and property.
6. (3.70) Marriage is a religious affairs
7. (3.03) Civil marriages are undersirable as they make

divorse easy.

8. (8.00) Tallying of horoscopes/stars does not ensure happy married life.
9. (8.56) Society should encourage widow remarriage.
10. (6.50) There is nothing wrong in a woman's taking initiative in a divorce case.
11. (7.38) No stigma should be attached to a single woman adopting a child.
12. (1.38) A widow should not put on any make up and coloured clothes.
13. (2.12) Abortion is immoral.
14. (1.43) Limiting of family is an interference with God's will.
15. (5.50) There is no harm in getting an unemployed boy married if his family is economically sound.
16. (1.33) A girl should be married before she attains puberty.
17. (6.37) An educated girl should be married to a boy having similar level of education.
18. (5.25) Joint family provides more security to its members than a nuclear family.
19. (7.05) After marriage sons should live separately from their parents.
20. (6 17) Joint families create more friction amongst family members.
21. (6.33) In a joint family the members are not free to take decisions for themselves.
22. (4.70) In a joint family, a man is more close to his mother and sister than to his wife.

SECTION - B

23. (2.16) Women's place is in home.
24. (1.40) Upbringing of children is strictly a women's job.
25. (8.14) Family responsibilities should be jointly shared by both man and woman.
26. (2.83) Man should have the final authority in family affairs.
27. (4.10) The family gets neglected if the woman takes up a job.
28. (5.59) Working woman should have complete control over her earnings.
29. (3.00) Women are unsuited for police and administrative positions in districts.
30. (7.40) Women should be economically independent.
31. (8.50) Women should get equal wages to men for similar work.

32. (8.25) Daughters should be given equal share in father's property.
33. (1.33) Purdah helps in providing protection and security to women.
34. (1.83) It is the duty of woman to pray and observe fast for the long life of her husband and son.
35. (5.20) There should be reservation of seats for women in the Government services.
36. (8.16) There should be no difference in the education of boys and girls.
37. (4.00) Girls should be taught home-science compulsorily.
38. (2.33) Co-education schools lead to sex permissiveness.
39. (8.50) Boys and girls do not differ in their intellectual abilities.
40. (7.73) Education is necessary for girls to establish the equality of both sexes.
41.(2.75) Highly educated girls find adjustment difficult.
42. (7.43) Education helps girls in looking after the house better.

SECTION - C

43. (7.70) Even with religion one can be good.
44. (5.50) True religion is nothing but faith in God.
45. (4.70) Prayers are very important in life for self purification
46. (8.61) Scriptures are man made and should change according to the changing needs of society.
47. (2.94) Drinking is a sin.
48. (2.20) Life is pre-destined and cannot be changed through efforts.
49. (6.87) Astrology should not have much importance in life.
50. (1.83) One is rewarded or punished according to his actions in the previous birth.
51. (3.05) Material gains are unimportant as they don't bring true happiness.
52. (2.39) Religious ceremonies and rituals are very important in life.
53. (8.20) All religions aim at achieving similar values.
54. (1.43) A religious man does more service to his country than a factory worker or farmer.
55. (1.33) Caste system should be preserved as it has the sanction of religion.
56. (4.30) Harijans as a class are necessary for the

service of the society.

57. (8.71) None can claim superiority on the basis of birth only.
58. (7.59) Caste system is the root cause of all our social evils.
59. (2.05) Priesthood is essentially the prerogative of persons belonging to high castes/certain families.
60. (8.50) Caste system needs to be eliminated for bringing social integration.

44A2 THE MODERNISATION SCALE

Authors : Raghavendra, S.Singh, A.N. Tripathi and Ramjee Lal.
Availability : National Psychological Corporation, 4/230, Kacheri Ghat, Agra.
Languages : English & Hindi.
Uses : To measure attitude of modernity of college students and adults.
Level : Literate - adolescents and adults.
Main features : 32 items scale based on method of summated ratings measuring attitude of modernisation in four areas viz., socio-religious, marriage, position of women and education.
Reliability : Split-half reliability °r' = .78.
Validity : Content validity of items determined on the basis of 100% agreement among judges. Concurrent validity established by correlating sub-scale scores with total scale scores, values of °r' ranged from .64 to .97. Factorial validity has been obtained with common factor contributing 46% to the total variance.
Time : No time limit but usually takes 20-25 minutes.
Norms : Under preparation.
Reference : Singh, R.S., Tripathi, A.N. and Lal, Ramjee. Development of modernisation scale for the study of social change. ISPT Journal of Research, Vol. V, No. 1, p. 37.

44A2 THE MODERNISATION SCALE

(The following items have to be checked on a 6-point of scale).

1. In Indian society, women need not be given more freedom than what they are already enjoying.
2. Sex education will corrupt the students.
3. It is better to have separate schools for boys and

girls.

4. Provision of remarriage of widows will upset the social system.
5. Like men, women should also be given the right to marriage.
6. Like men, women should be employed in all types of services.
7. Participation in sports, drama, etc. has adverse effect on studies.
8. Lack of strict control spoils the students.
9. There is no need of more modernisation of the present educational system.
10. Pilgrimage leads to the holiness of body and mind.
11. Women should be confined only to the house-hold activities.
12. The society can progress only if the women are given status equal to men.
13. Sex education should also be imparted to the students in schools.
14. Social progress is possible only after the eradication of caste system.
15. There is no need of Parda system for women.
16. Dining with lower caste people does no harm to one's religion.
17. It is better to dine only with the people of one's own caste.
18. For the smooth running of the family, women need to be only moderately educated.
19. Taking this world as Maya, is withdrawal from life, and cowardice.
20. The aim of education should be imparting maximum academic knowledge and not preparing a person for a vocation.
21. Marriage is a bond for whole life, therefore, it should be arranged according to the choice of boys and girls.
22. Meeting of boys and girls in loneliness before marriage, is a moral crime.
23. In elections, women should have no voting right because they have no sense of right and wrong.
24. Women should take part in politics.
25. It is better to have marital relation within one's own caste.
26. There should be co-education in all the schools.
27. Man is a puppet in the hands of God.
28. The marriage of boys and girls should be settled with the consent of their parents because they are more experienced.

29. Though it is an occasion of the highest pleasure, a marriage ceremony should be observed in a simple way.
30. Not man, but God does every thing.
31. This world is Maya; only God is true.
32. The marriage of boys and girls should be settled only after giving consideration to their horoscopes.

44A3 A SCALE TO MEASURE ATTITUDE TOWARDS FAMILY PLANNING

Authors : P.K. Dhillon, H.C. Ganguli and C.K. Basu.
Availability : 1st Author, Jesus and Mary College, New Delhi.
Languages : English & Punjabi.
Uses : To assess the attitude towards family planning of married men and women of rural areas.
Level : Adults - literates, married, single. It can also be used with illiterates with verbal instructions. it can also be used with college students.
Main features : Likert's scaling technique. The scale consists of 30 items.
Reliability : The split-half (odd-even) reliability was .96 and the test-retest reliability was .95.
Validity : The validity coefficient obtained by point biserial correlation was .33.
Time : It is not a time scale, but it takes about 10 - 15 minutes.
Norms : Norms are available on 450 married men and women.
Reference : The Indian Journal of Psychology, 1975, Vol. 50, Part-I, 25-32.

44A3 A SCALE TO MEASURE ATTITUDE TOWARDS FAMILY PLANNING

1. Birth control methods should be used by married couples.
2. Happiness in married life depends upon a planned family.
3. Limiting one's number of children is going against nature.
4. Family planning is one of the most effective ways to check the growing population.
5. Family planning is meant only for poor people.
6. A family limited to three children is an ideal family.
7. Display of family planning posters on the main road is repulsive.
8. Family planning is the pivot of all social and

economic planning.

9. Use of birth control methods brings discontentment in marital life.
10. To resort to birth control practices is a sin (against God, religion etc.).
11. Every married couple must practice birth control to have a small family.
12. Birth control has nothing to do with morality.
13. Birth control methods should not be used under any circumstances.
14. Proper spacing and limitation of children is a programme for family welfare.
15. Money spent on family planning propaganda is a waste.
16. Birth control techniques should be used throughout married life.
17. Use of contraceptives creates defects in the babies.
18. Family planning is not the answer to the problem of over-population.
19. Repeated pregnancies impair the health of the mother.
20. Widespread advertisements about family planning will make the boys and girls precocious.
21. To resort to abortion is a sin.
22. Emphasis on family planning is the correct measure to have healthier children.
23. The State should discourage family planning propaganda.
24. Girls and boys should not know anything about family planning until they are married.
25. One should have children of choice and not of chance.
26. Birth control methods are responsible for the increase of illicit sex relations.
27. Legalised abortion is one solution in the hands of a common man for keeping a family small.
28. Birth control practices are not given enough publicity in our country.
29. Contraceptive methods injure women's health.
30. Planned families can maintain a good standard of living.

44A4 MEASUREMENT OF AWARENESS OF CONGRUENCE

Authors : P.O. Ingle and U.G. Deshpande.
Availability : Author, Department of Agricultural Extension, Punjabrao Krishi Vidyapeeth, Akola.

Language : English.
Uses : To measure the awareness of existing congruity between old and new practice.
Level : Post-Graduate and higher studies.
Main features : Likert scaling technique used. Items -35.
Reliability : Split-half technique used and reliability coefficients worked out.
Validity : Content validity and construct validity borne out.
Time : Ten minutes.
Norms : Nil.
Reference : Ingle, P.O. "Study of congruence as a factor influencing adoption of agricultural innovation", unpublished Ph.D. thesis, P.K.V., Akola, Maharashtra, 1980.

44A4 MEASUREMENT OF AWARENESS OF CONGRUENCE

(The following statements have to be checked on a 4-point scale).

1. Sara method requires well drained soils.
2. Local method can be followed on ill drained soils.
3. Sara method requires black cotton soil.
4. Sara method necessarily requires well levelled soils.
5. Local method can be followêd on soils with less water absorbing capacity.
6. Method of preparation of layout is different in sara method and local method.
7. Sara Yantra is required for sara method.
8. Local method layout can be prepared by indigenous plough and pawada.
9. Sara method requires skilled labour for layout preparation.
10. Sara method requires technical knowledge for layout preparation.
11. Local method can be layed out by average labour/farmer.
12. Sara method of irrigation requires more time than local irrigation method.
13. Sara method can be followed with specific size of beds.
14. Local method can be followed with several sizes of beds.
15. In sara method water is delivered by special pipes.
16. In local irrigation water is directly flown in bed.
17. Sara method irrigates less area per day.

18. Per day more acreage is irrigated in case of local method.
19. Cost of operation is different for local and sara method of irrigation.
20. Local method is cheaper.
21. There is difference in nature of water conservation in sara and local method of irrigation.
22. There is difference in distribution of water in local and sara method of irrigation.
23. Distribution of water is speedy in local irrigation method.
24. Distribution of water is slow in sara method of irrigation.
25. Local irrigation lay out can not be prepared after the crop is sown.
26. Sara method lay out can not be prepared after the crop is sown.
27. Sara method is suitable for wheat.
28. Local method can be used for different crops.
29. Suitability to different irrigation sources is different in both sara method of irrigation.
30. Local method can be followed with any source of irrigation.
31. Water level in soil after irrigation is different in both sara method and local method.
32. Water percolates deep at the beginning of sara and remain shallow of the other end of sara.
33. There is difference in crop growth irrigated by sara method and local method of irrigation.
34. Crop irrigated by sara method and local method of irrigation grow uniform.
35. Crop irrigated by sara method do not grow uniform in all corners of sara.

44A5 CONGRUITY INDEX

Author : P.O. Ingle and U.G. Deshpande.
Availability : The Author, Department of Agricultural Extension, P.K.V., Akola, Maharashtra.
Language : English.
Uses : To measure congruity in different social and psychological aspects.
Level : Post-Graduate and Higher studies.
Main features : Twenty items.
Reliability : Split-half reliability worked out.
Validity : Content validity seen.
Time : Fifteen minutes.

Norms : Nil.
Reference : Ingle, P.O. "Study of congruence as a factor influencing adoption of agricultural innovations", unpublished Ph.D. thesis, P.K.V., Akola, Maharashtra, 1980.

44A5 CONGRUITY INDEX

(The following package of practices have to be rated in terms of its similarity and dissimilarity).

1. Soil quality.
2. Climate.
3. Plough used.
4. Number of ploughings.
5. Harrow used.
6. Number of Harrowings.
7. Seed quality.
8. Seed rate.
9. Implements for sowing.
10. Spacing.
11. Weeding.
12. Hoeing.
13. Quality of manures and fertilizers.
14. Doses of manures and fertilizers.
15. Pests.
16. Diseases.
17. Implements used for spraying and dusting.
18. Number of sprayings and dustings.
19. Duration of crop.
20. Harvesting and threshing.

44A6 A SCALE TO MEASURE THE DIFFERENTIAL PERCEPTION OF ADOPTERS AND NON-ADOPTERS

Authors : B.K. Murthy, C.M. Dudhani, K.M. Jayaramaiah, V. Veerabhadraiah and M.K. Sethu Rao.
Availability : Department of Psychology, University of Agricultural Sciences, Dharwar.
Languages : English/Kannada.
Uses : To measure the differential perceptions of adopters and non-adopters.
Level : Educated and uneducated farmers.
Reliability : Split-half (odd vs even item) reliability calculated by Rulon's formula = .79.
Validity : Construct and content validity is established.
Reference : Murthy, B.K. et al. A scale to measure the differential perception of adopters and non-adopters.

Mysore Jr. Agri. Sciences, 1973, 7, 282-292.

44A6 A SCALE TO THE DIFFERENTIAL PERCEPTIONS OF ADOPTERS AND NON-ADOPTERS

A. Background information of the respondent :

(1) Name of the respondent :
(2) Name of the village :
(3) Name of the taluk :
(4) Name of the district :
(5) Whether living in a joint family or divided :
(6) Age of farmer :
(7) Education of farmer :
(8) Land holdings : Dry, Wet, Garden.
(9) Annual income :
(10) Adopter or non-adopter :
(11) New practices adopted (in the case of adopter) :

B. Evaluative Perception Scale
The specified practice or idea :

Dimension-I : Practicability

1. New Skills
The adoption of the specified practice would involve :

(a) the learning of no difficult skills
(b) some easily learnable modifications in the existing skills
(c) not known
(d) the learning of a few difficult skills
(e) the learning of many difficult skills.

2. Marketability
The produce of the specified practice would be :

(a) most easily marketable
(b) marketable
(c) uncertain
(d) marketable with some difficulty
(e) marketable with utmost difficulty.

3. Supplies
The supplies for the adoption of the specified practice could be :

(a) obtained most easily

(b) obtained easily
(c) uncertain
(d) obtained with some difficulty
(e) obtained with utmost difficulty.

4. Resourcefulness for inputs for the adoption of the practice
The resources could be mobilised to enable me to command the inputs for the adoption of the specified practice :

(a) most easily
(b) easily
(c) not sure
(d) with some difficulty
(e) with utmost difficulty.

Dimension-II : Productivity

1. Improvement in income
The adoption of the specified practice would result in :

(a) immediate improvement in income
(b) improvement in income in reasonable period of time
(c) uncertain improvement in income
(d) improvement in income in future
(e) improvement in income in remote future.

2. Utilisation of the locally existing resources
The adoption of the specified practice :

(a) would make an effective use of many of the existing resources
(b) would make an effective use of some of the existing resources
(c) not known
(d) would make ineffective some of the existing resources
(e) would make ineffective many of the existing resources.

3. Interaction with the existing practices
The adoption of the specified practice affects the existing practices :

(a) most favourably
(b) favourably
(c) not known
(d) unfavourably

(e) most unfavourably.

4. Risk involvement
The adoption of the specified practice :

(a) definitely involves no risk
(b) seems to involve no risk
(c) not sure
(d) seems to involve some risk
(e) definitely involves a great degree of risk.

Dimension-III : Motivity

1. Temporal latitude of acceptance
The qualities of the specified practice should make it eligible for :

(a) immediate acceptance
(b) acceptance in the immediate future
(c) not sure
(d) acceptance after some lapse of time
(e) acceptance in the remote future.

2. Relation to other agricultural practices
The adoption of the specified practice would :

(a) develop all the other agricultural practices
(b) develop some of the agricultural practices
(c) develop or hinder-not known
(d) hinder the development of some of the other agricultural practices
(e) hinder the development of some of the other agricultural practices.

3. Improvement in social status
The adoption of the specified practice would :

(a) definitely improve the social status of the individual
(b) perhaps improve the social status of the individual
(c) improve or bring down-not known.
(d) perhaps not improve the social status
(e) definitely not improve the social status.

4. Relation to the living standard
The adoption of the specified practice would :

(a) definitely result in improving the living standard

(b) perhaps result in improving the living standard
(c) not sure
(d) perhaps not result in improving the living standard
(e) definitely not result in improving the living standard.

instruments with technical information **B**

44B1 MODERNIZATION ATTITUDE INVENTORY (MAI)

Authors : R.J. Trivedi and M.T. Patel.
Availability : The Author, A-57, Dhanlaxmi Society, Kareli Baug, Baroda.
Language : Gujarati.
Uses : To measure attitude towards modernization.
Level : Under-graduates, post-graduates and other adults.
Main features : The inventory is a 91 items Likert instrument consisting of eight sub-scales. Each scale has 10 to 14 statements that pertain to particular aspect of attitude towards modernization. The eight aspects within the inventory are : Attitude towards women-men equality, marriage choice, intercaste marriage, family planning, interstate migration, individual to nation, religion, and social dynamism.
Reliability : Reliability = .83 by split-half method and .62 & .54 by test-retest method.
Validity : Concurrent validity = .57 validated with rating of college teachers.
Time : About 40 to 45 minutes. There is no fixed time limit.
Norms : Norms are available with author.

44B2 MODERNITY ATTITUDE SCALE

Authors : C.L. Anand and M.A. Sudhir Kumar.
Availability : First Author, Department of Education, North Eastern Hill University, Shillong.
Uses : To analyse the social attitudes of the individuals.
Level : Social workers, researchers and scholars.
Main features : It is a five point Likert type forcing scale consisting of five sub-scales assessing the social attitudes of the subjects. The scale consists of 80 items measuring attitudes towards : religion, marriage, family, status of women in society and education.
Reliability : Split-half reliability = .76 (N = 100), and test-retest reliability = .72 (N = 100).
Validity : Validity assessed by correlation between the total scale score and the scores on each sub-scale using

product moment method.

Reference : Anand, C.L. & Sudhir Kumar, M.A. Developing a Modernity Attitude Scale. Indian Educational Review, 1982, 17(3), 28-40.

44B3 FAMILY PLANNING ATTITUDE INVENTORY

Author : M.B. Paliwal.

Availability : Indian Psychological Corporation, R.B. Lal Road, Lucknow.

Language : Hindi.

Main features : The inventory is a 25 items Likert type 5-point scale and measure the attitude towards family planning. The statements are in positive as well as in negative form.

Reliability : Split-half reliability coefficient (corrected by Spearman Brown formula) was found to be .81 and the odd-even reliability coefficient was found to be .70.

Validity : Content and face validity have been ensured.

Time : No time limit.

Norms : On the basis of the total scores.

44B4 A SCALE TO MEASURE LEVEL OF FARM MECHANISATION OF THE FARMERS

Author : Ranjit Singh.

Availability : Author, Department of Extention Education, Punjab Agricultural University, Ludhiana.

Language : English.

Uses : To measure level of farm mechanisation.

Level : Farmers.

Reliability : Test-retest = .923.

Validity : Validated by known-group technique.

Time : Twenty minutes.

Norms : Three categories on the basis of scores.

44B5 WOMEN SOCIAL FREEDOM SCALE

Author : L.I. Bhushan.

Availability : Author, Department of Psychology, Bhagalpur University, Bhagalpur.

Language : Hindi.

Uses : To measure desire for social freedom among women.

Level : Adolescent and adult females.

Main features : 24 items with two category (Agree-Disagree) responses including six negative items.

Reliability : Internal consistency - odd-even = .86, first vs 2nd half = .90 and temporal stability 'r' = .79.

Validity : Possesses criterion validity.
Time : About 20 minutes.
Norms : Available for married and unmarried college students.
References : Bhushan, L.I. Women Social Freedom Scale. Psychologia, 1982, 124 (4)

citations C

44C1 THE FAMILY ATTITUDE QUESTIONNAIRE

Author : Rita Ghatak.
Availability : Author, Zakir Hussain Centre for Educational Studies, School of Social Sciences, J.N. University, New Delhi.

44C2 PERCEIVED SOCIALIZATION PRACTICES INVENTORY

Author : M.L. Roy.
Availability : Author, Department of Psychology, University of Udaipur, Udaipur.

44C3 ATTITUDE TOWARDS SOCIAL CHANGE

Author : Beer Singh.
Availability : Rupa Psychological Centre, B-19/60, Deoriabir, Bhelupur, Varanasi.

44C4 SOCIAL PARTICIPATION SCALE

Author : Shashipuri.
Reference : Work roles and decision making patterns of farmer wives and husband. Ph.D. thesis, I.A.R.I., New Delhi, 1972.

44C5 ATTITUDE SCALE TOWARDS FAMILY PLANNING

Authors : M.A. Hakim & Y. Singh.
Availability : National Psychological Corporation, Kacheri Ghat, Agra.

44C6 A SCALE TO MEASURE FARMER'S ATTITUDE TOWARDS HIGH YIELDING VARIETY PROGRAMME

Authors : P.N. Jha and K.N. Singh.
Reference : Jha, P.N. and Singh, K.N. A scale to measure farmer's attitude towards high yielding variety programme. Indian Psychological Review, 1973, 10(2), 10-12.

adaptations D

44D1 VINELAND SOCIAL MATURITY SCALE

Author : A.J. Malin.
Availability : Indian Psychological Corporation, Lucknow.
Language : English.
Uses : To estimate the differential social capacities of an individual.
Main features : It is Doll's Vineland Social Maturity Scale adaptation used in Nagpur child guidance centre. It assesses the social and mental ages of children. Research work on the scale is still in progress.

5. Religion and Morality

instruments with technical information B

45B1 RELIGIOUS ATTITUDE SCALE (LIKERT TYPE)

Author : M. Rajmanickam.
Availability : Author, Department of Psychology, Annamalai University, Annamalainagar.
Language : English.
Uses : To measure religious attitudes of students and adults.
Level : School and college students and adults.
Main features : It is a Likert type scale consisting 30 items. The items are under six topics - the nature of God, future life, priests, the spirit world, personal religion, and formal religion. Each item has five alternative responses.
Reliability : Split-half (odd-even) reliability using Guttman formula = .98.
Validity : Criterion validity coefficient was found to be .86.

Time : No time limit.

45B2 RELIGIOUS ATTITUDE SCALE (THURSTONE TYPE)

Author : M. Rajamanickam.
Availability : Author, Department of Psychology, Annamalai University, Annamalainagar.
Language : English.
Uses : To measure religious attitudes of students and adults.
Level : School and College students & adults.
Main features : It is a Thurstone's type 17 items scale. The subject is asked to check any three statements which is taken as the individual score.
Reliability : Split-half = .86.
Validity : Criterion validity was obtained by correlating the scale values with the religious attitude scale and validity coefficient was found to be .86.
Time : No time limit.

45B3 MORAL JUDGEMENT TEST

Authors D. Sinha & M. Verma.
Availability : National Psychological Corporation, Agra.
Language : Hindi.
Uses : To assess moral judgement ot children.
Level : Children of 6 - 11 years.
Main features : The test consists of 50 items on 14 values . Ahimsa, Duty, Respect, Betrayal of faith, Purity, Forgiveness, Greed, Anger, Punnya (virtue), Lie, Revenge, Stealing, Truth and sin developed on the model of a general intelligence test. It has been divided into six parts : discrimination, incomplete sentence, analogies, best moral answers, moral reasoning and definition. Each item has only one correct answer.
Reliability : Split-half reliability by Spearman Brown formula = .93.
Validity : Scores on M.J.T. were correlated with the moral knowledge scores and indicated positive and significant relationship between the two.
Time : No time limit.
Norms : Percentile norms.
References :
(1) Moral Judgement in children. Paper presented at the 55th session of Indian Science Congress, 1967.
(2) Verma, M. Moral Development in Children. Thesis submitted for D. Phil. degree, University of Allahabad,

1968.

45B4 MORAL DEVELOPMENT TEST BATTERY

Author : A.S. Seetharamu.
Availability : Author, Department of Post-Graduate Studies and Research in Education, Mysore University, Manasgangotri, Mysore.
Level : 10+ to 13+ age group.
Main features : The test items consist of 34 situations involving moral judgement of which 24 are situational tests and the rest are story tests. The items are classified in 11 moral tracts such as honesty, responsibility, non-deceipt, non-lying, conformity to localised rules, kindness, fair play, dignity of labour, courtesy to an enemy, generosity and keeping a promise.
Reliability : Split-half = .88.
Validity : Face validity established.
Norms : Available with author.

6. Other Social Instruments

complete instruments | A

46A1 ATTITUDE TOWARDS COMPUTERS

Authors : Udai Pareek, A Ghose and D. Sarupria.
Availability : Author, Indian Institute of Management, Ahmedabad.
Language : English.
Uses : To measure attitude towards computers.
Level : Industrial workers.
Main features : It is a Thurstone type scale available in two parallel forms (A & B) each containing 20 items.
Reliability : Not available.
Validity : Not available.
Reference : Pareek, U., Ghose, A. & Sarupria, D. Perception of computers in the Indian industry : A study of image and attitudes in two textile mills. Indian Journal of Industrial Relations, 1979, 14(3), 339-378.

46A1 ATTITUDE TOWARDS COMPUTERS (A)

(The subjects have to tick mark those with which they agree).

1. Computer is not desirable now in the country because the majority of people may not be in favour.
2. Use of computers should be prohibited.
3. Computer helps to solve problems faster.
4. All industries would make use of computers as far as possible.
5. The use of computers can improve the quality of products within a short time.
6. With the help of computers employees of an industry can be relieved from repetitive (routine) types of jobs.
7. Because of the superior memory computers have great uses in industry.
8. If judiciously used computers can be useful in several areas.
9. The utility of computers is highly limited.
10. India is not ready for computers and will not be ready for quite some time.
11. Computer can solve complex problems which cannot be solved by human being.
12. Computers create more problems, and have little utility.
13. The use of computers goes against the interest of the employees and should not be encouraged.
14. Computer is economic if the industry used it full time, and this is not possible.
15. It is risky to depend upon the decisions suggested by computer.
16. Computer makes clerks redundant through mechanisation of clerical work.
17. Computers are a great boon to humanity.
18. Computers can be used to solve some problems, but not the major ones.
19. Computers will help employees learn new skills.
20. Computers can be helpful in solving several problems of industry.

Attitude towards Computers (B)

(The subjects have to tick mark those with which they agree).

1. Computers can be used to solve several problems, if properly used.
2. Computer does not supplant (substitute for) but supplements the clerical and other staff.
3. An industry should use the computer because it has superior memory compared to human memory.

4. Computer is too expensive for a country like India.
5. Computers might be useful but the results are not always encouraging.
6. All industries should make use of the computer for its development programmes.
7. Computer is good for management but bad for the clerical staff.
8. Computers can work more effectively than human beings.
9. Computer is more dependable than human beings.
10. The use of computer is a threat to the employees' position.
11. The government should pass a law to stop the use of computers in industries and other establishments.
12. Computers will help in ushering in technological culture in the industry.
13. Computer is useful for some purposes.
14. Computer can avoid labour-management problems.
15. Computer is the most remarkable achievement in the human industry.
16. Computer is very much helpful for management decision making.
17. The use of computer does not increase the productivity of an industry.
18. Computers can be used in India neither at present nor in the near future.
19. Computer creates a number of unavoidable problems for the management.
20. Computers are not useful in small scale industries.

46A2 A SCALE TO MEASURE ATTITUDE TOWARDS FATE

Authors : P.K. Dhillon, H.C. Ganguli and C.K. Basu.
Availability : Author, Jesus and Mary College, Chanakyapuri, New Delhi.
Languages : English and Punjabi.
Uses : To measure attitude towards fate.
Level :Literate : Adolescents and adults - married, single- in general of all professions, religions etc. It can also be used with illiterates - same groups but with verbal instructions.
Main features : Likert scaling method. The scale has 27 items.
Reliability : The split-half reliability (odd-even method) was .99 and the test-retest reliability was .95.
Validity : The validity coefficient obtained by the biserial correlation (believers and non-believers) was .97.

Time : 8 - 15 minutes.
Norms : Norms are available with the first author.
Reference : The scale is published in 'MANAS', 23,1,1976.

46A2 A SCALE TO MEASURE ATTITUDE TOWARDS FATE

1. Every man is the architect of his own fate.
2. Fate is the imagination of human beings.
3. Human beings are the puppets of fate.
4. Man proposes God disposes.
5. Opportunities are created in life, they do not come by themselves.
6. Fate is just a form of consolation for individuals, surrounded by sorrows and failures.
7. Whatever a man has today, is because of his efforts and not because of fate.
8. One is powerless, helpless against the overwhelming force of destiny.
9. Only unsuccessful people believe in fate.
10. People who don't want to make an effort, take consolation in fate.
11. Effort is mightier than fate.
12. It is better to be lucky than wise.
13. Number of children one has or will have is written in one's fate.
14. Fate is carved out by one's own hands.
15. Fate is just a superstition.
16. Every person is born with his fate already carved out for him.
17. To love or hate anyone is not in one's own hands but in the hands of fate.
18. Nothing is written in may fate, I will write it.
19. There is no such thing as fate.
20. Deaths are in the hands of fate.
21. No one has lost by his foolishness or gained by his wisdom.
22. With a lucky (fortunate) man all things are favourable.
23. Births are in the hands of fate.
24. Only weak, helpless people believe in fate.
25. Marriages are made in heaven.
26. What has been destined, one cannot increase it even by a particle by one's efforts.
27. Who has made a month, will give food; who has given life will also provide means of living.

46A3 A SCALE ON ATTITUDE TOWARDS GOVERNMENTAL FAMILY PLAN-

NING PROGRAMME

Author : P.K. Dhillon.
Availability : Author, Jesus and Mary College, Chanakyapuri, New Delhi.
Languages : English & Punjabi.
Uses : To assess attitude towards governmental family planning programme.
Level : Literate - adults and adolescents - married and single. It can be used with illiterates also with verbal instructions.
Main features : Likert scaling method. The scale has 11 items.
Reliability : The odd-even reliability coefficient was .88 and the test-retest reliability coefficient was .90.
Validity : The internal consistency of the scale argues for its validity and also scores on the first 9 items were correlated with scores on the last 2 items. The correlation coefficient was .80.
Time : Approximately 3 to 6 minutes.
Norms : Norms are available with the author.

46A3 A SCALE ON ATTITUDE TOWARDS GOVERNMENTAL FAMILY PLANNING PROGRAMME

1. Do you know of a family planning clinic in or near your village?
2. What do you think about it?
3. Do you like the work of the employees of the clinic?
4. Have you ever been there?
5. How do you or would you feel when going to the clinic?
6. What do you think about these types of clinics in general?
7. Do you think these clinics serve a useful purpose?
8. How do you feel about the posters of family planning on the roads?
9. What do you think about the propaganda of family planning?
10. What do the people of the village think about family planning clinics?
11. How do people of the village feel about family planning propaganda?

46A4 LIFE SATISFACTION SCALE

Author : P.K. Dhillon.
Availability : Author, Jesus and Mary College, Chanakyapuri, New Delhi.
Languages : English & Punjabi.
Uses : To assess satisfaction in life of married men and women.
Level : Literate - married men and women of all professions, religions etc. It can be also used with illiterate married men and women with verbal instructions.
Main features : Likert's scaling method was used. The scale has 13 items.
Reliability : The split-half reliability (odd-even) coefficient was .90 and the test-retest reliability coefficient was .94.
Validity : Face validity and correlation coefficient obtained between the total scores of the first 12 items with the last (13th item) item was .84.
Time : Four to eight minutes.
Norms : Available with the author.

46A4 LIFE SATISFACTION SCALE

(How satisfied are you with the following spheres of life).

1. The work or job you do?
2. Your children?
3. Your relatives?
4. Your husband/wife?
5. Your neighbours?
6. Your friends?
7. Your village?
8. The amount you earn/for wife - the amount of income you get in your house?
9. Your-in-laws?
10. Your leisure time activities?
11. Your health?
12. Your education?
13. Your life in general?

46A5 TEST OF SIBLING RELATIONSHIP

Author : Mohana Sekhar.
Availability : Author, Department of Education, University of Bombay, Bombay.
Language : English.
Uses : To measure cordiality of relationship among siblings.

Level : High School, College and University students. Adult male and female and professional college students.

Main features : Likert type rating scale consisting of 25 positive and negative statements. Rating scale uses four points to avoid the median value. Summated score on the test gives the degree of cordiality of relationship between siblings. Provision is made for assessing cordiality with younger and elder siblings.

Reliability : Test-retest reliability was found to be 0.78.

Validity : Against an external criterion of a single question in the form of a four point rating scale gave a value of 0.28.

Time : No time limit but usually takes 20 minutes.

Norms : Percentile norms for Bombay sample available with the author.

Reference : Sekhar, M. "A study of creativity in relation to home environmental factors". Doctoral Thesis in Education. Bombay University, Bombay, 1980.

46A5 TEST OF SIBLING RELATIONSHIP (YOUNGER AND ELDER)

(The following statements have to be checked on °yes° or °no°).

1. Do you have a younger brother/sister?
2. Age of my younger brother/sister is
3. I am fond of my brother
4. I pinch/slap my brother
5. I feel that my father/mother do not love me as much as my little brother/sister
6. I do not feel happy when my younger brother/sister gets good marks in the exam/wins prize in a competition
7. I feel proud of my younger brother/sister's achievements.
8. I feel that I should be a model to my younger brother/sister
9. I feel my mother/father cared for me more before my younger brother/sister was born
10. I do not play with my younger brother/sister
11. I do not like to teach my younger brother/sister bad things (to speak vulgar language, etc.)
12. I feel that whenever my parents go out I have to take the responsibility of looking after my younger brother/sister

(a) I feel happy to hold this responsibility.

13. When my mother finds that something is broken and scolds my younger brother/sister when it was actually done by me

    (a) I immediately confess that it was done by me.
    (b) I let my brother/sister get the beating.

14. I feel that I must do things which are different from what my younger brother/sister does
15. Do you have an elder brother/sister
16. Age of my elder brother/sister is
17. I feel that my elder brother/sister is not very friendly with me
18. I think I learn many things from my elder brother/sister
19. I do not disagree with my elder brother/sister
20. I fight with my elder brother/sister
21. When I get hurt my elder brother/sister gets concerned and applies medicine.
22. My elder brother/sister does not help me with my difficulties
23. I feel that I must do things which are different from what my elder brother/sister does
24. When my mother finds that something is broken and scolds my elder brother/sister when it was actually broken by me

    (a) I immediately confess it was done by me.
    (b) I let my elder brother/sister get the beating.

25. I feel proud of my elder brother/sister's achievements.

46A6 THE ALIENATION SCALE

Authors : Afzal Kureshi and Meenakshi Dutt.
Availability : Authors, Department of Psychology, Aligarh Muslim University, Aligarh.
Languages : English, Hindi, Gujarati, and Urdu.
Uses : To measure alienation of subjects.
Level : School and college samples, clinical and industrial samples.
Main features : The scale comprises 21 items to be answered by agreeing to one of the four alternative response categories according to the intensity of feeling. It measures factors like despair, disillusionment, psy.

vacuum, unstructured universe and narcissism.

Reliability : Split-half reliability = .85 (N = 100).

Validity : The scale is based on several scales measuring the dimension the validity of which had already been established. The items in the present scale represent the extracted factors, and so the validity of the scale is self-evident.

Time : About twenty minutes.

Norms : Norms for student samples and industrial sample are available with the authors.

Reference : Kureshi, A. and Dutt, Meenakshi. Dimensions of Alienation - a-factor-analytic study, Psychologia, 1979, 22, 99-105.

46A6 ALIENATION SCALE

(The following items have to be checked on a 4-point scale).

1. I feel I am not as happy as other are.
2. I feel if one can't face hard realities of life the only way is to keep busy with more pleasent things.
3. I feel our lives are governed by some discoverable laws.
4. I feel one is sometimes forced to take intoxicants to forget the troubles and miscries of life.
5. I feel it is safer not to confide in any one.
6. I feel there is no end to one's miseries, as long as one lives.
7. I feel disgusted to see others success as I know I could be far more successful had I been treated fairly.
8. I feel worried beyond reason over minor matters.
9. I feel one can be more contented by withdrawing from situations that are full of risks and uncertainties.
10. People sometimes put me in such a state of mind that I feel like tearing them to pieces.
11. I feel one is justified in hitting back as hard as possible, if provoked unreasonably.
12. I feel firm conviction and well founded ideologies are the hall marks of modern age.
13. I feel I am good for nothing.
14. I feel love and affection don't matter as much in life as working relationships.
15. I feel there are no well-defined objectives to guide me.
16. I feel dissatisfied even with my best performance.
17. I feel one is free to adopt his own way of life.

18. I feel the universe is governed by the principles of equality, fair protection and equality of opportunity.
19. I think I am the best judge of my actions.
20. I like to do things all on my own.
21. I feel it is not difficult for me to take a decision in the face of moral conflicts.

46A7 POLITICAL EFFICACY ALIENATION SCALE

Author : Abhimanyou Tambar.
Availability : Indian Psychological Corporation, Shanti Sadan, Rai Behari Lal Road, Lucknow.
Languages : English & Hindi.
Uses : To measure sense of political efficacy or alienation on any of its four dimensions i.e. powerlessness, normlessness, meaninglessness and isolation.
Level : All adult population.
Main features : The efficacy alienation scale comprises of four subscales i.e. perceived efficacy - inefficacy scale, normlessness scale, isolation scale, and meaninglessness scale. Combining these four yields a five point scale consisting of 33 items which tends to measure political alienation.
Reliability data : Split half reliability was completed, the details are given in the manual.
Validity : Cross validity and factorial validity were computed, the details are given in the manual.
Time : Approximately 45 minutes.
Norms : Not yet finalised.
Reference : Tambar Abhimanyou, A study of some psychological dimensions of political efficacy and cynicism; Ph.D. Thesis, University of Udaipur, Udaipur, 1977.

46A7 EFFICACY ALIENATION SCALE

(The following items have to be checked on a 5-point scale of agreement).

1. The policies of the ruling party which is controlling the administration in Delhi these days may seriously endanger the country's welfare any time.
2. I know my vote to this candidate or that candidate would not have made any difference.
3. More often the voters are governed by considerations a political.
4. I usually have confidence that the government will do what is right.

5. Our government which is organised and operating is hopelessly incapable in dealing with all crucial problems facing the country today.
6. Mostly the government fails to complete such important matters which are favoured by most of the people.
7. Elections have generally no meaning to me.
8. Political parties are so big that an average member has not got much to say about what goes on.
9. Politics and government are so complicated that an average man like me cannot really understand what is going on.
10. Activities and the policies of the central government is improving the condition of the nation.
11. It is not very important to vote in local elections.
12. It seems to me whoever you vote for, things are pretty much the same.
13. The activities of the municipality of my city are improving the condition of this city.
14. Nothing I ever do seems to have any effect on what happens in politics.
15. Some people or groups have so much influence over the government that interests of the majority are ignored.
16. This candidate or that candidate makes no difference to the voter in elections as they are conducted in our country today.
17. The majority has the right to abolish the minorities if it wants to.
18. Government is run by few big interest who usually have their own interest and neglect the common man's interests.
19. All the government laws are constituted for the benefit of the rich.
20. These days the government is trying to do many things including the few activities that they do not have the right to do.
21. Supreme Court does its job very well.
22. There are times when it seems better for the people to take law in their own hands rather than the machinery of the government to act.
23. I can understand the national and international issues facing the nation.
24. People like me have no say about what the government does .
25. Government waste a lot of money which we pay in taxes.

26. I can trust the central government in Delhi to do what is right for the people.
27. If any unjust and harmful regulation is being considered by the municipality of my city I will definitely try to oppose it.
28. In actual working the Supreme Court favours any particular group or groups in this country.
29. The laws of this country are supposed to benefit all of us equally but the fact is that they are all rich man's laws.
30. It is very important to vote even when so many other people vote in an election.
31. Most of the politicians can be trusted to do what they think is best for the people.
32. It is no use worrying my head about the public affairs I cannot do anything about them any how.
33. Most of the people who are running the government are a little crooked.

46A8 SOCIO-POLITICAL ATTITUDE SCALE

Author : S. Vasudevan.
Availability : Department of Psychology, University of Madras, Autonomous P.G. Centre, Coimbatore.
Language : English.
Main features : It is a 40 items scale divided into 6 subscales on casteism, libertarianism, religionism, socialism, reactionism and permissiveness.. The scale measures the social and political attitudes among the individuals.
Reliability : The reliability coefficient for all the subscale varies from .69 to .85.
Validity : Validity is established by employing item sum correlation method, significant at .05 level.

46A8 SOCIO-POLITICAL ATTITUDE SCALE

(The following statements have to be checked on a 5-point scale of agreement).

1. It is not wrong if workers spend more time during tea break.
2. Good character alone will not build the life of a worker.
3. Faith in religion facilitates man to work sincerely.
4. All government laws are helpful only to rich people.

5. Communists should not be given jobs in industries.
6. Government tax officials should have the authority to verify the accounts of an industry.
7. Workers should be selected for jobs on the basis of caste.
8. Religious institutions alone will help to develop moral character among the workers.
9. Rich people alone enjoy more government funds allotted for industrial developments.
10. Workers should be allowed to move freely among themselves.
11. If one meets loss in his industry, he think that it is an act of good.
12. During the time of scarcity it is not improper to sell goods at a higher rate.°
13. Faith in religion will not allow an individual to think independently.
14. An industry should manufacture the goods which yield more profit than the goods categorised by the governments as essential.
15. Workers have more immoral sexual contacts.
16. The ideas of priests and preachers should be accepted without any resistance (opposition).
17. Workers should be given freedom to criticise the decisions of the management.
18. Demanding wage increase is one of the routine acts of workers.
19. It is not illegal if an individual starts an industry even before obtaining the necessary permission from authorities.
20. Having no faith in God will not affect a normal individual.
21. At present the unrest among the workers is due to the loss of confidence in culture and tradition.
22. Associations on the basis of castes should not be banned.
23. The conduct of workers of industries is gradually (becoming bad) deteriorating.
24. Petty errors by the workers should not be considered seriously.
25. A honest man need not have faith in religion.
26. Government policies gradually take away our fundamental rights.
27. Government should not interfere in production and trade.
28. Having caste feelings is justifiable.
29. There are more differences among various castes in the ability of starting and running an industry.

30. To solve the problems of workers in industry it is good to follow new methods.
31. Government policies fail the satisfy the needs of the workers.
32. Political parties getting donations from the industrialists is not wrong.
33. Nationalisation of industries is not a correct way to improve efficiency.
34. The methods followed in business should not be compared with moral principles.
35. Workers are not machines; they do have freedom.
36. In business competition it is not wrong if one prevents other industries from getting raw materials.
37. In an industry, if workers belong to the same caste, they work efficiently.
38. Having participation in the administration of an industry by workers is not possible (The workers taking part in the administration of an industry is not possible).
39. Sometimes one will have many obstacles in his work, if he belongs to a particular caste.
40. Being a member of a particular caste will help him to improve his business.

46A9 POLITICAL AWARENESS TEST

Author : Virgin Sigamani.
Availability : Author, Department of Education, Madurai Kamaraj University, Madurai.
Language : English.
Uses : To find out the level of political awareness of the students.
Level : College students.
Main features : The questionnaire with 100 items consists of multiple choice questions and 15 questions on political behaviour of college students.
Reliability : Reliability was found out by using rational equivalence method.
Validity : Validity was determined by content analysis.
Time : No time limit.
Norms : No norms were established.
Reference : Virgin Sigamani, "Political awareness of college students ". M.Phil. Dissertation, Madurai Kamaraj University, Madurai, 1980.

(The respondents have to choose the correct one of the 4 responses).

1. Which of the following is one of the State Assemblies dissolved recently?

   (a) Kerala
   (b) Karnataka
   (c) Uttar Pradesh
   (d) Andhra Pradesh.

2. From which of the following electoral constituency has Mrs. Indira Gandhi been elected to the Parliament?

   (a) Chikmagalur
   (b) Medak
   (c) Tanjore
   (d) Delhi.

3. Who headed the commission to probe into the excess of emergency in India?

   (a) A.N. Grover
   (b) P. Jegamohan Reddy
   (c) J.C. Shah
   (d) A.C. Gupta.

4. Which of the following is the characteristic of dictatorship?

   (a) Electing the rulers by the adult citizens.
   (b) Concentration of authority in the hands of one man or in one party.
   (c) Decentralisation of governmental powers.
   (d) Decision by majority.

5. Who of the following is the Vice-President of India?

   (a) Mr. B.D. Jatti
   (b) Mr.V.V. Giri
   (c) Mr. M. Hidayatullah
   (d) Mr. R.V. Swaminathan.

6. The Chief Minister of an Indian State is appointed by

   (a) President
   (b) Governor of the State concerned
   (c) Prime Minister
   (d) Chief Justice of India.

7. Which statement about president of India is true in connection with a bill sent to him for his approval

   (a) He can reject it
   (b) He can send it back to the House for reconsideration
   (c) He can sign it with his own amendment
   (d) He can refuse to sign it.

8. What does adjournment of the House refer to in legislative practice?

   (a) Closing a debate on a bill
   (b) Suspending the Session
   (c) Dissolving the House
   (d) Postponement of the session to some other day.

9. What is veto?

   (a) It is a right of the person to vote in the elections to the Parliament.
   (b) It is a right of the person to vote in the elections of office bearers to an association.
   (c) It is a right of the person to hold a public office.
   (d) It is a right to reject or nullify decision, enjoyed by any single member of a Committee or Assembly.

10. Before the expiry of his term, the President of India can be removed from office by

    (a) Vice-President
    (b) Prime Minister
    (c) Chief Minister
    (d) Impeachment.

11. Who is the Chairman of the Indian Planning Commission?

    (a) President
    (b) Prime Minister
    (c) Chief Minister
    (d) Vice-President.

12. Under which Constitutional Amendment, Fundamental Duties for the Citizens have been incorporated in the Constitution of India?

(a) 40th (b) 41st (c) 42nd (d) 43rd.

13. A non-member of Parliament appointed as a minister in the Union Government of India has necessarily to become an M.P. within a period of- to enable him to continue as Minister

(a) 9 months (b) 6 months (c) 12 months (d) No fixed period.

14. What do you mean by °Coup d' etat'?

(a) Resignation by the Head of a State.
(b) Sudden overthrow of a government by force of violent means.
(c) War between two countries.
(d) A judicial term giving life imprisonment to a culprit.

15. Which of the following is not a function of the Election Commission of India?

(a) To advance loans to the poor candidates to fight elections
(b) To lay down general rules for election
(c) To allot election symbols to political parties and individuals contesting elections
(d) To supervise the conduct of elections.

16. Name the author of "Towards Total Revolution."

(a) Mahathma Gandhi
(b) Jeyaprekash Narayanan
(c) Morarji Desai
(d) Subash Chandra Bose.

17. The President of India has the same constitutional authority as the

(a) British Monarch
(b) President of U.S.S.R.
(c) President of U.S.A.
(d) President of France.

18. When can the President's Rule be imposed in a State of the Indian Union?

(a) During External Emergency

(b) During Internal Emergency
(c) Where there is failure of constitutional machinery in the state
(d) At no time.

19. Who of the following has the power to dissolve the Parliament of India?

(a) President
(b) Prime Minister
(c) Speaker of Lok Sabha
(d) Vice-President.

20. Who can declare the state of emergency in India?

(a) President
(b) Vice-President
(c) Governor of State
(d) Prime Minister.

21. Which of the following is not a regional party?

(a) D.M.K.
(b) A.I.A.D.M.K.
(c) Congress I
(d) Shiva Sena.

22. Who administers the oath of office to the President of India?

(a) Vice-President
(b) Prime Minister
(c) Chief Justice of India
(d) Speaker of Lok Sabha.

23. Which of the following is not a socialistic doctrine?

(a) Abolition of property in lands, rents to be used for public purposes
(b) Concentration of wealth in the hands of a few individuals
(c) Nationalisation of the means of transportation and commerce
(d) Abolition of all rights of inheritance.

24. The Indian Parliament can rename or redefine the boundary of a state by

(a) Amending the constitution

(b) Getting the consent of the Prime Minister
(c) Getting the consent of the Chief Minister of the state concerned
(d) Getting the consent of the concerned state legislature and parliament's approval.

25. In a parliamentary system of government like India the executive is responsible

(a) Directly to the people
(b) To the legislature
(c) To the judiciary
(d) None of these.

26. Who presides over the meetings of the Indian Rajya Sabha?

(a) President
(b) Vice-President
(c) Speaker
(d) Deputy Speaker.

27. Which of the following is not the member of U.N.O.?

(a) India
(b) People's Republic of China
(c) Taiwan
(d) Pakistan.

28. The cabinet in a parliamentary type of government like ours goes out of office

(a) When a vote of no confidence motion is passed against the entire ministry
(b) If a minister resigns his post or dies while in office
(c) When there is a big agitation
(d) If the opposition makes scathing criticisms.

29. Which of the following is not one of the Fundamental Rights provided in our constitution?

(a) The right to freedom of religion
(b) The right to freedom of speech and expression
(c) The right to equality
(d) The right to equal wage for equal work, both for men and women.

30. Who appoints the Governor of an Indian State?

(a) President
(b) Prime Minister
(c) Chief Minister
(d) Vice-President.

31. _________ is a Government of the people, by the people and for the people

(a) Welfare State
(b) Monarchy
(c) Democracy
(d) One party rule.

32. Finance Commission is set up in India after every

(a) 2 years (b) 5 years (c) 7 years (d) 10 years.

33. Which of the following may be classified as a Communal Party?

(a) Congress I
(b) D.M.K.
(c) Muslim League
(d) Janata.

34. Who is the constitutional head of the Government of India?

(a) Chief Justice of India
(b) Prime Minister
(c) President
(d) Attorney General.

35. The maximum strength of the Lok Sabha is

(a) 500 (b) 525 (c) 545 (d) 550.

36. Which of the following has the powers to declare a law invalid if it is passed against the Indian Constitution?

(a) Parliament
(b) Cabinet
(c) Parliamentary committee
(d) Supreme court.

37. What is the democratic method by which we can bring change in the government?

    (a) Revolution
    (b) Election
    (c) °Coup d' etat
    (d) None of these.

38. Who elects our President?

    (a) People of India directly
    (b) Parliament
    (c) State Legislatures
    (d) An electoral college.

39. The Vice-President of India is also the

    (a) Chairman of Rajya Sabha
    (b) Supreme Commander of the armed forces
    (c) Head of the Council of Ministers
    (d) Speaker of Lok Sabha.

40. What is the maximum period for which the Vice-President can act as President on account of resignation, death or removal from office of the President of India?

    (a) Six months
    (b) One year
    (c) Unexpired period of the term of the President
    (d) Indefinitely till the fresh election to the office of President is held.

41. At what age does one get voting right in our country?

    (a) 21 years (b) 18 years (c) 25 years (d) 20 years.

42. Which of the following party system is best suited for Parliamentary democracy?

    (a) One party system
    (b) Two party system
    (c) Multi party system
    (d) None of these.

43. The Government of USA is

    (a) Monarchical form

(b) Parliamentary form
(c) Presidential form
(d) None of these.

44. Citizenship means

(a) The membership of a state
(b) Citizen's partnership with others
(c) Ownership of property
(d) Citizen's membership in an Association.

45. In which case is a joint session of the Lok Sabha and Rajya Sabha convened by the President?

(a) To impeach the President and to pass a bill with two thirds majority
(b) When a bill is passed by the Lok Sabha and the Rajya Sabha with two thirds majority
(c) When the Rajya Sabha rejects a bill which is already passed by the Lok Sabha
(d) When an ordinance passed by the Lok Sabha but not by the Rajya Sabha.

46 Which of the following is not a state but a Union Territory of India?

(a) Himachal Pradesh
(b) Arunachal Pradesh
(d) Tripura
(e) Meghalaya.

47. In which organ of the U.N.O. do the Big Five powers enjoy the veto power?

(a) General Assembly
(b) Security Council
(c) Trusteeship Council
(d) Economic and Social Council.

48. Which party does the Deputy speaker of the present Lok Sabha belong to?

(a) Congress I
(b) D.M.K.
(c) A.I.A.D.M.K.
(d) Janata.

49. The Indian Constitution took effect from

(a) August 15, 1947
(b) August 15, 1948
(c) November 26, 1949
(d) January 26, 1950.

50. In which of the following country is only one political party allowed to exist

(a) India (b) USSR (c) USA (d) France.

51. The word °Secular' denotes

(a) Keeping away from all religions
(b) Freedom of religion and worship to all citizen
(c) Belief in one God
(d) Practicing different religions.

52. Who of the following is not appointed as the President of India?

(a) Prime Minister
(b) Vice-President
(c) Chief Justice of India
(d) An Ambassador.

53. For how long is the Vice-President of India elected?

(a) 3 years (b) 4 years (c) 5 years (d) 6 years.

54. Who was acting as the Prime Minister for the care taker government before Mrs. Indira Gandhi took over?

(a) Mr. Morarji Desai
(b) Mr. C. Subramaniam
(c) Mr. Charan Singh
(d) Mr. Raj Narayanan.

55. The seat of a member of India Parliament is declared vacant if he absents himself from all meetings of the House without the permission of the House for a period of

(a) 15 days (b) 30 days (c) 45 days (d) 60 days.

56. Who is the Chief Election Commissioner of India?

(a) Mr. M.H. Beg

(b) Mr. R.K. Hegde
(c) Mr. T. Swaminathan
(d) Mr. S.L. Shakdhar

57. In India the case of dispute in Presidential Election is referred to

(a) Chief Election Commissioner
(b) Supreme Court
(c) Parliament
(d) None of these.

58. Who administers the oath of office to the Governor of the State of India?

(a) Chief Justice of India
(b) President of India
(c) Chief Justice of the State
(d) Chief Minister of the State concerned.

59. To contest of the Vice-Presidential election in India, a person should have completed the minimum age of

(a) 30 years (b) 35 years (c) 40 years (d) 45 years.

60. What is the minimum strength of a Legislative Assembly of Indian States?

(a) 30 members
(b) 50 members
(c) 60 members
(d) No fixed limit.

61 How many countries are permanent members of the Security Council in the U.N.O.?

(a) 3 (b) 5 (c) 10 (d) All the members are permanent.

62. The Indian Parliament consists of

(a) Lok Sabha and Rajya Sabha only
(b) Lok Sabha only
(c) Rajya Sabha only
(d) President, Lok Sabha and Rajya Sabha.

POLITICAL BEHAVIOUR

Choose the correct answer and put the corresponding letter in the bracket.

1. Suppose you feel your college has an unfair rule

   (i) Do you think you will be able to influence in modifying the same so that justice is meted out to your fellow students?

   Yes, No.

   (ii) If you think you will be able to do so. What will be your mode of operation?

   (a) Negotiations with the principal
   (b) Approaching a ruling party man
   (c) An agitation.

2. College students do not have any °say' on what the government does.

   Agree/disagree

3. (i) Is your father a member of a political party?

   Yes/No.

   (ii) If your father is not a member, does he support or sympathise with any particular party?

   (a) Yes (b)No (c) Do not know.

   (iii) Do you tend to support the same political party as your father?

   Yes/No.

4. How do you identify yourself in political orientation?

   (a) Left (Socialist)
   (b) Moderate left (Liberal)
   (c) Moderate Right
   (d) Right.

5. (i) Do you attend political party meetings?

   Yes/No.

(ii) If so, how often?

Frequently/Occasionally.

6. Have you worked for a political party during an election campaign?

Yes/No.

7. (i) Are you interested in expanding your political knowledge?

Yes/No.

(ii) If you want to expand your political knowledge, what are the sources of your political information? Please tick the appropriate item(s)

(a) Newspaper
(b) Books on politics and current events
(c) Discussion with people interested in politics.

(iii) At the time of the recent General Elections where did you get most of your political news?

(a) Friends and family discussions
(b) Newspapers
(c) Radio.

(iv) Did you study "Modern Governments" as a main or ancilliary subject in your degree course?

Yes/No.

8. I participate in public demonstrations (protest type) organised by a political party

(a) Always (b) Often (c) Rarely (d) Never.

9. Do you feel that your college

(i) Union elections are fought on political party basis?

Yes/No.

(ii) Does any political party help the candidates financially to fight the college Union elections?

Yes/No.

(iii) Do you think that, only that candidate who is supported by a political party has more chance of victory

Yes/No.

(iv) Are you an office bearer in your college union?

Yes/No.

(v) If you are office bearer did you get the support of any political party in winning the election?

Yes/No.

10. Which aspect of a political leader appeals to you most?

(a) Gift of the Gab (Ability to speak effectively)
(b) Qualification and experience
(c) Administrative ability
(d) Impressive personality.

11. Do you read public affairs in the news papers?

(a) Nearly every day
(b) About once a week
(c) From time to time
(d) Never.

12. Is any of your relatives a legislative member or an active political leader?

Yes/No.

13. Do you intend to become a politician after completing your studies?

Yes/No.

14. How would you rate the level of political awareness of your fellow students?

(a) High
(b) Moderate

(c) Low
(d) Very low.

instruments with technical information B

46B1 TEST OF POLITICAL EFFICACY

Author : Abhimanyou Tambar.
Availability ; National Psychological Corporation, 4/230, Kacheri Ghat, Agra.
Languages : English & Hindi.
Uses : To measure feelings of political efficacy by using a TAT type projective measure.
Level : All adult population.
Main features : This is a TAT type projective test consisting of six pictures, the respondents are supposed to write a small interesting story based on each picture one by one. The six stories thus obtained, it is assumed, elicit political efficacy imagery (PEI). This PEI can be measured by using a scoring system, consisting of ten categories, the detailed description of which is given in the manual.
Reliability & Validity : Two sets of pictures, containing six pictures in each i.e. set °A' and set °B' were used. For each set of pictures two conditions aroused and neutral were used. Considering all aspects it was decided to use a 2 x 2 factorial design i.e. 100 subjects divided into four groups of 25 subjects in each group. The details of the data are given somewhere else.
Time : About 45 minutes.
Norms : Not yet finalised.
Reference : Tambar Abhimanyou; Measuring political efficacy through apperception, ISPT Journal of Research in Educational and Psychological Measurement, 1981, 5(1),11-27.

46B2 A SCALE TO MEASURE ATTITUDE TOWARDS THE MENTALLY RETARDED

Authors : P.K. Dhillon and Sadhana Chaudhri.
Availability : Authors, Jesus and Mary College, Chanakyapuri, New Delhi.
Language : English.
Uses : To measure the meaning of mental retardation.
Level : Literate - High School and College students, adults married and single of all professions.
Main features : The Semantic differential scaling technique was used. The scale consists of 21 bipolar adjectives.

Reliability : The reliability of the items ranged from .38 to .66.
Validity : Face validity established.
Time : Approximately take 10-15 minutes.
Norms : Norms are available with the first author.

46B3 NATIONAL INTEGRATION SCALE

Authors : A. Jamil Qadri and Mohd. Ghufran.
Availability : Department of Psychology, Aligarh Muslim University, Aligarh.
Languages : Hindi & Urdu.
Uses : To study factors which facilitate or hinder the process of national integration.
Level : Literate and semi-literate.
Main features : It is Likert's type scale. It consists of four sub-scales, viz., (1) Equality of opportunity (2) Composite versus unitary culture (3) Secular versus regional identification, and (4) National versus regional identification. Total number of items = 36 including six common items in some sub-scales.
Reliability : Reliability for four sub-tests is found to be (1) .86, (2) .71, (3) .87 and (4) .89.
Validity : In process.
Time : Thirty minutes.
Norms : Are being developed.

46B4 CITIZENSHIP SCALE

Author : Uma Varshney.
Availability : Faculty of Education, Banaras Hindu University, Varanasi.
Language : Hindi.
Level : College and University students.
Main features : The scale is divided into three parts A, B and C. Part °A' consists of 41 statements rated on a 5-point scale. Part °B' consists of 23 statements. Part °C' consists of 19 statements with five alternate responses. The scale measures one's opinion regarding government, political parties, politicians, election, duties, interests and national problems. Further details are available from the author.

46B5 PARENT-CHILD RELATIONS QUESTIONNAIRE (PCRQ)

Author : Ram Ashish Singh.
Availability : Author, Department of Psychology, Jagdam College, Chapra, Saran, Bihar.

Language : Hindi.
Uses : To measure the relationships existing between parents and children during childhood which forms the main basis of human development.
Level : Mainly developed for high school students (13 to 16 years), but can be used on any sample.
Main features : The PCRQ consists of M-form and M-form containing six sub-scales in each with a total items of 60 in both the forms.
Reliability : Reliability ranges from .64 to .85.
Validity : Face validity established.
Time : Thirty minutes approximately.
Norms : Not available.
Reference : Singh, R.A. Academic achievement as a function of parent child relationship. Unpublished Ph.D. dissertation, Bihar University, Muzaffarpur, 1981.

46B6 PARENT-CHILD RELATION TEST

Author : Govind Tiwari.
Availability : Agra Psychological Research Cell, Agra.
Language : Hindi.
Uses : To measure quantitatively the attitude of parents towards their children.
Level : Father and Mother.
Main features : The present test measures the attitude of fathers and mothers towards various aspects of their relation to the child. Eight areas of parent-child relation have been taken. These are : Acceptance-Rejection; Dominance-Submission; Encouragement-Discouragement; Trust-Distrust; Reward-Punishment; and Tolerance-Hostility. The responses of the father or mother may come in eleven alternatives.
Reliability : (1) The split-half reliability (N = 300) was found to be .79. For the M-Child relation (N = 297) and F-Child relation (N = 292) the °r' was .89 and .86 respectively.
(2) The test-retest reliability (N = 120) was found to be .78. For M-Child relation (N = 112) and the F-Child relation (N = 117) the °r' was .76 and .80 respectively.
Validity : Validity was established against the valid tests on parent - child relation.
(1) °r' between the present test and the Indian adaptation of parental attitude research instrument was found to be (N = 100) = .69.
(2) °r' between the present test and the Indian adaptation of children's report of parental behaviour inven-

tory was found to be (N = 100) = .74.

Norms : Percentile norms for mothers and fathers are separately given in the manual.

References : (1) Tiwari, G.P. Dropouts - its importance at the primary level. Indian Education, 1969, 8 (5-6).
(2) Tiwari, G.P. Family dynamics of dropouts at the primary level. Unpublished Ph.D. Dissertation, Agra University, Agra, 1971.

46B7 LIFE SATISFACTION SCALE

Authors : Q.G. Alam & Ramji Srivastava.

Availability : Authors, Department of Psychology, S.N. college, Azamgarh.

Language : Hindi.

Uses : To measure individual adjustment and self fulfilment.

Level : Adults.

Main features : Sixty items, covering six areas of satisfaction - health, personal, economic, marital, social and job.

Reliability : Test-retest reliability coefficient = .84.

Validity : Established.

Time : About twenty minutes.

Norms : Available with authors.

46B8 VICHAR-MAPNI (PHILOSOPHY OF LIFE SCALE)

Authors : Om Prakash Srivastava & R.K. Naidu.

Availability : Authors, Department of Psychology, University of Allahabad, Allahabad.

Language : Hindi.

Uses : To measure attitudes and beliefs which would determine appraisal of an event.

Level : Physically handicapped subjects. Can also be used on other groups.

Main features : This scale measures attributed causes of suffering (Part-A) and consequences of suffering (Part-B).
Part-A : Eight causes of suffering were postulated. They were : (i) Members of his family, (ii) Others belonging to society, (iii) His misfortune, (iv) Deeds of his present life, (v) Deeds of his past life, (vi) Neglect by government, (vii) Circumstances and (viii) God.
Part-B : Consisted of 20 items. Ten positive and ten negative, which were intended to measure constructive or destructive consequences of suffering as perceived by

the individual.
Reliability : Not reported.
Validity : Not available.
Time : Fifteen minutes.
Norms : Not available.
Reference : Srivastava, O.P. Stress and coping mechanisms of physically handicapped children. D.Phil. Thesis, University of Allahabad, 1981.

46B9 SOCIAL SUPPORT SCALE : AFFIRMATION BY PARENTS AND PEERS

Authors : R.D. Caplan & R.K. Naidu.
Availability : Second Author, Department of Psychology, University of Allahabad, Allahabad.
Languages : English & Hindi.
Uses : To measure person-environment fit among university students.
Level : University students.
Main features : Affirmation can be computed by measuring the absolute difference between the students' perception of their parents' or peers' position on locus of control and their own self-stated position on control. The obtained difference measures the degree of incongruence between the opinions of the students on the one hand and the opinions of the parents and peers on the other. The item content for the self, parent and peer versions are identical. Scale (i) includes ten items rated on a 5-point response scale : Do not agree very little, Agree somewhat, Agree much, Agree very much.
Reliability : Coefficient alpha the coefficient of internal consistency was computed. Correlation between items was also computed. Three indices were found and °r' values ranged from .38 to .67 and the alpha values ranged from .55 to .80.
Validity : Not available.
Time : Average fifteen minutes.
Norms : Not available.
Reference : Caplan, R.D. & Naidu, R.K. Stress, coping and social support : A study of University students in India.

46B10 SOCIAL SUPPORT FROM PEERS SCALE

Authors : R.D. Caplan & R.K. Naidu.
Availability : Second Author, Department of Psychology, University of Allahabad, Allahabad.
Languages : English & Hindi.

Uses : To measure person-environment fit among University students.

Level : University students.

Main features : Consisted of 6 items designed to measure social support from peers. Each item was rated on a 5-point response scale : Never, Sometimes, Often, Very often, Almost Always.

Reliability : Coefficient alpha the coefficient of internal consistency was computed. Correlation between items was also computed. Two indices were found and °r' values ranged from .38 to .71 and alpha values ranged from .77 and .83.

Validity : Not available.

Time : Average three minutes.

Norms : Not available.

Reference : Caplan, R.D. & Naidu, R.K. Stress, coping and social support : A study of University students in India.

46B11 SOCIAL SUPPORT FROM PARENTS SCALE

Authors : R.D. Caplan & R.K. Naidu.

Availability : Second Author, Department of Psychology, University of Allahabad, Allahabad.

Languages : English & Hindi.

Uses : To measure person-environment fit among University students.

Level : University students.

Main features : Consisted of 10 items designed to measure parental behaviour in terms of what they do for the subject. Each item was rated on a 5-point response scale. Never, Rarely, Often, Frequently, Always.

Reliability : Coefficient alpha the coefficient of internal consistency was computed. Correlations between items was also computed. Three indices were found and values range from .42 to .65 and alpha values range from .66 to .79.

Validity : Not available.

Time : Average five minutes.

Norms : Not available.

Reference : Caplan, R.D. & Naidu, R.K. Stress, coping and social support : A study of University students in India.

46B12 SUPPORT SCALE

Authors : Om Prakash Srivastava & R.K. Naidu.

Availability : Authors, Department of Psychology, University of Allahabad, Allahabad.

Uses : To study support systems among physically handicapped children and adolescents.
Level : Physically handicapped children and adolescents.
Main features : The scale measure three aspects of support : (1) Source of support (i) Family, (ii) Friends, (iii) Teachers, (iv) Fate, (v) Circumstances and (vi) God, (2) Amount of support and (3) Kind of support (i) assisted in control of anxiety, (ii) assisted in understanding and analysis of the problem & in the formulation of a course of action, (iii) assisted by providing the requisite material resources.
Reliability : Test-retest reliability = .68 (N = 40).
Validity : Not available.
Time : Fifteen minutes.
Norms : Not available.
Reference : Srivastava, O.P. Stress and coping mechanism of physically handicapped children. D.Phil. Thesis, University of Allahabad, Allahabad, 1981.

citations C

46C1 ATTITUDE TOWARDS DIVORCE/WIDOW REMARRIAGE

Author : M.M. Kamala.
Availability : Author, Department of Post-Graduate Studies and Research in Psychology, University of Mysore, Mysore.

46C2 ATTITUDE TOWARDS NATIONAL PROBLEMS

Author : Uma Varshney.
Availability : Author, Faculty of Education, Banaras Hindu University, Varanasi.

46C3 THE RETARDATE ATTITUDE QUESTIONNAIRE

Author : Rita Ghatak.
Availability : Author, Zakir Hussain Centre for Educational Studies, School of Social Sciences, J.N. University, New Delhi.

46C4 SEX BEHAVIOUR ATTITUDE SCALE

Author : Y. Singh.
Availability : National Psychological Corporation, Kacheri Ghat, Agra.

46C5 A SCALE OF ATTITUDE TOWARD WAR

Authors : R.B. Tripathi & R.N. Singh.
Availability : Rupa Psychological Centre, B-19/60-B Deoriabir, Bhelupur, Varanasi.

adaptations D

46D1 PERSONAL REACTION INVENTORY

Authors : Afzal Kureshi and Rahat Ali Khan.
Availability : Department of Psychology, Aligarh Muslim University, Aligarh.
Language : Hindi.
Uses : The M-C SD Scale is a measure of social desirability and also an indirect measure of approval motive which reflects a self-evaluative style brought into play in the testing situation.
Level : It can be used with literate male and female subjects.
Main features : It is a Hindi adaptation of the Marlowe-Crowne Social Desirability Scale (1960). Scale comprises 33 items of a self-reporting nature of which 18 items are keyed true and 15 in the false direction. Checking a true item as true and false item as false is to be scored as I, and is indicative of social desirability.
Reliability : The split-half reliability of the Hindi version of the M-C SD Scale is .64 (N = 192).
Validity : High scorers on the SD Scale showed improvement following positive evaluation of their performance, whereas low scorers were unaffected by positive evaluation. Reverse was the case with negative evaluation. On the Rod & Frame Test high SD scorers were more field-dependent than low SD scorers.
Time : Twenty-five to thirty minutes.
Norms : Norms for Indian samples are in process of development.

46D2 PARENTAL ATTITUDE RESEARCH INSTRUMENT (PARI)

Author : Uma Saxena.
Availability : Agra Psychological Research Cell, Agra.
Language : Hindi.
Uses : To measure the attitude of the parents towards various aspects of child rearing.
Level : Father and mother.
Main features : It is the Hindi adaptation of PARI developed by Schaefer and Bell (1958). The present PARI consists of two forms (Father's and mother's) separately. The Hindi version of father's PARI consists

of 100 statements which comprises of 20 scales. Each scale consists of five statements. Mother's form of PARI consisting 115 statements which comprises the 23 PARI scales. Each scale consists of five statements.

Reliability : (1) Split-half reliability of mother's form (N = 200) = .83.

(2) The test-retest reliability for the same was found to be (N = 100) = .78.

(3) The split-half reliability (N = 200) of father's form was calculated to be .79 and the test-retest (N = 100) was found to be .77.

Validity : Concurrent validity (r = .81 for father's PARI and r = .78 for mother's PARI) was found out using Hindi and English versions of PARI on father's and mother's.

Norms : On the basis of the responses to the PARI, the subjects (both mothers and fathers) can be categorised as high, medium and low on each scale.

Instrument Index

Author Index